3. THE POWER OF LABYRINTHS – USING YOUR LABYRINTH

3.1.   Wishing Tree
3.2   Sensory Labyrinth Walks
3.3   Experiencing the Labyrinth Differently
3.4   Insights into Impermanence
3.5   Insights into Pilgrimage
3.6   Drama – Theseus and the Minotaur
3.7   Science & Labyrinths - Understanding your Heart
3.8   Number and Labyrinths – developing counting methods
3.9   Using Pacing and Averages to measure the Labyrinth Path
3.10   Labyrinth Clock – Constructing a Sundial

4. FOREST SCHOOL – STARTING OUT

4.1   Sticky Paper Quests
4.2   Crowns for the Seasons
4.3   Willow Towers
4.4   Tree Bark Rubbings
4.5   String Journey
4.6   Clay Beasts and an Animal Ark.
4.7   Soft Toy Town
4.8   Stone Age Bling
4.9   Bird Nests
4.10   Bug Hotels
4.11   Gypsy Trail
4.12   Blindfold Trail
4.13   Camouflage Game
4.14   Magic Carpets
4.15   Bats and Owls

5. FOREST SCHOOL – INTERMEDIATE

5.1   Fire-lighting
5.2   Whittling a Toasting Fork and Making Toast
5.3   Charcoal Pencils
5.4   Making a Whistle.
5.5   Wizard's Staff
5.6   Witches Broom
5. 7   Making a Drop Spindle and Spinning Yarn
5.8   Weaving with Natural Materials
5.9   Dream Catcher
5.10   Free Shelter

6. ADVANCED FOREST SCHOOL –EQUIPPING A FOREST SCHOOL AREA

7. ART IN NATURE

8. STORY AND LANDSCAPE

THE POWER
of
OUTDOOR LEARNING

*107 Lesson Plans & Projects
for Schools*

Chris Trwoga

SOMERSET NATURAL LEARNING ACADEMY

www.snla.co.uk

The author is happy to provide further advice and guidance for any of the projects in this book.
Contact Chris at:
learning@snla.co.uk

British Library Cataloguing in Publication Data
Trwoga. C.
The Power of Outdoor Learning

A CIP record for this book is available from the British Library.

Printed and bound in Great Britain
by Berforts Information Press, Stevenage.

Editing, layout and design by S. M. Parsons

Published by **Winding Road Books**
www.windingroadbooks.com

Making a willow labyrinth

ACKNOWLEDGEMENTS

Gwyneth Harwood for her primary liason work.

Our outdoor learning team - Gwyneth, Kevin Ball and Ingrid Crawford.

The Glastonbury Trust for their financial support.

NHS Somerset for their financial support.

Fiona Moir, Public Health Advisor, NHS Somerset.

Kate Bennett, Cluster Manager, CLASP Schools, Somerset.

Gwyneth Harwood, Kevin Bull, Ingrid Crawford, our Outdoor Learning team.

We wish to thank the following schools for being our 'guinea pigs' and letting us develop our ideas with their students. Our thanks also go to the schools who provided us with photographs and obtained parental consents.

Ansford Academy, Shepton Mallet.
St. Benedict's V.A. C of E Primary School, Glastonbury
Castle Cary Primary School.
Crispin School, Street.
St. Dunstan's Academy.
Evercreech Primary School, Shepton Mallet.
Fairmead School, Yeovil.
Hindhayes Infants School.
Rockwell Green Primary School, Bridgwater.
St. John's Infants School, Glastonbury.
North Cadbury Primary School.
Tintinhull Primary School, Yeovil.
Upton Noble Primary School, Shepton Mallet.
Winsham Primary School, Chard.

Our special thanks go to the children and young people themselves, who have shown so much energy, enthusiasm, initiative and sheer joy in their outdoor learning.

CONTENTS

I. FIVE REASONS FOR LEARNING OUTDOORS

The spiritual, social, and emotional benefits of Outdoor Learning.

II. BEING PRACTICAL

Risk, Safety Routines, Dressing the Part, Tools and Materials.

1. SPECIAL PLACES

2. THE POWER OF LABYRINTHS – MAKING LABYRINTHS

9. MATHS & SCIENCE

9.1   Earthworm Populations
9.2   Insect Distribution Maps
9.3   Making Insect Habitats
9.4   Studying Tree Health
9.5   The Science of Tug-of-War
9.6   Playing Field Planetarium
9.7   Making a giant Compass and Clock
9.8   Fairground Probabilities Challenge
9.9   Investigating the earth at our feet
9.10   Hinged Counterweight Trebuchet and Missile Trajectories
9.11   Making a mini Ice-House.
9.12   Coordinates Game.

10. CRAFT TECHNOLOGY

10.1   Arrows-Making
10.2   Miniature Willow Bridges – Arches and Suspension Bridges
10. 3   Hurdles
10. 4   Travois Races: Native American Transportation
10.5   Raising Water: Shadufs
10.6   Getting Rid of Water: Soakaway
10.7   Moving Water: Mill or Marble Race
10.8   Holding Water: School Pond Project
10.9   Rope Bridge
10.10   Cob Bread Oven.

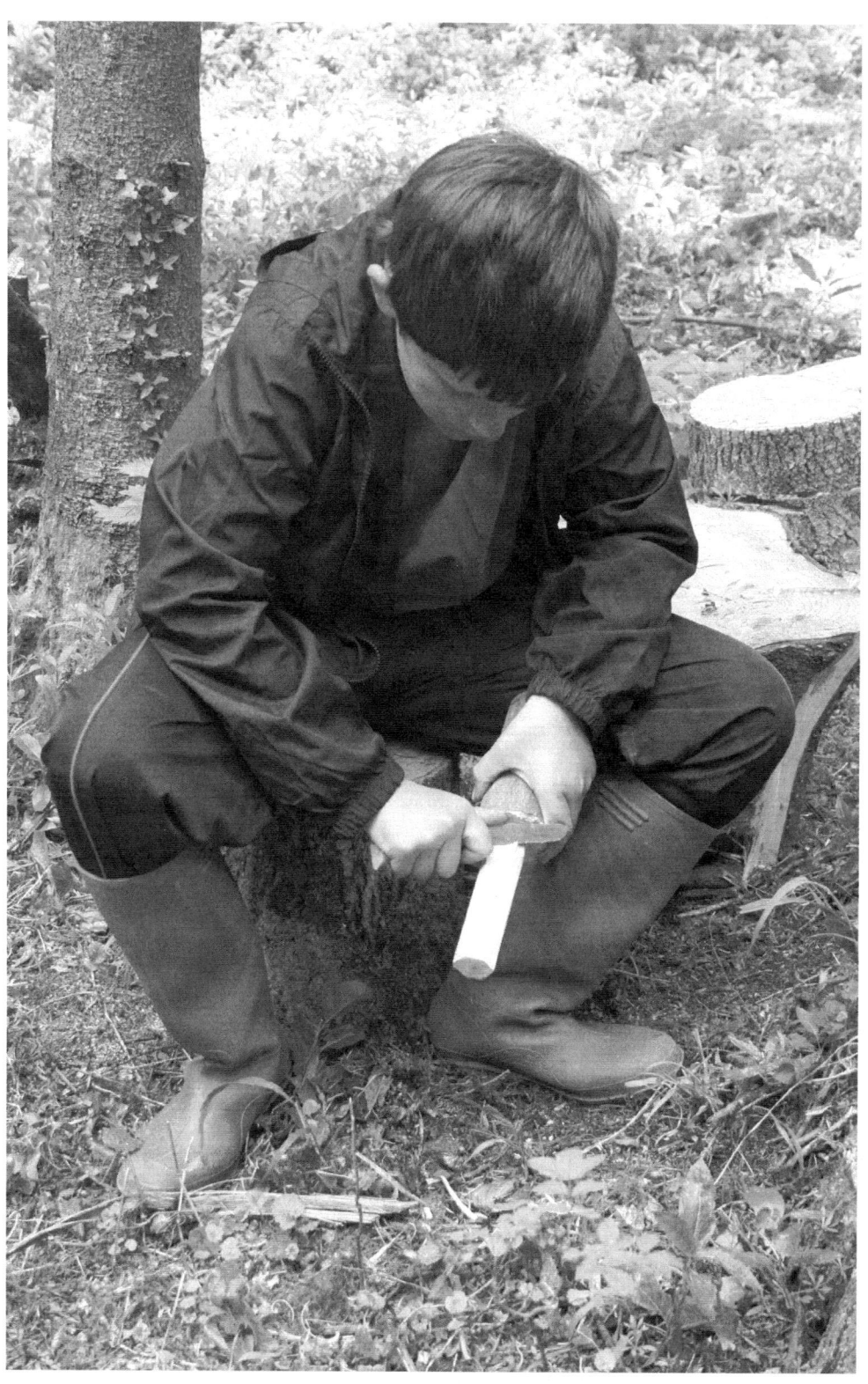

PREFACE

This book is written in the belief that God did not design children with classrooms in mind.

If you are as old as I am, you may remember sloping wooden desks with fixed bench seating set out in serried rows facing a blackboard and teacher's podium. The appearance and psychological effect was not dissimilar to church pews and pulpit (where I also spent many unhappy childhood hours) and are a product of a Victorian educational system.

Fixed desks fossilized teaching and learning styles in the same way that pews fossilized forms of worship. The pew offered a sloping ridge for the Book of Common Prayer and fixed focus on the pulpit, in the same way that the desk provided for pen and ink and focused on the teacher as fount of all wisdom. Children were deemed as learning best in the arid, unstimulating environment of a whitewashed classroom.

Fast-forward 140 years and the blackboard is interactive, pen and paper a tablet and the book, the internet. The daydreams of the bored Victorian child are replaced with the under-desk portable media gadget, complete with store of games and music and the capacity to endlessly text your mates. Church and pew may be gone from the lives of children, but the media envelope of celebrity culture and must-have materiality is far more pervasive, persuasive and oppressive than the church ever was.

Children are not just auditory and visual learners. Children have bodies, and learn through their whole body, or "soma", in a way that many adults have forgotten. Children learn by moving, touching, tasting, seeing and smelling. They were designed by God to learn through experience and to draw their conclusions about the world from the outcome of their endeavours. Nowadays, children are in danger of becoming screen readers instead of somatic beings. In denying children the right to roam, the opportunity to connect with natural environments, and to enjoy the company of their peers in the flesh instead of through a screen, we risk stunting them not just physically, but emotionally and spiritually too.

I believe that the well-being of children is dependent on deep engagement with others and with the physical world. It is about experiencing things in a physical and visceral sense. It is about sharing experience with others in the same, palpable way that a group of youngsters enjoy playing football or building a den in a woodland space.

It is about connecting.

Research indicates that a person's ability to connect with and enjoy the natural world is shaped by childhood experiences. Our capacity as adults to enjoy what nature provides can be damaged by the absence of that store of memory, that enriches the lives of those who routinely experienced natural environments as children. Using the language of Edward Wilson, children who are denied experience of the natural world can see their innate Biophilia (love of nature) become Biophobia (fear of nature). Not only can we lose the spiritual and emotional capacity to enjoy nature to the full, we risk losing the physical capacity too, because we are no longer fit enough to walk over rough terrain, cope with inclement weather or navigate without the aid of an electronic device.

Thinking and research from across the globe is calling for a return to nature for our children, and to nurture them deliberately and consciously as spiritual and somatic beings. This book is my contribution to that call.

FIVE REASONS FOR LEARNING OUTDOORS

"Our children no longer learn how to read the great Book of Nature from their own direct experience or how to interact creatively with the seasonal transformations of the planet. They seldom learn where water comes from or where it goes. We no longer coordinate our human celebration with the great liturgy of the heavens."
Wendell Berry[1]

"Individuals do not exist as isolated, discrete or separate entities, but as interconnected beings whose growth, well-being and transformation are shaped by dynamic and fluid relationships between friends, family, the global community and Higher Spirit within the Universe. The ancient abiding human quest is for connectedness with souls, with one another, with nature."
Raisuyah Bhagwan[2]

We begin with happiness.

A turning point in my own thinking about well-being came 15 years ago on a Scottish Mountain. On a bright, but bitter October day I ascended Buchaille Etive Mor with a party of twelve young teenagers. Buchaille Etive Mor is a steep, rocky mountain that overlooks Scotland's Glen Coe to the north, and the vast, boggy wastes of Rannock Moor to the south.

After a two hour sharp, scrambly ascent we reached the summit and gazed across what looked like half the world. A quiet jubilation rippled through the group. One girl in particular stood out. She was looking down at her asthma inhaler, realizing she hadn't needed it for the entire ascent. One boy declared that it was the best moment of his life. As I looked at the faces of the youngsters, I realized that such experiences are more life-enhancing than anything they could possibly experience in the classroom. You might choose to disagree. But I remember it, fifteen years on, and I have no doubt that many of the young people in that group remember it too.

They did that. It was their Everest. It was a moment of self-discovery, of something done that is real and tangible, now and always.

But you can't take twenty-eight kids up a mountain every day and it would be wrong to think of learning outdoors being all about 'peak' experiences. Learning outdoors is not about adventurous training or an adrenalin rush. It's about opening the classroom door, taking the kids out to the school field, and doing stuff in the sun, the wind and the rain. It's about learning strategies that enable kids to connect positively with themselves, each other and the natural world.

Why? What's to be gained by peeling kids off the computer and kicking them out of a nice, warm classroom? How does parking their backsides on wet grass make them better?

We are told that children in the UK and the USA are the unhappiest in the developed world. A UNICEF report published in 2007 put Britain and the USA at the bottom of the well-being league.[3]

One of the issues UNICEF reports on is family breakdown. The UK and USA are bottom in terms of the numbers of children living with one parent or step parents. The UK is also at the bottom in terms of children finding their peers 'kind and helpful' and the USA is not far behind at third from bottom. The report gives a picture of relational disintegration in the home spilling out into poor relationships with peers and a loss of any sense of being part of a community. This absence of trust creates a climate of insecurity, and we are told insecurity is one of the biggest triggers of unhappiness.[4]

The report also talks about levels of physical exercise and obesity, where the UK and USA score badly. The UK is bottom of the league when it comes to teenage drunkenness and underage sex, and close to the bottom with smoking and cannabis use amongst the young.

Perhaps most telling are the statistics for 'subjective well-being' – how children feel about themselves. Of all the developed countries surveyed, UK youngsters were at the bottom in terms of their feelings about their own physical health, about school and their satisfaction with life in general.

The UK government spent £2,000,000 on a 'Happiness' survey in 2011, asking people how 'happy' they are, how anxious they feel, and whether they feel their life is worthwhile. Unsurprisingly, most people felt okay and came up with a long list of 'things that make them happy', most of which cost money. It affirmed a kind of vague 'cuddles and consumption' road to well-being.

Draw back from the snap survey, take the long view, and another picture emerges that blasts this cosy outcome. The average level of contentment in the UK is no better than the early 1950s when we had just emerged from a world war, were a whole lot poorer and households had far fewer material possessions.[5]

Whatever David Cameron's happiness index may say, sixty years of economic growth has not taken us one step forward in the happiness stakes, and given the breakdown of family and community life, some would argue we are a lot worse off.

Audit tools for 'emotional health and well-being' in schools are just as depressing. A child's 'emotional health and well-being index' is measured, amongst other things, in terms of "decrease in behavioural incident reports, decrease in fixed term exclusions, decrease in persistent lateness, decrease in children who soil themselves and improvement of personal hygiene."[6]

All these outcomes are important. All of them are manifestations of a child's ability to cope in an ever more complex and stressful social and emotional milieu. But do they equate to what we understand as 'well-being'? Is a high functioning, academically achieving, punctual, well-turned out (and affluent?) child necessarily happy? A coping child is less of a problem to the system and enables us to tick lots of evidence for well-being boxes. But reduction of absenteeism, lateness, poor behaviour, playground accidents and bullying incidents does not necessarily mean we have tackled the deeper malaise. Yes, children are being taught coping strategies and to be 'emotionally intelligent'. But maybe we should be doing something about the whole, damnable, nasty world we've made for them.

So what can we do about it?

In a lecture delivered in December 2009, Stephen Rogers, Director of the University of the First Age, began by posing the question 'Why are we doing education. What are we preparing learners for?' In responding to his own question he used the words 'Autonomy, Connectedness and Transcendence'.

By 'autonomy' he meant enabling learners to take responsibility for their actions, for the direction of their lives and working towards financial independence. By 'connectedness' he meant the ability to live alongside others and with their environment in a harmonious way. By 'transcendence', he meant the capacity to bring meaning and purpose to their lives and become conscious of the 'mystery of things'. Transcendence, he said, is about the human capacity to rise above the mundane and reflect upon and experience the endless possibilities of the human spirit. He summarized by saying that education is about 'learning to know, learning to do and learning to be'.

In education there has been far too much emphasis on 'learning to know' and scant attention given to 'learning to be'.

In order to achieve these things children need opportunities to deconstruct the environments that formalize and fossilize existing relationships of which the archetype is the classroom. The built environment is a reminder of embedded status and values, including greed, wastefulness and social relationships based on material acquisition. Even if children can't articulate these things they feel them. Natural environments create opportunities to strip away the norms and open up new possibilities for being and doing.

In the winter of 2008 - 2009 a significantly heavy snowfall closed down hundreds of schools and prevented many thousands going to work. It elicited the comment in the press and on TV that the snowfall could cost the nation many tens of millions in lost earnings. Other commentators noticed that it had brought whole communities out to play together, united families in snowy adventures and, all too briefly, created a kind of healing within communities and with nature. What price do you put on a family having a joyful day together experiencing a winter landscape at its best?

Classrooms are part of the problem. They are sedentary environments designed for learning in a particular way. "Learning to do and learning to be" means that kids need some kind of a journey. They need new permutations of activity and opportunity that enable them to locate themselves and to re-evaluate their relationships with each other and their environment. Kids who don't cope in the classroom do just fine in Forest school. Get the villains playing a game of football on a wet, windy afternoon and they ain't villains any more.

And doing stuff that makes them feel better is far more effective than teaching children to analyze and articulate why they are unhappy. Teaching children to analyze their feelings all the time is to introduce them to one of the more significant social diseases of the Western world. Helping kids experience wellness through physical engagement with nature is to give them tools that build emotional resilience.[7]

Think, reflect. How many kids do you know who behave completely predictably in your classroom? You don't break the mould by breaking the kid. You break the box that confines him.

BIOPHILIA

The biophilia hypothesis was first proposed by Edward Wilson, in his book, *Biophilia: The Human Bond with other Species,* back in the 1980s.[8] The biophilia hypothesis is an evolutionary theory, defined as "the innately emotional affiliation of human beings to other living organisms. Innate means hereditary and hence part of ultimate human nature". In other words, Wilson says that 'love of nature' is part of our genetic make-up. We are designed to respond to natural environments in a way that helps us survive and thrive. Natural environments help us function more effectively.

Wilson argues that Biophilia is not a single instinct or emotion, "but a complex of learning rules … from attraction to aversion, from awe to indifference, from peacefulness to fear-driven anxiety". These responses have shaped human behaviour and culture. Our dependency on nature goes beyond the material and physical, and sustains us aesthetically, intellectually, cognitively and spiritually. [9]

Thus, the primordial and eponymous myth of the Loss of the Garden of Eden, expresses a deep, subconscious sensibility of a oneness with nature fractured by the mistaken belief that we are somehow different or above nature. Wilson explores this combination of innate, instinctive sensibilities and cultural evolution through the symbol of the snake.

Snakes, he says, cause sickness and death in primates and other mammals. This is manifested in the behaviours of primates, where a powerful, instinctive fear is combined with a necessary fascination. Thus, the instinctive response is not to run from the snake but to observe closely until the danger has passed. This long-developed survival strategy of fear and fascination has moved from the instinctual to the cultural and is manifested in many religious and mythic contexts. It has become what Jung described as an archetype, present in our myths, symbols, dreams and phobias. [10]

Thus, nature is not only the setting in which our innate, instinctive responses are formed; it is also the backdrop to our cultural evolution. We might argue that we cannot make sense of what we are and what we have become, when we are separated from nature.

In his influential book, *Last Child in the Woods*, Richard Louv makes the same observations. He coined the phrase 'nature deficit disorder', not so much to identify an actual medical condition (he denied that was ever his intent), but to lament the loss of a whole realm of experience that enriched his own childhood and past generations of Americans. Nonetheless, the damage to our children is real and he relates nature deficit disorder to attention-deficit hyperactivity disorder (ADHD), stress, depression and anxiety, not to mention childhood obesity.[11]

Sue Palmer, author of *Toxic Childhood, How the Modern World is Damaging our Children and What We Can Do About It*, says that boys in particular need the play opportunities and the rough-and-tumble of wild spaces and this need for nature is hard-wired.

"Boys have a deep biological need to be out and about. According to evolutionary biologists, the brains of newborn human babies haven't changed significantly since Cro-Magnon times, so infant males are still born with the genetic encoding of Stone Age hunters. As they grow, their bodies yearn to rehearse this masculine role: they need to run across fields, clamber through undergrowth, fashion tools and weapons, push boundaries, take risks. If they don't fulfill these needs, they're likely to suffer in terms of development – physically, emotionally, socially, cognitively." [12]

If you work with children outdoors you know all this. Younger children constantly demonstrate a fascination with natural things. Just watch what happens when a creepy-crawly makes an appearance when you're planting bulbs with a reception class. Playing in an unkempt and overgrown patch of garden, exploring a wood, the textures of sand, shell and stone on a beach, the fascination with mud, sticks, hedgehogs and rabbits, making dens, all exert a deep fascination with children. There are exceptions to biophilia. I have also observed children who are fearful of dirt and the uncertainty of the woods or what lies under the earth and are disgusted by creepy-crawly things. We might call this biophobia – where clean, scrubbed and over-protected children are taught to avoid 'germs' and anything unfamiliar in the same way that stories like 'Hansel and Gretel' were used to warn past generations of children about the dangers that lurked in the forest.

William Bird[13] argues that the harm done to children deprived of contact with nature can be life long, resulting in what he describes as an "extinction of experience". The adult ability to enjoy natural environments is conditioned by childhood experience. Depriving children of the magical experiences of play in woodland and other natural spaces may be depriving them of the deep satisfaction of immersion in nature for the rest of their lives.

A deep experience of natural environments, on the other hand, provides the child with "a source of independence and inner strength that can be drawn upon during stressful situations for the rest of their life."[14]

SPIRITUAL GROWTH

In 2005 we began work on 'The 6 Schools Project', a programme of experimental work to explore the relationship between emotional well-being and spiritual practice in several local schools. Our method was to observe and record the impact on a child's perceived sense of wellness following spiritual exercises drawn from the great religious traditions. The spiritual exercises included periods of stillness, meditation, basic yoga and reflection.

At the same time we were supporting Forest School in our local area and began making observations of Forest School sessions. Out of our observations and practice both in and out of the classroom, we came to the conclusion that childrens' spiritual development is more readily nurtured outdoors.[15]

Despite the fact that 'spiritual development' is enshrined in the opening lines of the UK National Curriculum, the educational inspectorate have yet to come up with a satisfactory definition of what they mean by 'spiritual development'. Too often, educationalists have described it as some kind of intellectual quest for meaning that belies the actual experiences of most young people. 'Spiritual development', for most of us, is not about being able to express our angst about the meaning of life in a vast and impersonal universe. It lies in the depth of our relationships – being at peace with ourselves, learning to love others, caring for our world and finding meaning in purpose and fulfillment.

In his PhD thesis on spiritual health, John W. Fisher[16] describes spiritual wellness in terms of relationships. He identifies four categories. These are relationships with self, relationships with others, relationship with the environment, and our relationship with the transcendent.[17] According to Fisher, spiritual wellness manifests in the extent to which people live in harmony with themselves (self-esteem, fulfillment, purpose), their relationship with others (belonging, caring, shared purpose) and the environment (caring for the natural world, a sense of being immersed in it and inspired by it).

Fisher points out that the Western spiritual tradition has neglected the environmental aspect of spirituality. Western spirituality has often manifested an ambivalent, even negative attitude to Nature. God is described as revealing himself through Philosophy and Revelation, not the natural world. Western Christianity regarded Nature as a kind of necessary evil, born out of our sinful nature. The Gnostics went so far as to regard Nature as the work of the Devil. Our spiritual relationship with the natural world is something we are having to re-learn from indigenous peoples and has become a core feature of alternative spiritualities in the developed world.[18] It is through immersion in Nature that we, and particularly children, gain true insightfulness into the transcendent. When children are absorbed in studying the richness and variety of life in the school pond or the bug-box, it is their souls that are being fed, as well as their scientific awareness.

David Hay[19] states that a deepening awareness of their relationship with the 'other' has the potential to provide children with the kind of peak experiences that can inspire them through life. It is this heightened sense of experience – the deep forest, the mountain top, the sunrise and the gathering storm that lies at the heart of many so-called religious experiences.

For Hay, spiritual development, in terms of connectedness, has a vital role to play in a child's moral development. Positive relationships generate the emotional force that underpins moral outlook and behaviour. Connecting with Nature produces an ethical response in terms of a desire to care for the environments that give us joy. Emotional indifference (disconnection), on the other hand, can produce a careless or even destructive attitude to the environment.

Out of this emerges a theory of spiritual development where spiritual and emotional wellness (the goal of spiritual development) is rooted in the quality of our relationships with each other and the natural world. In a community where shared spiritual values are strong (and this is not the same as shared religious beliefs), individuals thrive. The values of social cohesion and environmental responsibility implicit in this model are increasingly being recognized, including the shift of emphasis in the teaching of R.E. in UK schools to the promotion of shared values, mutual understanding and community cohesion.[20]

 "A natural environment can strengthen the community by increasing the amount of contact people have outdoors. The natural environment is inclusive of all ages, which helps to engage all parts of a community. A sense of place describes an attachment to a place that is an important part of someone's sense of identity and creates a feeling of belonging. The natural environment has a strong influence on peoples' relationship with place, and is consistently stated as their preferred place. The natural environment is therefore important in creating a sense of belonging and identity...."[21]

'FLOW' AND SPIRITUAL WELLNESS. Professor Csikszentmihalyi[22] argues that tasks in which we become completely absorbed can produce a kind of ecstasy. He uses the term 'flow' to describe the experience. Flow is the creative ecstasy of the musician or sculptor. It is the heart of all the great martial arts traditions where single-mindedness and focus is the key to success. Flow is absorption, where we are oblivious to distraction and become lost in the activity. At the higher levels of engagement we can become unconscious of the more mundane aspects of what we are doing such that our brains are able to focus entirely on the creative dimension.

Flow can be compared with the Buddhist experience of *no self*. Through deep meditation we may briefly experience the disappearance of self, a brief extinguishing of the ego. In this state it is possible to experience ecstasy, a glimpse of nirvana, if you like. Equally, with true absorption we experience a falling away of the ego. I become the task and Chris Trwoga, as an ego, has become the hands and eyes that mould the clay. And when the sculpture is complete so am I complete. In considering what creativity means we might distinguish between the actor who becomes the character in the play and the celebrity who sees all creativity as a form of self-promotion.

The attainment of mindfulness or 'flow' is supported by outdoor environments, particularly for vulnerable youngsters. Some recent work I did with a group of Year 7 boys might suffice as an example. The occasion was a Forest School day for a group of young teenagers with behaviour management issues. By early afternoon, they had made a most creditable and serviceable trestle table from timber harvested that morning. They had stuck at the task for more than 4 hours without a break.

These were youngsters who would struggle to stay focused on a task for 10 minutes together in the classroom.

Spirituality is about authentic engagement with others. It is something we do with others and not through others. Children grow spiritually and emotionally through personal experience, not the vicarious experience of philosophical narrative or the cyber-experience of the computer. It elicits the kind of knowing that can only come through first-hand experience.

And what about the transcendent? Through deep engagement with the world children have the capacity to be intrigued, fascinated, awed by little things – unusual insects, the veins of a leaf, the structure of a snowflake To know what snow is a child touches, tastes, handles, shapes into snowballs or snowmen, looks at a snowflake through a magnifying glass, watches the snow fall and feels the cold. The child experiences snow. The child comes to understand snow as a personal perception. The child connects to snow and through snow with the deeper nature of things. And the child morally engages with snow in deciding when and if to lob the snowball at the unsuspecting passer-by!

Defining spiritual wellness in terms of the nature and depth of our relationships with self, other, the natural world and the Cosmos, provides a pedagogy for spiritual development. It enables us to identify approaches to working with children that promote relationality.

We look, therefore, to activities that celebrate common purpose and common values. The ideal approach will serve to connect children not just with each other but with their environment. One strategy that expresses this pedagogy is our work with labyrinths, where children are brought together to create sacred space in a natural setting, whilst making a gift to the whole community.

Natural settings have a marvelous capacity to help children enjoy being children again. It does this in innumerable subtle ways. Dress codes vanish away beneath the waterproofs and the muddiness. The structures that reinforce behavioural conformity are gone, and relationships become more fluid and natural. One of my first recollections of observing young teenagers doing Forest School was the return to childhood forms of play: girls on an improvised see-saw, boys on a swing, games of hide-and-seek – doing stuff that would be seriously uncool anywhere else. Children become absorbed in their environment and their activities. Self-expression shifts from body image to the work of their hands.

For kids, particularly young children, spirituality is about doing stuff that helps them feel better. They feel better because they're connected and absorbed. It's about affective learning. Here, in this space, I'm engaged with my friends and teachers, we're doing stuff that lets me express myself and my creativity and I know that I'm helping others. I don't need to analyze whether or not I'm better. In this moment I know I'm well.

In enabling joyfulness, celebration, connection with nature and creativity a school opens the door to a sense of purpose, love and immersion in life that is the foundation for an enduring sense of purpose. Relational spirituality is outward looking and shifts the pedagogy away from the sterile, inward-looking 'quest for personal meaning' towards an outward-looking, communal sense of shared values and purpose.

COMBATING SEDENTARY LIFESTYLES

Life in school tends to reflect life in the wider world. As working environments and entertainment become screen based, so has education. Schools are proud of their serried rows of computer terminals. Companies working on computer-based learning programmes make their products attractive to children by designing them to replicate the formats of familiar computer games. The outdoor learning movement, popularized by the Learning Outside the Classroom Manifesto of 2006, is fighting against the tide. The level of disconnection with the world *out there* grows for all of us as our cyber lives become all-encompassing.

Why is it a problem?

Video game addiction was identified as a problem, particularly amongst males, as early as the late 1970s and early 1980s, with dependency also a major issue. [23] Those who demonstrate addictive tendencies do less well at school, show increased tendencies towards aggression and have problems with homework. There is evidence for social dysfunction, with gamers often socially marginalized as they find their online relationships more successful.

The growth of the video game is symptomatic of a general shift towards sedentary entertainment, learning and employment. Children don't play like they used to. In part, this is a consequence of parents being more fearful of their children playing outdoors than they once were. A child's opportunity and indeed ability to range independently in urban and non-urban environments has shrunk dramatically. In a much reported story released by the Daily Mail, one family's experience showed how the grandfather had ranged several miles on foot, unsupervised, to play, fish and go to school. The grandson in 2007 was limited to the immediate streets near his home - a range of 300 yards.[24]

The same applies for every aspect of a child's life. Busy parents deliver their children to school by car, where past generations might walk to and from school each day. There have been spasmodic attempts to reverse the trend, with 'walking bus' schemes, where parents organize to walk children to school in groups, but these have proved a fad, rather than a growing trend. And the problem is not confined to the UK. Health experts in the USA, Australia and many other developed countries express similar concerns. Urban lifestyles are also impacted by changes in housing conditions. Housing built since the 1970s often has unfenced front gardens and very small rear gardens. There has been a growing trend towards replacing grass with timber patios, gravel and decorative concrete slabs. Outdoor play equipment in the domestic setting limits imaginative play. Parks with play equipment are now considered spaces where responsible parents do not let their children play unsupervised.

For the past 3 years we have been supported by National Health Service Somerset, as part of their Healthy Schools project, to address some of these issues in schools. The focus is the endemic problem of obesity in children and the aim of our work was to encourage teachers to get children out of the classroom and mobile as much as possible. It was less of an issue with infants. Most schools have nurseries designed to encourage free play and movement between indoor and outdoor spaces. By the end of the primary stage the situation is very different. A mere 2 hours a week of physical activity from KS2 onwards is far from unusual. During the winter months a substantial proportion of children in UK schools have no significant outdoor activity, with school fields closed because they are deemed unsafe or out of condition.

The overall picture is a depressing one in which we are all complicit. The more that teaching and learning approaches are pushed into high tech realms the more schools reflect the home-based experiences of youngsters, where play and social interaction takes place through a screen. And whilst childrens' lifestyles become ever more sedentary we are told by the medical profession that the consequences in terms of obesity, incipient diabetes and circulatory diseases are life-long.

Sedentary lifestyles have significant impact on a child's ability to learn. Teachers and students have stressful lifestyles and may experience stress in a number of ways. One casualty is on our ability to learn and remember things. Stress produces significant hormone imbalances that affect the way our brains work. It becomes harder to concentrate when our adrenalin levels keep us in 'fight or flight' mode.

Physical exercise has immediate physiological benefits in promoting deep breathing and blood circulation. It has a calming effect by balancing adrenalin and endorphin levels and encouraging the manufacture of dopamine which is vital for learning. Dopamine also enhances goal directed behaviours and creativity.[25]

Being outdoors helps relieve stress even without the exercise. Scientific research demonstrates that for many people there is an immediate positive response to views of nature. The response causes a rapid reduction in stress as measured by a lowering of blood pressure, muscle tension and pulse rate, usually within minutes of entering the natural space. Natural environments also help restore our ability to concentrate and to learn. In work environments full of distractions (think of the average classroom full of teenagers) there is concentration fatigue from having to work continually at blocking out the 101 things going on in the room that are crying out for our attention. Nature provides an effective restorative environment. Research indicates that even looking at a natural landscape can help our brain resume direct attention. [26]

One hardly needs the work of a scientist to demonstrate this. Every teacher knows that youngsters confined to the school building through extended periods of bad weather become excitable, unsettled and much tougher to teach. And the hour a week of P.E. doesn't necessarily help. My own experiences of supervising P.E. lessons in the secondary context brought the point home. Often sandwiched between two classroom based lessons, P.E. involves a dash to locate P.E. kit and then across the school to the changing rooms. A 50 minute P.E. session was rarely more than 30 minutes of actual sport allowing for movement from the classroom, changing and sorting out of P.E. equipment. There was no warming down at the end of the session, but another quick change (without a shower because there wasn't time), followed by a dash to the other end of the school for a period of French or Maths.

Every school has a duty to its children and young people to quantify the time they spend engaged in physically demanding activities. They also need to quantify the amount of time that children and young people spend in front of screens. Learning outdoors should not be an occasional treat, alongside an hour a week of games or P.E., but an integral entitlement of not less than 20% of all curriculum time.

IMPROVING THE LEARNING ENVIRONMENT

"Children learn better in the environment that best suits the learning activity"

As a child I experienced an essentially Victorian learning environment. We sat at fixed oak topped, iron-framed desks, complete with ink pot. Teacher sat at a raised desk at the front and we spent a great deal of time copying down information from the chalkboard. The cane sat astride teacher's desk as an ever-present reminder of the need for diligence and good behaviour. Mine was a town centre school, built in the shadow of cotton mills and a nearby brewery. The heady smell of hops was a regular distraction and we walked home on winter's evenings along cobble streets illuminated with gaslights. Yes, that was education in a northern mill town in the early 1960s. I still have a great fondness for our querky heritage of Victorian school buildings of which thousands survive across the country. I am less fond of the dreary flat-roofed, multi-story, office-building type schools that are usually less child-friendly than their single storey Victorian counterparts. I digress.

The classroom is a box. The subject-based curriculum is a collection of boxes. Information is stored in boxes. We keep our teaching artefacts in boxes. Interactive whiteboards and computers do not mark a learning revolution but a technological advance that brings threats as well as opportunities. One of the threats of computers, as we indicated above, is that learning becomes an ever more sedentary. They may make our classrooms look high-tech but they don't make classrooms any less of a two-dimensional commodity. Movement in a classroom is necessarily confined and the physicality of the learning experience limited.

On teaching training courses we are told about learning styles. One of the better known models proposes that children have a preferred learning style. Some children are auditory learners, others aural (listeners), others visual or kinaesthetic learners. Much is made of the problems we create for children if our teaching focuses too intensively on one learning style – too much talk, for example, or two much visual stuff. Children become more effective learners if their particular learning style is identified and catered for through personalized learning approaches.[27]

The whole concept of individual learning styles has been questioned by some educationalists, including the neuroscientist, Baroness Greenfield.[28] The arguments against the rigid application of personalized learning styles are numerous, but two in particular demand our attention.

Firstly, topics should be taught in the learning style that suits the required skills and the lesson content. If, for example, we are teaching children to recognize the shapes of countries and continents, the teaching style needs to be predominantly visual. The teaching style adopted by a teacher, is therefore topic dependent to a significant degree. In that sense, the teacher needs to consider the context of each curriculum theme or topic and to choose the learning setting most likely to provide the appropriate stimulus. Do we teach children to read maps indoors or outdoors?

Secondly, the idea of separating children into different types of learners is problematic, given the many variables that impact on a child's receptivity for learning. What is important is to recognize the capacity of the learning environment to stimulate and motivate, and to have the adaptability to meet the learning needs both of individuals and the group. Learning is about stimulation and about gaining knowledge and skills through all the senses. Photographs can help us interpret a map, but this is still partial experience and partial knowledge. To move through a landscape using a map is to truly understand what a map can tell us.[29]

The outdoors offers greater opportunities to develop learning skills. Well-constructed outdoor tasks allow for students to experiment, take risks, tolerate failure in an individual or group context, as well as to approach practical problems from a range of different perspectives. Most of the activities in this book are collaborative, requiring a pooling and sharing of skills within a group. Success is dependent on structured discussion, followed by decision-making based on shared information. Outdoor learning activities are generally physical, with three-dimensional outcomes that demonstrably work or don't work. As such they also provide transparent opportunities for reflection, both of the process and of the outcomes.

Children need stimulation through all the senses and to learn through real, physical engagement with the world. Teachers fret about the development of gross motor skills in infants. As Forest School leaders, we fret about the fact that some teenagers are handling basic craft tools for the first time when they come to us. All children are auditory, visual and kinaesthetic learners because their brains are designed to work in three-dimensional environments and where the skills they learn transform materials and physical space. We're back to heredity. The classroom doesn't figure in our evolutionary history.

Schemas. Some infant schools use schemas to support infant learning development. The schema concept is that infants demonstrate patterns of learning/play behaviours that can be readily identified. These behaviours include trajectory (throwing things), transporting (moving objects about), enclosure (e.g. den-building), enveloping (covering or hiding), rotation (circular and swinging movements) and connection (linking things and recognizing similarities). Natural, outdoor play environments, not only extend the opportunities for children to home in on the play opportunities that suit their current needs, but provide broader opportunities for imaginative play and skills development. A pile of sticks and pieces of tarpaulin do not carry the pre-determined play forms of toys or playground equipment manufactured by adults. The trunk of a fallen tree, for example, might be a bridge to cross, a shelter, a horse or a space rocket.[30]

In the final analysis, learning outdoors is about providing balance. Natural environments offer a canvas on which children can manifest wellness and spiritual growth. They offer opportunities to release energy, be creative, learn 'in the round' and to be still and reflective away from the computerized drivers of urban life. Children have manifold opportunities to develop their social and co-operative skills in environments that allow for greater freedom of movement, action and experience.

PRACTICAL MATTERS

Risk, Safety Routines, Clothing, Materials, Tools, the Cost.

All the activities and projects in this book have been developed directly with children and young people. Stuff we tried that doesn't work isn't in the book. Stuff that does work has been adapted and refined by watching the kids do the activities.

Activities for all ages. You will notice that there are few references to age or key stages in our activity descriptions. The decision not to divide this book up into activities for five-year-olds and activities for thirteen-year-olds is based on our experience of working right across the age range. We like the idea that everyone, regardless of age or ability, has something they can contribute to the building of a labyrinth or the digging of a pond. For example, we have made seven circuit rope labyrinths with thirteen-year-olds and we have made them with seven-year-olds. We also make them on weekend courses with adults. The seven-year-olds generally need plenty of support and guidance (but still do all the making) and thirteen-year-olds can often be left to figure it all out for themselves. Adults may experience the whole task as a spiritual exercise. The task is the same – but the learning outcomes are different. Teachers know their kids best and will be able to select and adapt activities to suit their groups. This doesn't apply to every activity in this book, but we like to think that the majority of activities can be accessed at some level. If not, infants can enjoy using a mill race or a shaduf and learn things from it, even if it has been constructed by older children in the school.

Children, construction and tools. Many of the activities described in the book involve basic construction work and the use of a range of tools, some of them sharp.

You may well be saying: "I don't have these skills to make these things myself. I'm not qualified to do sawing with children. We don't have the tools or materials in school. This isn't for me."

I will be the first to say that teachers must work within their competences and experience. It helps a great deal to have a member of staff who can provide the experience, support and guidance, in the safe management of groups using tools. It doesn't take a lot, nor need cost the earth. A single, trained and experienced Forest School coordinator on a school team can support the delivery of every activity in this book.

It's about pooling experience across school staff, in-house training, supportive school policies, practice, confidence and clear guidelines and procedures. It is also about individual members of staff bringing together sets of materials and adding them to the pool of available resources within the school. A set of 40 or 50 pre-cut hazel poles, a bundle of withies, a bale of 2 ply string, a couple of rubber mallets and some safety scissors costs less that £100, takes an hour to order online and provides all the materials you need for the majority of construction tasks in this book. As for experience, many of these projects began life in my own back garden, as I tried things out before inflicting them on the kids.

If you are still uncomfortable with the thought of putting sharp tools and children together, it is still possible to delivery many of these activities without anything nastier than a pair of safety scissors. In the shaduf making or shelter building activities, for example, we often use pre-sawn poles. There is still all the teamwork, problem-solving and construction issues to deal with but children need not handle anything sharper than a rubber mallet.

The risk versus benefit debate. A couple of summers ago, I observed an Information Technology lesson, where they were in the last stages of planning a barbeque. They had worked out the costings on spreadsheets, and designed menu cards and invitations on a publishing package. It was June and we were enjoying a spell of excellent weather. I asked the teacher when the barbeque was taking place. She told me she had decided, in consultation with her head of department, that to run a barbeque was too "risky". I asked what she meant by "risky"? What followed was a list of potential accidents. Children burning themselves, food poisoning, cuts from sharp cutlery, allergic reactions, insanitary conditions in the school garden. Was she correct in her decision?

The same school took youngsters to Italy every year for a skiing holiday. There had been skiing accidents in the past involving broken limbs. There was the annual camp with the eleven-year-olds doing canoeing, abseiling and rock climbing. Why the different attitudes to risk in one school? You will know the answer. The trips to Italy and the annual camps were run by external providers. The school's risk management involved obtaining local authority consents, doing a pre-visit, satisfying themselves that the company offering the service were qualified to do so, were on the list of registered and approved providers of adventurous activities, and had a good reputation.

This pattern of buying in external providers of outdoor learning is repeated in schools across the UK. A plethora of companies have sprung up in the last decade to meet a rapidly growing need. Most of these companies provide excellent, well-tailored products. But they are expensive and schools are fortunate if parents are prepared to pay for expensive outdoor services much more than once or twice a year. Government research shows that the average parent already spends nearly £80 per year on school trips at primary level and just under £300 at secondary level.

The sad thing is that the use of external providers and the decline in teacher led outdoor learning has not arisen as a consequence of an increase in accidents. Yes, there have been a number of fatalities as a result of carelessness, ignorance or downright incompetence in the past quarter century, but they are statistically tiny. Guardian Education calculated the risk of a child dying on a school trip as 1 in 8,000,000 – slightly greater than the chance of being struck by lightning.[1] If you take out the tragedies where children have drowned, the odds become truly insignificant. It isn't about increases in deaths or serious injury. When you talk to schools and local authorities you discover that risk aversion has grown because of fear of litigation. I worked at a school several years ago where a single parent had successfully sued the school twice in as many years as a result of minor injuries to her accident prone daughter. These accidents happened in the classroom. Such stories send ripples of panic through the teaching community. But the reality is rather different.

In 2009 The Guardian obtained actual litigation figures for the UK. I quote from their article:

"Of the millions of individual school trips taken over the past 10 years in the 138 local authorities that responded to requests under the Freedom of Information Act, only 364 ended in legal action and in fewer than half of cases – 156 – were schools found to be culpable and ordered to pay compensation. Between 1998 and 2008 the total compensation paid out was £404,952, meaning on average local authority paid out just £293. 44 a year following problems on school trips."[2]

The article goes on to say that in a survey of teachers carried out by the Countryside Alliance, 76% of teachers felt the main barrier to venturing out of school was "concerns about health and safety."

The reality is there isn't a culture of litigation out there, but, to quote Beth Gardner of the Council for Learning Outside the Classroom, "a culture of fear". The problem has been compounded by some of the teaching unions advising their members against running trips and off-site activities.

Nonetheless, any activity involving additional risk needs justifying. Running an activity with very young children using steel spades and wheelbarrows can't be justified if the learning objectives can be met using plastic trowels and rubber buckets.

Let's return to our IT barbeque lesson with the class of twelve-year-olds.

The IT teacher doing the barbeque lesson argued against the barbeque from the point of view of risk. She could just as easily have said that her learning outcomes did not require the children to run the barbeque. Her course is about Information Technology, not lighting a barbeque or slicing onions safely. If it had been a Food Technology activity, the risk/benefit analysis would look very different – and, of course, the staff would be more likely to feel competent to manage the activity safely.

I will use the example of young children and bow saws. We use bow saws with children as young as 7. They work in teams of three and there will be an adult supervising a maximum of two teams. Although this produces a ratio of 1:6 there are only two bow saws in use at any one time and the methodology is such that children have to break with procedure in a highly visible way to put themselves or others at risk. Children grow enormously in confidence as a result of their experience, their gross motor skills improve in a very short space of time, as do their team skills and group co-ordination. I consider teaching young children to use saws safely well worth the residual risk.

We have had no children cut themselves with saws, having worked with literally thousands of children. Risk management should be such that accidents don't happen if procedures are followed. If accidents do happen and the procedure is being followed, then the procedure needs changing.

By comparison I have banned the use of tree swings in our wood. Observations showed that the risk of injury, though statistically slight (we had one slight concussion which prompted the ban), was potentially considerable. Use of the swing was a repetitive activity that may have been 'fun' but taught no more skills than could be acquired in a children's playground. It drew children's attention away from more valuable and creative forms of play. The risk, however slight, outweighed the benefits of children enjoying free play. In all cases you need to be able to justify risk, however slight, in terms of benefits, including learning outcomes.

Competence. In 2000, two schoolgirls, Hannah Black and Rochelle Cauvet, were swept to their deaths by a river in spate, whilst on a school field trip led by teachers. The local authority was prosecuted under the Health and Safety at Work Act. It is clear from the records that those leading the school party lacked awareness of the lethal risk posed by fast-flowing water that a canoeing or mountain walking qualification would have provided. Put simply, they lacked the competence to manage that type of activity safely. A badly managed road-crossing with a group of children, a disorganized digging party in a school garden, or allowing children to run wild in a wood all have the potential to cause serious, even fatal accidents.

Most local authorities and insurers now require that teachers leading adventurous activities off-site have appropriate qualifications and experience – a Forest School Leader's BTEC Level 3 certificate, for example, to work with children in woodland. The situation on-site for schools is far less defined, and individual teachers must refer to the established policies of their school with regard to outdoor activities. Our own guidance is that a teacher should be demonstrably competent on the basis of experience. Take lighting a fire as an example. If a teacher has worked alongside a Forest School Leader for a number of sessions, or has other relevant and demonstrable experience, observation of safe practice on a number of occasions by a designated person should be sufficient to determine competence. Schools need their own internal procedures based on best practice to verify competence – usually a formally qualified member of staff who can provide training to others and evaluate practice. Schools should consider the appointment of an Outdoor Education Adviser to provide support and guidance for on-site activities and to supplement the work of the Educational Visits Coordinator.

Risk Assessments. A risk assessment is a tool for identifying hazards and formulating strategies to minimize the risks they pose. Many authorities use an online system that provides a centralized approval mechanism, often through a point scoring mechanism. A risk assessment is also a working document that communicates the strategies to minimize risk to all participants in the activity. This includes the students as well as staff. Activity leaders should be visible in communicating the safety procedures. For example, if you are on a welly walk and your risk assessment requires a head count every ten minutes, do it visibly and vocally. If working with fire, the leader should remind other adults and the students of the required safety procedures each and every session, as well as indicating the location of the fire safety equipment. It gives students and staff confidence, is part of preparing youngsters for the world of work, and provides witnesses in the event of an incident that you have done your job.

Site Risk Assessments. The outdoors are an ever-changing environment, where weather, third party access, general wear and tear and unpredictable events like vandalism, make regular checks a must. Typically a site assessment includes tree health, vegetation checks (hazardous plants), condition of working materials, such as poles used for shelter building, surface conditions (grass wearing away, ground becoming hard or muddy, dangerous litter), pond edges, fencing, condition of any shelters and so on. By monitoring the outdoor learning environments in this way and producing a written record, it becomes possible to manage and maintain the sites on a basis of need. A site that has become muddy, for example, can be rested.

Safety Routines. Safety with groups of children is best ensured by routines that are fully understood and practiced without exception. Even with regular groups the introductory safety talk should take place at the start of every session – including, for example, reminding everyone of the 'Lost Child Procedure' with off-site activities. Other routines might include reminding students that the fire area is 'out of bounds' if an adult isn't present, even if no fire is burning. If we are using our fire area for Circle Time, for example, the safe entry and exit procedure is used whether or not the fire is lit. We have a blanket ban on children carrying sharp tools unless blades are covered. Children are taught the routine of asking for a tool and asking again for it to be taken from them. They are also taught to report an incorrectly discarded or placed tool, rather than deal with it themselves. That way they are involved in policing the safety procedures without being put at risk. All schools should have a Code of Practice that sets out the Outdoor Learning safety routines. Thus a common standard is practiced by all and can be communicated to the students without the challenge of inconsistency.

Dressing the part. You will probably be familiar with the outdoor learning mantra "there is no such thing as bad weather, only bad clothing". Often, the first barrier that a school has to overcome in pushing forward an outdoor learning policy is the recognition that learning outdoors takes place in all weathers. Dealing with challenging weather is an important part of the outdoor learning experience. With this in mind, schools may need to educate parents as well as staff, and make provision within schools for the use and storage of wellies and waterproofs. Personal experience teaches that training students in the rapid deployment of protective clothing is integral to outdoor learning. Reception teachers will know it can take twenty minutes to get a class of infants into wellies and waterproofs. It is, however, part of the learning process and great for developing gross motor skills.

We keep a stock of **safety helmets** as part of our clothing kit. Currently, they can be bought online for as little as £3 and store nicely in a large box. They are used with activities where there is enhanced risk of head injury. This might include the use of heavier poles for shelter construction, woodland activities involving removal of overhead branches, digging holes with steel spades and any work of head height and above. Again, the use of safety gear of this kind is great practice for a multitude of future working environments.

Many activities require the use of **gardening gloves**. We store them in sized class sets in flexible buckets. We use sturdy gardening gloves made of canvas and leather at around £3 per pair. Our standard rule is that hands must be gloved for handling wood, digging and sharp tool use.

Attitudes to safety clothing, overalls and wet weather gear are formed in youth. It is a depressing observation that so many children and young people do not possess suitable clothing for anything more than a trip to the shops. Waterproofs and overalls are unglamorous and it can be a struggle getting teenagers to wear protective clothing when they have not had the experience of their use at home or primary school. Covering up for rain isn't the only problem. In this sexualized age of boys leaving their underpants exposed to the rear and girls displaying too much midriff, youngsters working in woodland spaces run the risk of ticks, nettle rash, laceration from brambles, and bites from horseflies and mosquitoes. With Lime Disease in the ascendant, **overalls for youngsters** working in woodland and open countryside is a wise move. Part and parcel of encouraging both adults and young people to spend more time outdoors is re-discovering the role of clothing as protection instead of fashion statement. When this barrier is broken, children and young people can find clothing that allows them to get wet, scruffy and dirty a joyful and liberating experience.

Materials. Many of the activities in this book require little more than bundles of sticks or poles and a ball of string. Our stock-in-trade material for construction activities are long, straight hazel poles, green withies (willow sticks) and elder. If you don't have the wherewithal to get hold of these things many of the activities in this book won't be open to you. You will need, as a school, to stock up. It makes a huge difference to planning outdoor learning knowing you've got several dozen hazel poles, bundles of withies, bales of string, lots of rope and all the tools you need for your outdoor learning stored in the school lock-up. Even better if you've got a designated outdoor learning area set up and ready.

But you tell me that you work in an inner city school and these materials just aren't available. We get through too many poles to source them from our own wood or beg them from a local Woodland Trust. Like everything else, we buy online. Type in 'Willow Fencing' or 'Willow Hurdles' and look for a supplier that makes willow fencing. Contact your nearest supplier and ask if they can supply hazel poles and willow withies. Someone will say yes, particularly if you explain you are a school. Don't expect to get them for free - it can make re-ordering embarrassing - but ask about discounts, or, more importantly, free delivery. We currently pay £50 for a hundred good straight hazel poles averaging 3 metres in length and 3 cms in diameter, and £15 for a bundle of a hundred 2 metre long willow withies. This may sound expensive but these materials can be used again and again. Making mini-structures with withies is great fun and your 100 withies or hazel sticks will last a couple of years before they become too brittle to use.

Our staple for sawing activities with infants and very young children is elder. Elder has the quality of being easy to cut with a mini hacksaw and has a soft pith centre that can be pushed out with a steel tent peg, resulting in a bead, wheel or tube for a whistle or bug hotel. The problem nowadays is finding the stuff. This is a plant that no one grows commercially and most people regard as an unpleasant weed that refuses to die. It is generally found in hedgerows, and if you have parents with gardens it is always worthwhile putting out an appeal. Otherwise contact parks departments or local landowners. Believe me, people are only too glad to get rid of the stuff or invite you in to prune it out of their hedgerows.

Knowing you have these materials to hand is half the battle. Keeping them in accessible order is the other half of the battle. Tie poles and withies tightly into bundles and store upright or on shelves or racks. If there isn't the space for standing materials, use blocks of wood or a pallet to get them off the floor. An airy, draughty store is better than an enclosed, damp space. Wood contains a great deal of moisture and will make everything in a badly aired space damp.

Kids love sawing and it is too easy to see your entire stock of poles reduced to firewood in a matter of weeks. We always utilize students in cutting timber to length, but once cut, the saws disappear to conserve supplies. We have our hazel poles tied up in shaduf kits, ballista kits, travois kits, tipi kits and so on. That way students can come to the activity area and with nothing more than rubber mallet, string and scissors and do some very complicated structure building in the space of a single lesson. The other advantage of limiting sharp tool use is that fewer adults are needed to supervise the activity.

Rope and string. We buy rope and string online in bulk. Having someone in school to coordinate purchase of materials is the sensible way to manage this. A 300 metre bale of two-ply sisal twine costs £7 online and we buy 10 bales per annum in a single purchase. A 220 metre coil of 14mm sisal rope will cost about £85 and is enough to make two rope bridge kits and leave you with lots over for making shelters. Buying string or rope from your local D.I.Y. store will cost you several times as much. A tangled rope is unusable, so storing ropes properly is vital and activity leaders may need training in the various methods of coiling ropes. We manage our ropes by using empty garden hose reels bought on Ebay

to make it possible for children to lay out and wind in ropes with far less risk of tangling. The message is to solve the problem before you run the activity with kids. I've seen rope bridge activities ruined by having youngsters attempt to unpick a messy coil of rope left by a previous group. Don't be afraid to allocate a significant proportion of activity time for tidying up ropes. It's part of the learning process and essential for successful multiple use of your outdoor learning equipment.

Tools. Having the right tools and clear, documented procedures for their use is vital to safety. You will find regular reference in the activities to 'safety knives' and 'safety scissors'. By 'safety', we usually mean tools without a blade capable of causing a puncture wound. We use Opinel No. 7 round-tipped safety knives with a blade-locking collar (available online at around £10). Our bill hooks also have any pointed tips ground away to make them safer to use. Ensuring that your tool kit is free of tools capable of inflicting deep puncture wounds is important. A student may lacerate themselves, producing a cut that bleeds heavily. A tool with a sharp point, on the other hand, can pierce a major blood vessel or vital organ. A laceration can usually be dealt with by good first aid. It's about stopping the blood flow. A deep puncture wound involves the complication of internal bleeding and may be beyond the capacity of an ordinary first-aider to tackle.

This does not mean the working edge of a knife or saw should be blunt. The working edge of every tool should be maintained in optimum condition. A student struggling with a blunt knife or a saw with the teeth in need of sharpening or re-setting is more likely to injure themselves than someone using a well-maintained tool. Working edges should be kept free of rust, oiled regularly and kept covered when not in actual use. A bow saw blade cover, for example, should be replaced the moment the saw is no longer in use.

Tools that suit little hands. I have already mentioned that I much prefer trowels and buckets with infants, rather than spades. It's easier for the kids and much more fun. The same applies to little saws. We introduce children to sawing activities with mini hacksaws. Their first activity is always bead making. The mini hacksaw needs to be fitted with a wood-sawing blade (they are usually sold with a metal-cutting blade) and should have a handle that is similar in shape to that of a tenon saw. Don't get the junior saws with the in-line steel handles. They're uncomfortable and much harder for infants to use. The mini hacksaws can be bought for around £5 each. A packet of 10 wood-sawing blades can be bought for just under £2.

Measuring things. Many of these activities require some basic maths and tools for measuring. One basic piece of kit which we use a lot is the 'right angle' or 'square'. We make these in two sizes. The smaller consists of a one metre piece of 2 x 1 timber attached to a 50cm piece of 2 by 1 to form a right angle. The two pieces are reinforced by a corner brace to make what looks like a miniature gallows. They are illustrated in the labyrinth chapter. The larger size is 1.5 metres by 75cms. They cost a couple of pounds in materials each and a competent D.I.Y. person can make one in 20 minutes. We have a stock of 8 to cope with large group activities, but 4 is enough for a typical school situation. Other measuring is done with a rope taped at 1 metre intervals, and a standard 25metre tape.

The Cost. I haven't done the adding up, but I guess by the time you have bought class sets of wellies and waterproofs, and all tools and materials it is into four figures and looking scary. Unless you are very fortunate you will need to prioritize and build your provision over time. Nonetheless, the whole lot, including a couple of class sets of waterproofs, will not come to much more than the cost of a couple of decent computers or a single weekend residential for a dozen kids. There are lots of outdoor activities that require minimal materials and don't require specialist training.

The real sticking point is the confidence and the will to do it.

His favourite occupation seemed to be strolling outdoors by himself, looking at the grass, the trees, the flowers, the vistas of light, the varying aspects of the sky, and listening to the birds, the crickets, the tree frogs, and all the hundreds of natural sounds. It was evident that these things gave him a pleasure far beyond what they give to ordinary people. It had not occurred to me that any one could derive so much absolute happiness from nature as he did.

Dr. Bucke, describing the poet, Walt Whitman[1]

1. SPECIAL PLACES

Talking about special space, Finding my special space, Memory bag, Personal shrine, A special home, Making a tipi, Celebration focal point, A quiet space outdoors, Visiting places of worship, Living willow garden structure.

We shape our buildings; thereafter they shape us.
Winston Churchill

The word *temenos* was used by the Greeks to describe those special places where the gods feel close. Originally, these places were natural – mountains, high cliffs, deep caves. Over time men learned to create space to evoke the deep and special feelings Rudolf Otto referred to as the *numinous*. Stone circles, burial mounds, the temples of Karnak, the Parthenon, Benares and Ankor Wat manifest form and space designed to invoke deep feelings and responses.

The layering of myth and history in the landscape also sets space apart as special or sacred. Aboriginal sacred sites, for example – perhaps the most famous being Uluru - are layered with stories of the Dreamtime. To use the phrase adopted by Christopher Tilley, they become sedimented with meaning. It is the investment of, myth, memory and experience that makes space special.[2]

At the domestic level, we adapt our surroundings, not only for utility and comfort but to create a space that feeds our need for security, belonging, ownership and identity. The spaces we make can be an expression of our sense of who we are. This applies particularly to sacred space, which expresses deeper feelings about who we are as individuals and communities.

At the same time, most of us, at some time or another, experience working and living in space that feels cold, friendless, even hostile. I reflect back to my university days working in the brutalist architecture of 1960s modernism or walking through the high-rises of Moss Side and Hume in my native Manchester. Some of the schools I worked in during the 1970s and early 1980s, when cash-strapped local authorities left schools ill-maintained and undecorated for years on end, were cheerless spaces to work in.

Special spaces don't have to be 'sacred' in any formal sense. What matters is that they are special to us. It can be a special walk or view – or it can be a place that we share with friends, to celebrate, to remember, to have fun. Special spaces live in the memory as somewhere we can visit in our imagination and find peace.

Last year we made tipis with children at a Somerset primary school. They were made outdoors and designed for outdoor use. Visiting the school recently, we discovered they had been in almost continuous use – indoors – having been set up in various classrooms or the school hall to provide special space for story-telling and Circle activities. They had become special space.

It is vital that children and young people have a stake in their environment. They feel more connected with landscape and community for having played some role in shaping the spaces in which they live and work and welcome opportunities to transform and take ownership of space, be it a bedroom, classroom wall, or the colour schemes used in a school environment. It applies particularly to transforming outdoor spaces and investing energy in permanent features, such as the planting of trees.

By providing students with an opportunity to engage physically and experientially with their landscape, to invest in 'altering the earth' we enable them to experience meaning and value in that relationship with form, structure and landscape. This principle is most clearly expressed in our work with labyrinths (see the special chapters on labyrinths and their use).

Young People and Sacred Space. Sacred space can be a difficult concept to explain to children – although many will identify with the idea that there are spaces in their school or neighbourhood where they feel safe or peaceful, or where they prefer to play.

The ideas we might wish to discuss with our students can be summarized as follows: -

— Understanding that some spaces (or places) can give rise to special feelings.

— That we can alter space to express how we feel, to invoke memory or express what we believe.

— That spaces can invoke the full range of feelings (happy, fearful, alone, peaceful, safe etc).

— There are spaces where we feel we belong.

— A place may be special for a while – say for a festival or in the aftermath of a death, and cease to be special afterwards.

— Some spaces have become special to millions of people and have been so for thousands of years (Jerusalem, Makkah, the Ganges –Yamuna confluence, Stonehenge).

— The importance of respect for the special spaces of others because of the powerful feelings they evoke.

These are some of the functions of sacred/special spaces:

A Place to be Alone. A space for 'time out'. It can help to have a place where we know we can be alone. Where do we go to get away from the things that make us angry or sad – at least for a while? Do you have a space like this in your life? Is there a space in the school like this?

A Quiet Place. Sometimes it helps to be quiet. A place without ipods, mobile phones and too much chat. Being quiet helps us be calm and think. It can help us to see things more clearly when we are away from the influence of others. What quiet places do you know? How do you feel about silence or just being with natural sounds?

A Place of Stillness. A place of stillness, particularly when the world is such a busy and restless place, can be a real help. Being still in our bodies can help our minds to become still. A place of stillness helps us to reflect. We can't always be doing.

A Place for Sharing. We share best when we are encouraged to listen. The pace of talk is slow and we try to say things that mean something instead of chatting about nothing in particular. Most of all, we try to be honest. If we can give some kind words, some encouragement, even love, so much the better.

A Place for Connecting and Belonging. Special places can be natural spaces. Sometimes it is good to feel grass, or sand, or dirt – even mud – between our toes. It reminds us of who we are and where we come from. Ancient peoples, such as the Aborigines of Australia or Native Americans feel very close to the natural world. They understand that we are part of Nature, not the owners of it. Sometimes a place is so special it lives long in our memory. We can travel to it in our daydreams and it helps us find a bit of happiness on a bad day.

A Place for Celebration. We need somewhere special to celebrate the big moments in life, in particular, the rites of passage – birth, coming of age, marriage and death. Increasingly, people are using spaces for ceremony that are not traditional places of worship. Getting married on a beach, for example. A school or local community decorate a particular space to celebrate a special event – an important birthday, national event or a traditional festival.

A Place of Remembrance. Someone is killed in a road accident. Shortly afterwards flowers appear at the roadside. Mementoes appear too. Cuddly toys for a child, a team shirt for a football supporter. It has become a familiar sight on our roadsides. The space becomes a shrine. For a time it is sacred space. Students will sometimes create sacred space unprompted. Some children, for example, will create their own ritual for the burial of a loved pet and create a shrine thereafter.

A Place to talk to God. Believers experience God in different ways. As a feeling or an emotion it might be the sense there is something out there that is special, creative, powerful and good. Someone or something that cares for us and protects us and listens to us. These experiences rarely come in busy, noisy places. For many it is the peace of a garden, a stormy sea, a high mountain or the halls of a great temple that will help them speak to God and feel the divine presence.

1.1 Talking About Special Space
– Bringing In The Outdoors

Aim. To encourage students to talk about how they feel and respond to different kinds of space.

In Brief. Students study pictures of landscapes and talk about which pictures they like best and why.

What you will need:

Photos of different places - e.g. an empty beach, a quiet country lane, a path through a wood, a park with play areas, a town centre square, a riverside that might be used for fishing, a modern cityscape, a mountain landscape etc.

Drawing pins / blue tack.

Method.

1. Give each image a suitable name, such as 'Woodland Walk' or 'A Quiet Beach'.

2. Pin your images up around the room.

3. Divide the students into groups and give them time to look at the images.

4. Ask each student to choose the picture that most appeals to them and talk about it in their groups.

5. Discuss how their chosen image makes them feel.

6. Why did they choose that location and not others? If it is a wood, imagine the sound of birds, the scents of dead leaves and musty earth, the smell of flowers. Hear the birdsong. If it is a beach you can hear the sound of crashing waves and the call of seagulls - and there is always that special smell of the sea!

Reflection. Think about your favourite picture. Imagine walking into the scene. Perhaps there is a path to follow. Imagine yourself walking slowly, relaxing, breathing easy. What is the weather like? Imagine a warm, sunny day. Why not sit down and relax? Enjoy the warmth. For a few moments we will enjoy where we are in silence. We will use our imagination to listen to the sounds of our special place.

1.2 Finding My Special Space

Aim. To help students to be aware of their feelings about spaces that feel safe or help them feel peaceful or relaxed. To encourage the enjoyment of moments of quiet and be aware of the sights, sounds and smells around them.

In Brief. On a woodland or park walk, students locate a space that feels special to them and enjoy a few moments of quiet reflection.

What you will need:

Access to an outdoor space - e.g. a woodland park, school garden, churchyard, park or similar. The area needs to be sufficient to enable the students to be at a little distance from each other. *

Suitable clothing so that students will not feel uncomfortable during a few minutes of relative stillness.

This activity should not be attempted on a first visit to an unfamiliar place. It is best done after a couple of visits, when a place no longer feels strange, but is not yet completely familiar.

Method.

1. Explain to the group that they are going to find a 'special place' where they can listen to sounds and observe what goes by. Explain that we don't always see animals and birds because the noise we make scares them off. By being still and quiet in our own special place we may see and hear things that we would otherwise miss. What is most important is that they should feel comfortable and safe in the space.

2. Invite them to wander the chosen area and find a space that feels good to them. It should be a space away from other students and where they cannot make eye contact. They simply need to make a choice and be clear that they have a preference.

3. When they have found their space begin the period of silent observation; this can be themed to things like listening to birdsong, or observing cloud shapes. A special sound, such as the ringing of a small bell, can mark the begining . The time should end with the same sound.

4. Young students may find this difficult and even a bit scary to start off with. Accompanying adults should therefore be visible and the time limited to one or two minutes in the first instance. With older students a group can go to five minutes or even ten when weather and the mood of the group is right.

Reflection. Sit in a circle and share your experiences. Why did you choose your particular space? How did your space feel? What did you see and hear? Was it pleasant or hard to sit still on your own for a few minutes? Even if we don't always enjoy being on our own for a short period is it something we should do?

1.3 Medicine Pouch / Talisman

Aim. To enable students to connect with a special outdoor space when they are back in the classroom or at home.

In Brief. Students collect three small items that remind them of their special place and use them to create a talisman.

What you will need:

A small pouch - either made by the class or bought in (e.g. a cheap velvet jewellery bag.)
Access to an outdoor space - woodland or park is best.

Method.

1. Discuss the role of souvenirs and the part they play in our lives. Talk about special things the students have made, found or purchased that remind them of a special place. They could bring in a souvenir from home to share their experiences with their fellow students.

2. Explain that they are going to find something they could carry in their pocket that will remind them of a special place. Encourage them to think about small, distinctive pebbles, mollusc shells, fragments of dead wood etc. that somehow capture the spirit of the place where they will be.

3. Share your own special 'found' objects. For example, I have a small collection of what I call 'Dragon Sticks' that I share with students. They are pieces of dead wood, where there is a natural 'dragon face' or form visible in the wood.

4. Give students a small, clear, re-sealable bag to store their finds and head off to your chosen site. Aim to collect no more than four items. Encourage them to discuss their chosen items with their companions to support their choice and reinforce memory. When they have chosen their special items they should return one of the items (ideally something durable like a pebble) to the environment where they think they can find it again, perhaps tucked amongst the roots of a tree.

Reflection. Can you remember the exact spot where you found your objects? Can you describe the place? What about the object you left behind? Can you close your eyes and go to the place where you left it? Think about your special object and where you left it. Try to imagine you are there now.

Handle the items you brought back. Remember the things that made you choose them. Now share those thoughts with the person next to you. Place them in your special pouch and carry them with you. Use them to connect with your special place.

1.4 Personal Shrine

Aim. To explore ideas of individual significance and spirituality by making a portable shrine or memento box. To encourage the students to reflect on the things that are important to them.

In Brief. Students make a portable shrine, utilizing a small box or similar container and a display of special items.

What you will need:

A small cardboard box for each student - child size shoebox is ideal. *

Coloured crepe paper, newspaper, PVA mix.
Leaves, petals and other small gathered natural items.

A more ambitious shrine can be created with a timber frame or small wooden box.

Method.

1. Explain how a shrine can be made out of a collection of special mementoes, photographs, objects you find beautiful like feathers or crystals – in fact anything that makes you feel good or helps you deal with daily life. The collection can be things that remind them of something important or special - a pebble from the garden at home, a shell from a beach, leaves from a wood, a photograph etc. Students can be asked to articulate or share what they have brought.

2. The teacher can support the process by bringing in objects of their own to share with the group.

3. Once assembled the items are made into a small display by mounting them within the box.

4. Objects might be added to the collection for all sorts of reasons – feathers that represents flight or dreams, a small souvenir, a badge, an item of jewellery such as a friendship bracelet.

5. The shrine or icon may well be very personal and the child or young person may not wish to share the outcome with a group. It might be easier to share with a friend in a paired situation.

Reflection. Personal shrines are a way to show the sacred in our lives. As we collect the materials and images to make a shrine, as we paint and glue, insights arise. Assembling a shrine is an act of love. It can also be a prayer. Consider how your shrine is a miniature special place. Choose one item from your box to share with a friend. Tell them about where you found it or obtained it and what it means to you. How many of your objects are natural and how many are man-made? Which is your most important object and why?

1.5 Home

Aim. To explore the idea of dwellings as 'special space'. To celebrate diversity of lifestyle and to reflect on why people make the choices they do when they choose a place to live.

In Brief. Students explore a variety of images of homes from countries around the world to gain an insight into what they tell us about lifestyles and values.

What you will need:

A variety of photographic images or drawings of different types of dwelling. Laminate to pass round or on display boards. They should represent a range of cultures and lifestyles.

Suggesstions include:	
a typical 1930s semi-detached house	a southern African kraal
a terraced house	an Indonesian longhouse
Buckingham Palace	a straw bale eco-dwelling
a gypsy caravan	a rainforest tree house
a narrowboat or barge	a tipi or yurt,
	a Bedouin tent etc....

Method.

1. Discuss what it would be like to live in the different types of dwellings and how they might affect the way people live as a family, such as sharing a single space and very limited personal possessions. What about homes that have no electricity or homes that generate their own?

2. Discuss construction materials, decoration, significant household features such as clay oven or fire.

3. Ask students to find out more about the homes and lifestyles that interest them and write or draw creatively about what it would be like to live in such spaces.

Reflection. Think about your own family and the home in which you live. What is important to you about your home? Think about all the things a home provides. Some houses are far bigger than people need. Why do some people like big houses? Think about the kind of home that appeals to you the most. Why does it appeal to you?

1.6 Making a Tipi

Aim. To learn how to make a simple shelter and explore aspects of nomadic culture.

In Brief. Students use hazel poles and a tarpaulin to make a tipi (*see fig. 1.6*).

What you will need:

6 to 8 pupils (7 or 8 years-old onwards) . Ten 3m hazel poles around 3 – 5cm thick.

A 4 by 6m tarpaulin or canvas per tipi.
A rubber mallet. 12 tent pegs per tipi. 2 mini hacksaws (wood blades) if poles need trimming.

Measuring tape. A bale of sisal twine. A roll of carpet / gaffer tape. Pair of scissors.

Method.

1. Using twine, loosely tie the poles about 50cm from the top. Stand them up and spread out to form the conical tipi shape. Measure from the ground to where the poles are tied together (top of the cone) and add 10cms to your measurement.

2. Peg down the uncut tarpaulin flat to the ground. Check that the width of the tarpaulin is at least twice the distance measured from the ground to where the tipi poles are tied; e.g. if tipi is 2 metres high, the diameter of the semi-circle is 4 metres. Put a steel tent peg through the eyelet at the centre point of the tarpaulin edge (or the edge of the fabric if there is no eyelet).

3. Tie a marker pen to a piece of string and fix the string to the tent peg. Adjust the string length so that it reaches the near left hand corner of the tarpaulin. The pen and string can now be used as a giant compass to mark a semi-circle on the tarpaulin. Use strong scissors to cut out the semi circle.

4. To strengthen the cut edges turn over 2cm and staple. At regular intervals around the semi-circular edge of the tarp attach 12 neat squares of tape. This can be done front to back for extra strength. The holes for the tent pegs will be cut through this. Now make the holes. This is best done with a hole-punch. It can also be done with an eyelet maker (any hobby shop) – but ensure the eyelet is wide enough to take your string. Attach a loop of string to each of the eyelets.

5. Now use a 2 metre length of string attached to the centre of the straight edge of the tipi cover to haul it into place. Drape the cover round the pole frame to form the tipi and peg down.

6. The last task is to close the upper part of the front or entrance. This is done in the traditional way. Make 4 pairs of 2cms slits to the top front of the tipi opening. Thread an attractive stick through each of the pairs of slits. By winding string round each stick and pulling, the two flaps of the tipi will be pulled together. This will leave an opening wide enough to go in and out. Furnish interior with a square of tarp and bits of old carpet.

Reflection. Find out about the Plains Indians of America and how they lived in tipis. Discuss what it would be like to live in a temporary house that folds up and goes on a travois to be pulled by horses or human energy. People use tipis today for ceremonies, events and holidays. What makes tipis feel special? Discuss what it feels like inside the tipi - both alone and with friends.

Fig 1.6   Building a Tipi

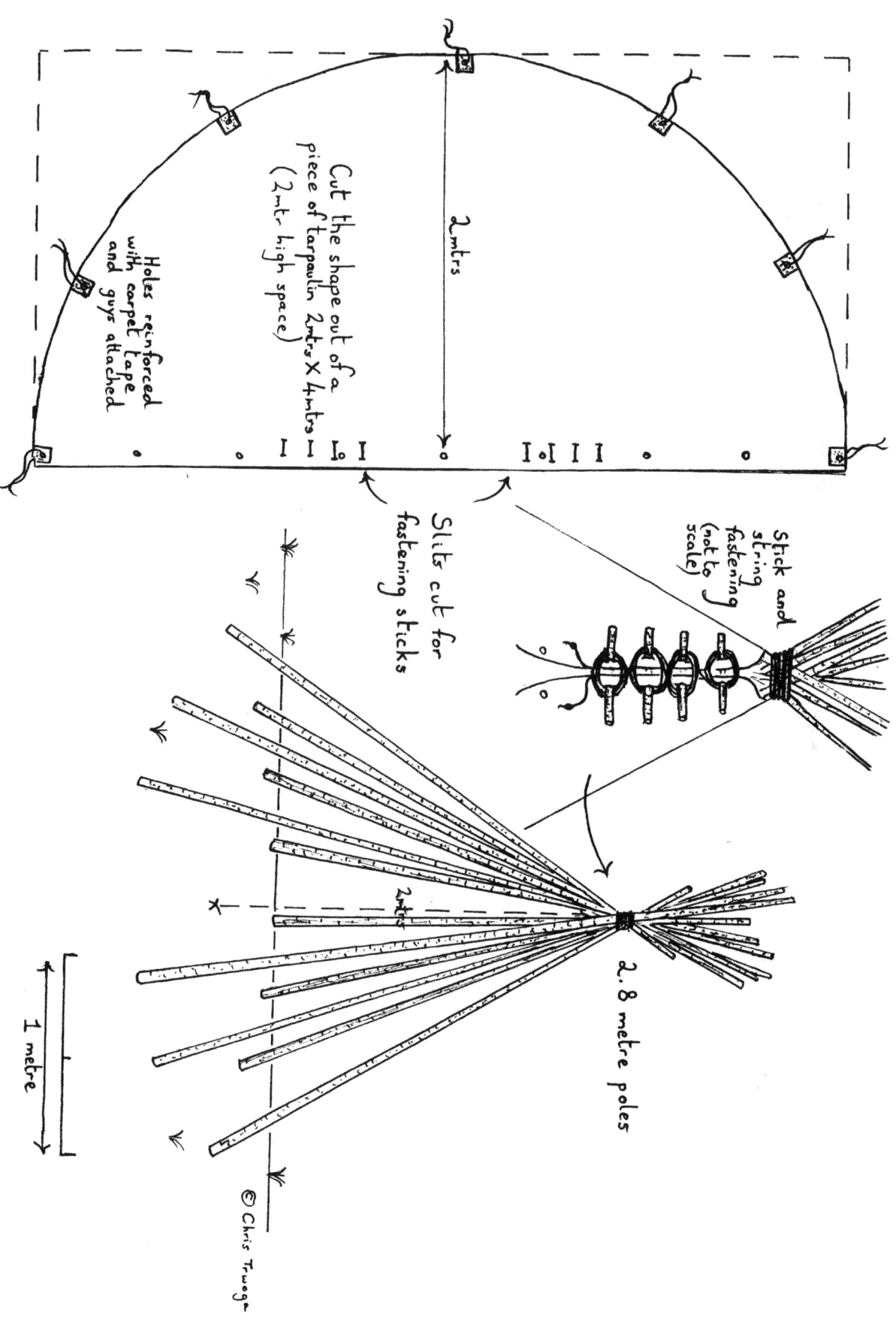

Holes reinforced with carpet tape and guys attached

Cut the shape out of a piece of tarpaulin 2mtrs X 4mtrs (2mtr high space)

2mtrs

Slits cut for fastening sticks

Stick and string fastening (not to scale)

2mtrs

2.8 metre poles

1 metre

© Chris Truogu

1.7 Celebration Focal Point

Aim. To help students understand the idea of special, or 'sacred' space by maintaining a 'Place of Reflection' in the classroom or as a focal point in the school.

In Brief. Students and teacher create and maintain a focal point within the school that celebrates or memorializes significant events in the life of the school.

What you will need:

An accessible public space within the school large enough to take a table, with a wall space behind it suitable for displays.

Method.

1. Discuss the idea of a 'Celebration Focal Point' or special space with your group. Produce a list of the things it might be used for – celebrating birthdays, festivals, special school events, achievements, remembering people who have left etc. Discuss the places in the school where it might go.

2. Go on a tour of the buildings to evaluate different locations. It should have a flat wall space behind it that can be appropriately decorated and provide an attractive space to display work, photographs and so on. Equally, it should be accessible and a place where young people can gather.

3. Locate a suitable table, ideally of wood, and different from the standard school furniture. Plan and bring together materials for your first display – perhaps a bowl of seasonal natural finds, and information and a display for the next significant annual festival. Collect information on birthdays and achievements. Where schools have a cycle of assemblies it can also be used to display the theme of assembly for that day or week.

4. If the class has 'quiet time', a 'time of reflection' or special 'circle time', it is useful to have a candle which is lit to make the special space a focus at particular times in the day or week. Refresh the shrine routinely so that students maintain an interest in it.

5. The special space can be used to mark a loss or the anniversary of a loss for the community. Where a space is routinely maintained and refreshed to reflect events it becomes easier and more natural for students to take ownership of such a space and to choose what is special and important to them.

Reflection. What have we changed on our special space this week? Why have we made those changes? What does our special space help us to remember? What good things have happened this week that we can celebrate for individuals in the group and for the school as a community?

1.8 Planning A Quiet Space Outdoors

Aim. To enable students or young people to enjoy a special outdoor space for quiet enjoyment.

In Brief. A small area of the school grounds is set aside as a quiet space and transformed in keeping with a collective vision of the space.

What you will need:

A suitable area within the school grounds. A small garden space is ideal. *

Where space and resources are at a premium, it might be no more than a bench in a quiet corner, decorated with pot plants. At the other end of the scale a special garden space might be created, involving a landscaping project. In between the two, an idea that works well is to create a living willow arbour that has space for one or two benches (see activity 1.10).

Method.

1. This activity should involve wider consultation than an individual class group. The more energy the school community as a whole puts into it, the more successful it will be.

2. Discuss the idea with your students. You may wish to do a survey to see how many would welcome a 'quiet outdoor space' and when they might make use of it. Visit different spaces within the school grounds. Which spaces look and feel right? What are the practical issues of using those spaces? Visit the proposed area with clipboards, drawing paper and pencils. Collect thoughts of how it might look. Make sketches of the area and add the features.

3. Talk about the following as part of designing the space:

    •   Does it have the feeling of privacy without creating problems for supervision?
    •   How much seating should there be? Too much and it becomes a meeting point
    •   Does it have an attractive outlook? If not what can be done to provide a visual focus - a screen of plants, a willow structure or other attractive feature.
    •   Can we encourage wildlife? Visual evidence for caring for other living things, such as nest boxes and bird feeders express the wider spiritual value of connecting with nature.
    •   How will it be cared for? Ownership by the students and the awareness that people care about the space will ensure that it is respected.
    •   Will the space feel sufficiently different for us to feel we have moved apart from the everyday space we call school?

4. Now get a plan together (this in itself is a brilliant class project) which involves as many members of the school community as possible and bring the project to fruition! See activity 1.10 for an idea which worked really well for us.

Reflection: Reflecting on a special outdoor space, for the use of the community as a whole, is a suitable theme both for assemblies and staffroom discussion. Do we need such a space? Who might use it and why? What does it say about us as a community if we don't think a 'quiet space' is a good idea? What are the opportunities for 'quiet' and 'stillness' in our day? What can I/ we do to help make the space as a gift to the community?

1.9 Visiting a Church, Gurdwara, Mosque, Synagogue or Temple

Aim. To sensitize students to the ways that 'places of worship' formalize function and enable specific ritual or ceremony to take place. To understand the importance of respecting the sacred spaces of others. To reflect on the importance of formal sacred space to those who use it.

In Brief. Students visit a place of worship to reflect on the use of formal sacred space by believers and to experience the special atmosphere of sacred space for themselves.

What you will need:

Access to a sacred site that is suitable for a visit by students. It is better if it is still in use, rather than a redundant or ruined site, unless still used as sacred space.

Method.

1. As a lesson on spirituality this is not just about being able to interpret the function and symbolic content of a 'place of worship'. Rather, it is to get a sense of the meaning and significance of such places to believers.

2. Students should both experience the space as a worshipper might (quietly, respectfully) and, as part of the process, interrogate the more obvious and universal symbols employed.

3. They should pay particular attention to how both internal and external spaces work for them.

4. They should explore the interplay of constructed and natural features (water, flowers, light, with landscaping, sculpture, open and closed spaces). Bring them into the sacred space. If you have not already done so as part of any preparation explain the features that are of special significance to the believer. You are providing a focus for their own thoughts.

5. Explain that you want them to experience the space as a believer might through quiet reflection.

6. Encourage the group to continue to explore and reflect on the space from where they are sat or stood. Allow a few minutes of quiet time to absorb the spirit of the place.

Reflection. How did the space make you feel? What aspect or feature of the sacred space has stuck in your memory? Do we need 'formal' spaces like this, or would any quiet, attractive space serve the same purpose? What did the space tell you about the people who use it?

1.10 Living Willow Garden Structure

Aim. Students design and construct their own special or sacred space, using living willow.

In Brief. Students use living willow to construct an arbour, archway, dome or sacred symbol to act as a focal point in their special outdoor space.

What you will need:

Freshly cut willow * (if you can't use it straight away store it in buckets of water, with the thicker root end submerged). For a 2m high arbour you will need withies of 3m in length or more.	
Secateurs for trimming (*teacher use only*)	Rubber mallets.
Wooden stakes (made with a short length of hazel sticks or similar with a profile thicker that the willow) to make holes in the ground	Steel stake and lump hammer if the ground is hard or stony.
Spades, weed barrier, membrane pegs, tree bark mulch.	
Late autumn to early spring is the best time to plant willow.	

Method.

1. Discuss the role that a willow structure might serve, how it is planted and how it will change as it grows. Explore the school grounds or garden for a suitable site. Consider the use to which it will be put. Students can then envision the structure with on-site discussion and sketching before coming to a consensus about how it might look.

2. From rough sketches produce a scale plan. The plan should indicate the area to be de-turfed. Work out the number of withies required (then order them!). Students mark the design on the ground with string and pegs.

3. De-turf the marked out area and peg down the weed barrier over the surface. A small cross arch arbour for example, will need four 40cms squares cut in a square formation 1.5 metres apart. Once the design is cut out, water the ground well (this makes planting much easier).

4. Students plant withies using a wooden stake and mallet to make the holes to a depth of about 20cms. Push the withies into the ground from the base (teacher can use a steel stake and lump hammer if ground is too hard).

5. Once planted use green garden sisal string to tie the structure into shape.

6. Cover the weed barrier with tree bark mulch to retain moisture and improve appearance. Take the students out regularly to water the willow. Remember that leaves will shoot before roots develop and watering must continue for several weeks after leaves have appeared if rainfall is limited.

Reflection. Visit the space when the willow has started to grow. Think about the leaves that have sprouted and the roots that are spreading beneath your feet. Think about the fact that you planted the willow and helped it grow. Reflect on the fact that what you have made will not just be enjoyed by you but by many others – perhaps even by students not yet born. How does it feel to give something to the future?

2. THE MAGIC OF LABYRINTHS

Drawing a Layrinth, Making a Finger Labyrinth, Choosing a Location for a Labyrinth, Making a 3 Circuit Pebble Labyrinth, Making a Labyrinth for People with Disabilities, Making a 7 Circuit Rope Labyrinth, Making a Living Willow Labyrinth, Decorating a Labyrinth, Fabric Labyrinth, Scavenger Labyrinth.

PART 1. MAKING LABYRINTHS

What, exactly, is a labyrinth? A labyrinth is a circular path that has a single entrance and is followed inwards towards a centre or 'goal'. It has 'walls' to define the path but these are symbolic in nature. A labyrinth can be a path traced on paper with your finger or a path on the ground wide enough to walk. The classic labyrinth has seven circuits, but some have as few as three. The important thing to understand is that a labyrinth is not a maze. A maze offers a confusion of routes and is meant to be a puzzle. A labyrinth, on the other hand, has one path and a single destination – the goal at the centre of the labyrinth.

Walking (or running) a labyrinth is supposed to be a relaxing, therapeutic and mindful experience. It allows the 'rational' part of our brain to relax and the emotional and intuitive faculties to take over. That's the theory anyway.

Labyrinths have been around for millennia. Examples found carved on rocks in Galicia, Spain, date back to the Stone Age. They are found in the mosaics of ancient Greece and Rome. A thousand years ago Norse sailors made cobble labyrinths close to the sea to capture evil spirits that might bring bad luck on their voyage. I have seen labyrinths carved on the walls of ancient Hindu Temples and laid into the floors of churches. They are one of our most universal and recognizable sacred forms.

Labyrinths have grown in popularity in recent decades, with schools, churches, hospices and local community groups working with labyrinths. They have found a new status as a tool for well-being and spiritual development.

I first worked with labyrinths in 2004, when I became involved with planning a community labyrinth for Glastonbury, in Somerset. I built a labyrinth the following year with thirteen-year-olds. It was the enthusiasm and enjoyment of the teenagers, working on their labyrinth that convinced me that there was much more to labyrinths than a gardening exercise.

At first sight laying out a full-size labyrinth looks complicated. That is why learning to draw a labyrinth first is so important. Once you are able to draw a labyrinth without reference to an image you are halfway to being able to lay one out on the ground. When we run courses with teachers the skills associated with laying out a labyrinth are readily acquired during an afternoon.

Our work demonstrates that labyrinths work best if students make their own. The labyrinth becomes an expression of a community coming together to create a special space that all can enjoy. By comparison, labyrinths spray-painted onto tarmac by a paid professional are routinely ignored. It is not the form that matters; it is the creation of special or sacred space by the folk using it.

Labyrinths as Sacred Space. Labyrinths can be regarded as a kind of universal sacred space, a structure that is accessible to people of every faith and none. The word 'sacred' need not be specifically religious. 'Sacred' implies 'special', 'set apart', reserved for a different purpose to ordinary or 'profane' space. Such spaces don't have to be permanent. They can be like the images and shrines of Hindu festivals, set up for the festival and cast into the sea to dissolve away when the celebrations are over. To enable a group of people to create their own sacred space to celebrate the turning year or other special event is peculiarly powerful.

Labyrinths and Community Cohesion. What labyrinths have in common with sacred spaces the world over is the community effort that goes into their making and the shared beliefs and values they represent. When we make a living willow labyrinth every student in the school plants a willow. The joy when the willow began to grow is truly special. When we make temporary labyrinths, we encourage the schools to invite in parents and other members of the community to enjoy the space whilst it is there. They create a time of joy and celebration.

Children like to run labyrinths, some like to take their shoes off and feel the grass under their feet, some want to walk them quietly. I have even seen youngsters flee to the heart of a labyrinth to sulk after an altercation with a teacher or a friend. Part of their value lies in the capacity to be different things to different people. But whatever they mean to the individual, their value as a space that is set apart insinuates itself into the life of the community.

And try leaving any kind of labyrinth down in a public place. In no time at all complete strangers will be walking it. Last year we constructed a huge cobble labyrinth with a primary school group on Charmouth beach in Dorset. The moment it was finished and the students had broken for lunch people came over to ask if they could walk the labyrinth.

What kinds of labyrinths can we make? The labyrinth construction methods offered in this chapter are tried and tested, don't cost much and most of the work is accessible to children of primary school age. With a permanent willow labyrinth, for example, plastic trowels and rubber buckets enable nursery children to contribute to the digging or laying the tree bark.

Full-size labyrinths can be made from almost anything. A temporary labyrinth can be painted onto mown grass with line marking paint or laid out with sprinkled flour. They can be made with pebbles, cobbles, ropes, tea lights in paper lanterns and so on. Permanent labyrinths can have walls made of tree bark, pebbles, living willow, inset bricks or stone, even a continuous flower bed.

As for costs, it is all a matter of what is available and what you can afford. We use brightly coloured 16mm nylon ropes to make temporary 7 circuit labyrinths. The materials to make a rope labyrinth, including reels to store the rope, 250 steel pegs and 120 metres of quality rope costs about £120. Three buckets of polished pebbles provide the materials to make a three circuit cobble labyrinth and this can cost just a few pounds. In autumn, stacks of wet leaves provide a good material and cost nothing.

2.1 Drawing a Labyrinth

Aim. To introduce students to the labyrinth form.

In Brief. Students learn to draw three circuit and seven circuit classical labyrinths *(see fig. 2.1 & 2.1a overleaf)*.

What you will need:

A wall display of labyrinths to show the students.

Paper and pencils.

Crayons, colouring pencils, felt tips, paints or similar.

Method.

1. Provide or show pictures of labyrinths / mazes big enough to be traced with a finger.

2. Can they spot the main difference between the two? What happens when you walk round a maze? How might a labyrinth feel different to walk round?

3. Now demonstrate how to draw a 3 circuit labyrinth, starting with the seed pattern for the students to copy (see fig 2.1). Ensure they start at the centre of the page and give them some idea of the scale to draw to.

4. When ready move onto the seven circuit labyrinth (see fig 2.1a). Once the method is mastered, students can produce a coloured and decorated labyrinth or maze painting to decorate the classroom display boards.

Reflection. What does it feel like to run your finger round the labyrinth? Labyrinths are found all over the world. Why do you think people are fascinated by labyrinths? What do you like about them?

Fig 2.1   Drawing a 3 circuit classical labyrinth

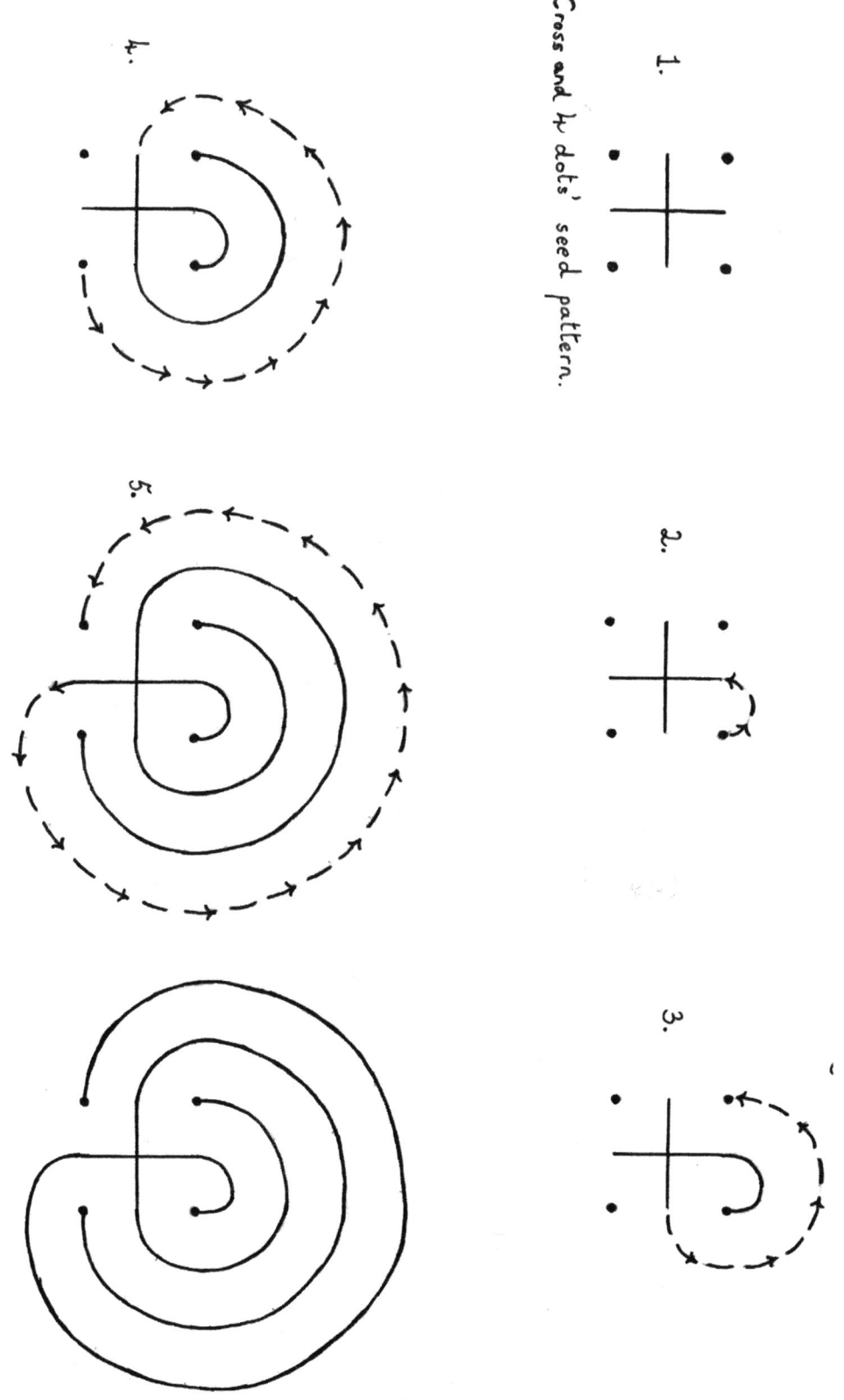

'Cross and 4 dots' seed pattern.

1.

2.

3.

4.

5.

Fig 2.1a Drawing a 7 circuit classical labyrinth

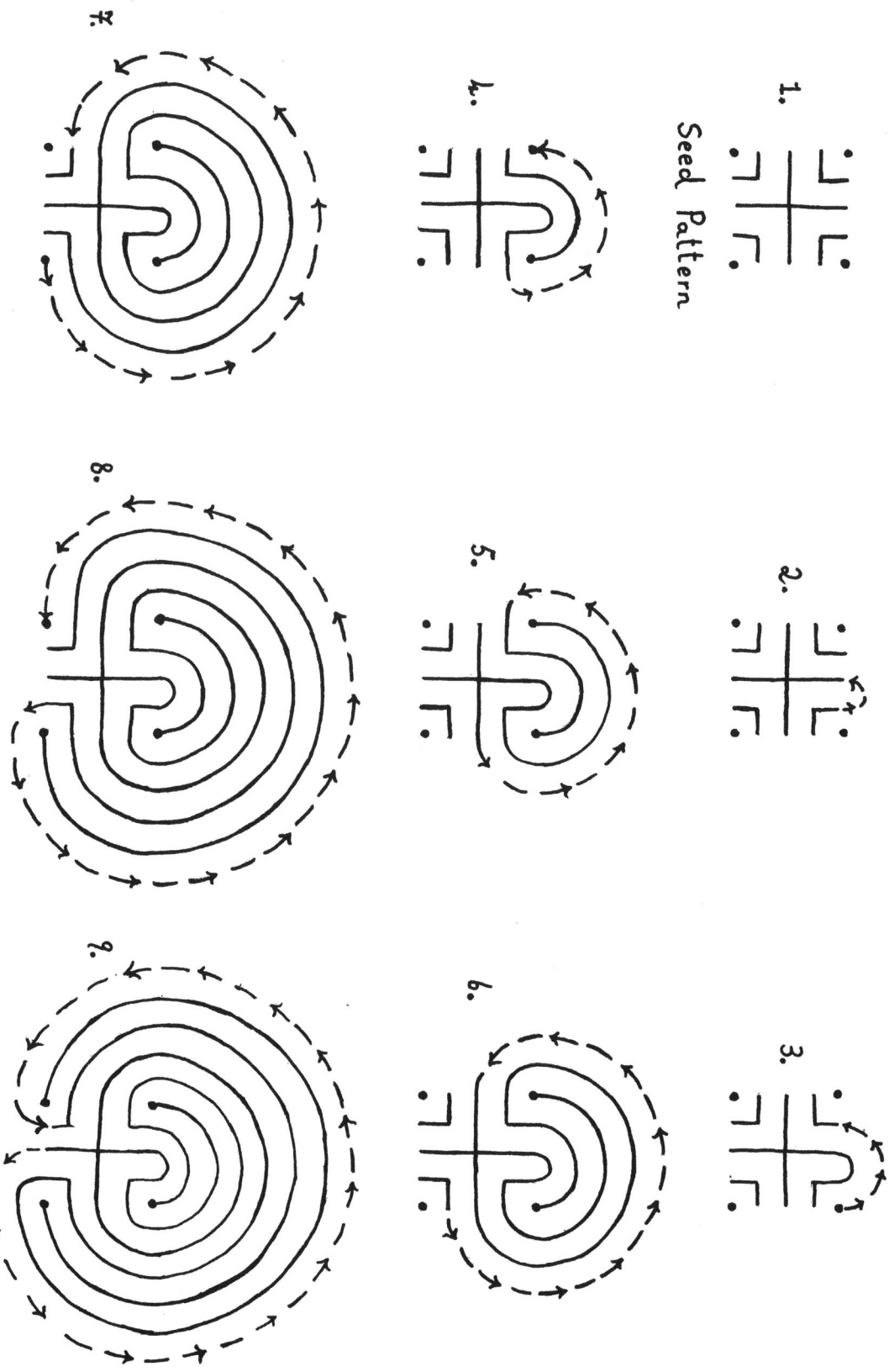

2.2 Making a Clay and Papier-mache Finger Labyrinth

Aim. To enable students to experience the labyrinth form by creating three-dimensional finger labyrinths.

In Brief. Students use modelling clay, papier-mache and other materials to make a finger labyrinth for use and display.

What you will need:

Papier-mache. and clay - a 10 kilo bag of air-drying clay is enough for the average class	A board base (4mm thick or similar). About 30cm sq per student (alternatively they can work in pairs or threes).
Glitter, magazine pictures, natural materials such as feathers, leaves, snail shells - brought in by students	
Powder or acrylic paints and paint brushes.	
An alternative to clay or papier-mache is cord, wools or fabrics. These can even be sewn onto a fabric base.	

Method.

1. Discuss finger labyrinths with your class. Explain their use as a kind of relaxation tool (think of doodling!).

2. Practice drawing a seven circuit labyrinth big enough to trace with your finger.

3. Encourage the students to think of a theme for their labyrinth. A collage of favourite magazine pictures can be used to decorate the board or it can be painted like a landscape. One of my favourite finger labyrinths was made in the shape of a heart, painted pink and decorated with pink feathers from a cheap feather boa. Another was themed on African wildlife and the labyrinth was made against a background of African landscapes and animals.

4. Get students to sketch out their ideas.

5. They are now ready to begin construction! A reasonable labyrinth might take a number of hours to complete and drying time will be needed between the various stages of construction.

6. Once complete, students write a brief article about their labyrinth to display alongside their work.

Reflection. Share your work with the rest of the group. Describe your design and what it means to you. What do you like best about your work? What were the difficulties and how did you overcome them?

2.3 Choosing the Right Location for a Full Size Outdoor Labyrinth

Aim. To enable students to make informed choices in a significant planning decision.

In Brief. Students choose a location for a temporary or permanent labyrinth.

What you will need: *(per group)*

A clipboard, paper, ruler, pencil and magnetic compass.	Access to 25m tape measure.
A rubber mallet, a dozen steel tent pegs.	A 1m length of string.

Method.

1. Discuss location. Does it feel right? Is it an attractive part of the school? Ideally, it is quiet, not in constant use and not part of a running track or other sports facility Is there a special tree that you want to work into the labyrinth landscape? Can young children be supervised there? It should be dry with plenty of natural drainage.

2. Different groups explore the school grounds and come up with 4 or 5 suggestions. They then select one location and check what's under the turf by hammering in (and removing) their tent pegs around the site. If they go in smoothly and easily you have a good location for a rope or permanent labyrinth. Change location if the ground is unsuitable.

3. Choose the alignment. A classical labyrinth begins by marking a cross on the ground. The main axis aligns the mouth or entrance of the labyrinth with the goal or centre. This alignment is what you see as you begin your journey. This can then be orientated towards one or more of the following:

   - *A significant visible landmark* - e.g. a building, large tree, hill etc.
   - *A Ley* - use a map or Google Earth to align with distant features in the landscape like churches, ancient monuments, bridges etc.
   - *The cardinal points of the compass.*
   - *A celestial event* such as sunrise at midsummer or spring equinox.
   - *A sacred place* such as Jerusalem.

4. Once a group is satisfied with location and orientation, they use the string and 4 steel pegs to mark out the centre of their labyrinth and its orientation. The groups can now visit each other's sites. Individuals from each make a brief presentation explaining their choices. Finally, the class review all the sites together and make a single, final choice.

Reflection. What are the important things about choosing the right space? Why is it good to share ideas and compromise? What are our thoughts on the alignment? Many sacred sites are orientated on the cardinal points of the compass (churches are usually east-west), or fixed on significant celestial events (e.g. summer solstice sunrise at Stonehenge or winter solstice at Maes Howe, Orkney). Churches, mosques and synagogues are also built along an axis that has special meanings, such as the direction of Jerusalem or Mecca.

2.4 Making A Temporary 3 Circuit Cobble Or Pebble Labyrinth
'Cross and Dot' Seed Pattern

Aim. To learn a simple technique for making a three circuit classical labyrinth.

In Brief. Students use pebbles, stones or cobbles to make a small temporary labyrinth.

What you will need: *(for a labyrinth with 3 circuits and a 50cm path)*

A space at least 4m in diameter. Grass mown fairly short.
A pair of timber right angles (see pic p71). 1m by 50cm.
Six buckets of stones/pebbles per labyrinth (either purchase from a garden centre or get class to collect over time). Flexible two handled builder's buckets are best (we recommend Rhino for durability, cheaper ones tend to fall apart).
Laminated diagrams of 3 circuit labyrinth (use fig 2.1).

Method.

1. Practice drawing three circuit labyrinths with the students.

2. With appearance and potential users in mind, choose a suitable site. A slight slope can improve visibility. Consider the shade of a tree or incorporate a sapling/narrow trunked tree (but with no low branches) into the centre. With infants, make a winding path of pebbles from the labyrinth to a special place (e.g. a tree) where they make a wish.

3. *Lay out the cross.* Lay the right angle stick on the ground and place the stones/pebbles along its length to create a cross with 1m arms intersecting at 50cm. Mark the centre with a large stone or small cairn.

4. *Lay out the 4 dots.* Use the angle stick to mark out the corner dots thus making the corners of a square with 1m sides. Use a large stone for the 4 dots or build 4 small cairns.

5. *Lay out the goal.* With a graceful curve of pebbles link the top right hand dot to the top arm of the cross. Get the goal shape right as the half-circle you create here determines the shape of the entire labyrinth.

6. *Lay out the 3 circuits.* The first wall circuit runs from the right hand arm of the cross, round the goal, to the top left hand dot. To achieve a neat curve the students use two right-angles with the arms positioned 50cm apart and lay the stones between the ends of the two sticks. This may take a little practice. The second circuit runs from the lower right hand dot round to the left hand arm of the cross. The third and final circuit runs from the bottom arm of the cross (the arm closest to the mouth or entrance) and round the labyrinth to link with the lower left hand dot. Students often make mistakes on the first go, usually because they have used the right angles incorrectly. Over time they will learn to lay out 'by eye'. With pebbles/stones mistakes can be quickly remedied.

7. Once complete, students walk their labyrinth.

Reflection. Walk your labyrinth slowly. Try not to talk. How does it feel? What problems did you encounter making the labyrinth? How did you solve them? What is special about the shape?

2.5   Making a Pebble Labyrinth for People with Disabilities
'Square and 4 Circle' Seed Pattern

Aim. To encourage research and reflection on the needs of others.

In Brief. Students make a large pebble or cobble labyrinth to a plan that facilitates use by partially sighted or wheelchair bound users (see fig. 2.5).

What you will need: *(3 circuits, 75cm path)*

A space at least 4 m in diameter. Grass mown fairly short. 4 tent pegs. 4m length of string.

A pair of timber right angles (see pic p71). 1.5m by 75cm.

10 small buckets of stones/pebbles (purchase from a garden centre or collect over time). For a partially-sighted group use stones which provide a strong visual contrast with the grass.

Laminated diagrams of this labyrinth design (use fig 2.5). Paper and pencils for drawing.

Method. (refer to fig 2.5 opposite)

1. Discuss the issues of people with disabilities using a labyrinth.

2. In goups, students practice drawing the labyrinth. Discuss why this design has gentle corners and lots of space in the centre.

3. Choose a location. Discuss the need for disabled access to the labyrinth.

4. *Lay out the square.* Use the string, 4 steel tent pegs and right angles to mark out a square with 1.5 metre sides.

5. *Lay out the circles.* Use either a 75cm length of string or your 75cm right-angle to mark out a 1.5 metre diameter circle in pebbles using the top right-hand corner of the square as your centre. Leave a 5cm space between each pebble. Now do the same with the remaining 3 corners of the square. You should end up with 4 'dotted' circles, 1.5 metres in diameter that touch the adjoining circles at two points but do not overlap.

6. *Lay out the goal.* Fill in the line of pebbles around the top half and bottom left quarter of circle A. Remove the pebbles from the lower right-hand quarter of circle A to form the entrance to the goal.

7. *Lay out the 3 circuits or "walls" with pebbles/stones.* The inner wall curves round from the bottom of circle A anti-clockwise all the way to the centre of circle D. The middle wall begins at the centre of the lower right-hand circle (B) and sweeps round the inner wall anti-clockwise to join the lower half of circle D. The final and outer wall travels round the lower half of circle B anticlockwise and then sweeps round the outside of the labyrinth all the way to the centre of circle C. Referring to the diagram, remove excess pebbles from circles

8. If appropriate, adorn the central space. A decorative pebble pattern works well.

Reflection. You were thinking of others when you made your labyrinth. How well do you think you met their needs? Why is it important to think about people with limited mobility or sight in designing public spaces? Has your school been adapted to meet the needs of people with limited sight or mobility?

Fig 2.5 'Square and 4 Circle' pebble labyrinth with 75cm paths

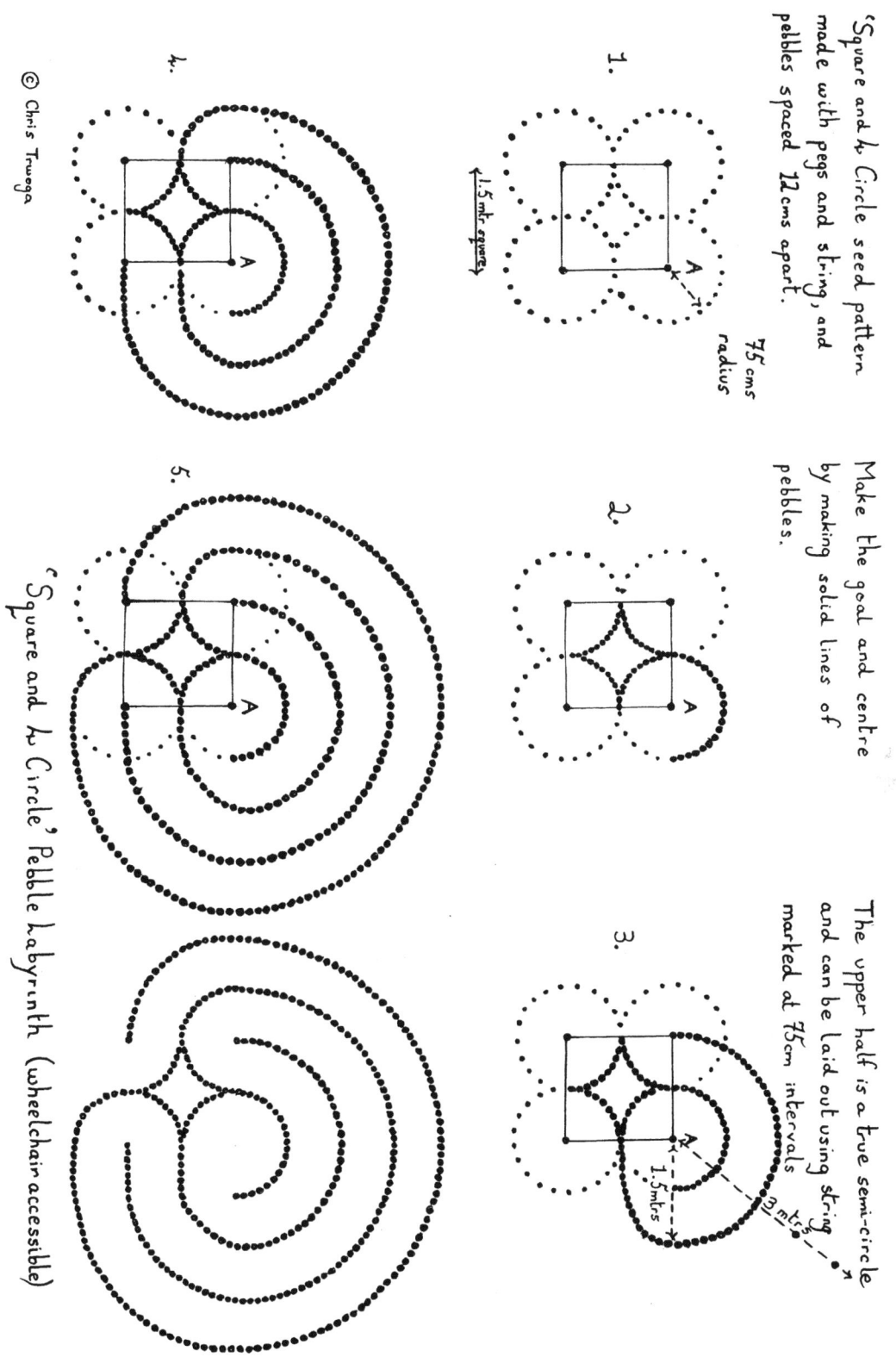

'Square and 4 Circle seed pattern made with pegs and string, and pebbles spaced 12cms apart.

1.

1.5 mtr square

75 cms radius

Make the goal and centre by making solid lines of pebbles.

2.

The upper half is a true semi-circle and can be laid out using string marked at 75cm intervals

3.

1.5mtrs

3 mtrs

4.

5.

© Chris Truega

'Square and 4 Circle' Pebble labyrinth (wheelchair accessible)

65

2.6 7 Circuit Temporary Rope Labyrinth
50cm Path 'Cross, Right Angle and Dot' Seed Pattern

Aim. To develop spatial awareness and measuring skills in younger students. To develop skills in interpreting and applying plans in older students.

In Brief. Two ropes of different colours are used to make a labyrinth on a grassy surface.

What you will need: (based on groups of 8 students working in rotation)

A suitable site (see activity 2.3) at least 10m in diameter.	Pliers to straighten bent pegs. 3 rubber mallets.
Two laminated cards of fig 2.6 with the ropes shaded in as per actual rope colour.	2 timber right angles (see pic p71). 1m by 50cm.
250 x 7" steel tent pegs with looped ends.	25 metre measuring tape to check your space is 10m in diameter

Pre-cut lengths of 16mm rope as follows:
* Two x 2m lengths (1 of each colour) to make the central 'cross'
* Four x 1m lengths (2 of each colour) to make the 4 right angles
* Four x 50cm lengths (2 of each colour) to coil and make the 4 'dots'
* Two x 60m lengths (1 of each colour), stored on 50 metre garden hose reels.

Method. (refer to fig 2.1a to learn the form and fig 2.6 to peg out on the ground)

1. Teach students how to draw a 7 circuit classical labyrinth without reference to a diagram - see fig 2.1a. This makes a huge difference when laying out on the ground.

2. Demonstrate the materials and explain the task. If your students are already familiar with pebble labyrinths explain that greater care and accuracy is needed when working with ropes. A mistake at the start can mean undoing an hour's work and starting again.

3. ***Peg down the central cross***. Use your two 2m lengths of rope (1 of each colour) to make the central 'cross'. Check all arms are of equal length and at right angles to each other.

4. ***Peg down the 4 right angles***. Use your four 1m lengths of rope (2 of each colour) to make the 4 right angles. Use your timber right angle tool to ensure that they are 50cm from the related cross arms at all points. Ensure the colours are in the correct relation to each other.

5. ***Peg down the 4 dots.*** Tightly coil your four 50cm lengths of rope (2 of each colour) to make the 4 dots. Fix in place with with several pegs. The right angles and the related dot would, if joined, form a square with 50cm sides.

6. Check that the correct colour rope has been used for each part of the seed pattern. and check all measurements – the clearance between all features should be 50cm.

7. ***Form the goal.*** Use a short piece of spare 'plain' rope to join the top arm of the cross with the top of the right-angle to the right. Ensure that this rope creates a neat semi-circle. This rope will be removed later.

8. You are now ready to lay out the walls! For the purposes of this guide, the ropes will be referred to as the 'hatched and the 'plain' rope as per fig. 2.6. In actuality they will, of course be different colours. Have the Seed Pattern diagram to hand (fig 2.6).

Fig 2.6   Making a 7 Circuit Rope Labyrinth

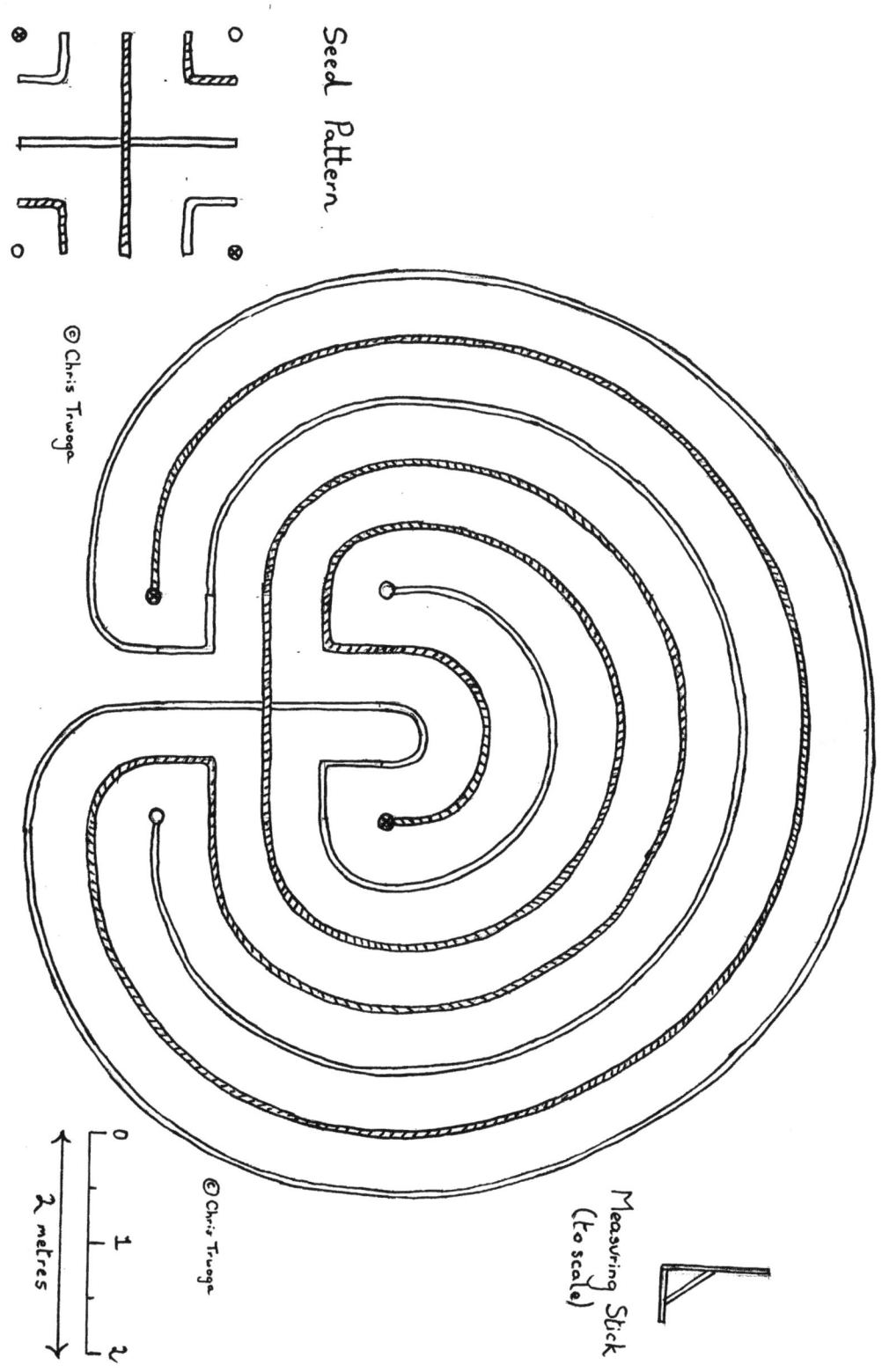

Seed Pattern

© Chris Truога

© Chris Truога

Measuring Stick
(to scale)

0
1
2

2 metres

9. **Peg out the 'hatched' 60 metre rope.** Take the rope from the top hatched right-hand dot anti-clockwise to the top left-hand hatched right angle and peg down. Peg the rope alongside the hatched right-angle and loop it back clockwise around the left hand 'plain' top dot to the right-hand 'hatched' arm of the cross. Note that the distance between the two circuits of the hatched rope is 1m - this allows the plain rope to run between them. Next, peg the rope left along the hatched arm of the cross and loop it round clockwise to the lower hatched right angle. Note how the distance between the inner circuit of the rope and the next circuit of the hatched rope is 1m. Again, this is because the 'plain' rope will start between them. Finally, peg the hatched rope round anti-clockwise to the lower hatched dot. Peg any surplus rope back on itself.

10. **Peg out the 'plain' 60m rope.** Unpeg the temporary rope placed around the top of the goal. Start the plain rope at the top left-hand plain dot. Peg it between the hatched rope circuits clockwise to the lower arm of the plain right angle that forms the right side of the goal. Re-make the goal shape with the rope and then peg alongside the plain rope that forms the left-hand side of the goal. The plain rope then follows the course of the plain arm of the cross downwards, then follows the outermost hatched rope anti-clockwise. It sweeps right round the labyrinth anti-clockwise to join the lower plain right angle. From the lower plain right angle, the plain rope then sweeps clockwise to form the third wall in, sweeping round the labyrinth once more to end at the plain dot below and to the right of the goal. Peg the remainder of the rope back on itself to complete the labyrinth.

11. Ensure all pegs are hammered home and there are no loose or unpegged lengths of rope that may become a trip hazard. The labyrinth is now ready for use!

Reflection. Walk the labyrinth slowly. Think about the distance in and out of the labyrinth. What is unusual about the way you move round a labyrinth? How successful was the team effort that went in to making your labyrinth? What aspects did you enjoy most about the work?

2.7   Making A Permanent 3 Circuit Living Willow Labyrinth
'Square and Four Circle' Seed Pattern

Aim. To foster student initiative and independence. To enable students and young people to take responsibility for a significant school improvement project.

In Brief. A permanent labyrinth is made by cutting away the turf and then planting the trench (labyrinth wall) with living withies.

What you will need: (for a 3 circuit labyrinth with 80cm path and 20cm wall)

3 to 4 bundles of 100 cut withies, 3m in length (check that the withies are about 1.5cm in diameter at their base, tapering to not less than 7mm for the first 1.5 metres).	50 steel tent pegs. 3 rolls of green sisal garden twine.
20 m² of weed barrier. 250 weed barrier pegs (buy online). 12 bags of tree bark mulch.	Yellow or white washable powder paint or grass line paint, mixed in a bucket with a couple of 4cm paintbrushs.
3 spades of identical blade width 20cm. 6 builders waste buckets (soft rubber - *Rhino* brand small size are best). 12 high quality trowels (*plastic if working with young children*). 3 rubber mallets. Gardening gloves for 12 students. 50 metres of brightly coloured (not green) twine.	2 right- angles with a 1m long side. The 1 metre is marked out 20cm/ 80cm. A stick marked out 40cm – 10cm – 10cm – 10cm – 40cm, to correctly space out the withy planting. 3 sharp wooden stakes of 1.5cm diameter to make holes for withy planting. Steel spike and lump hammer for hard ground (***adult use only***) for making planting holes in hard ground.

Time required. We typically construct a 3 circuit living willow labyrinth with 80cm path and 20cm wide walls in three days, working on it for 4 – 6 hours a day. Bear in mind that turf cutting is heavy work and children of primary age will need adult support with this. *Any young person using a steel spade should wear shoes or wellies with reinforced toe-caps.*

Method.

1. This is a permanent labyrinth and will be with the school for some time. It is therefore important to raise the profile of the project and to involve as many students as possible. Get all groups active from the planning stage and ensure they are familiar with the design. If they have worked with temporary labyrinths it means they can do a lot more of the laying out with less adult intervention.

2. Have the area mowed but don't cut the grass too short as it will be walked on intensively during construction. Choose a site that is reasonably well drained. We say 'reasonably' because willow likes damp conditions, so don't go for anything too dry. See also activity 2.3 for more advice on where to site a labyrinth.

3. Mark out a square with pegs and twine with sides of 2 metres. Now mark out four 1.9m circles with pegs and twine using the corners of the square as the centre of each circle. The resulting circles will not touch but will be 20cms apart. Once you are satisfied with your 4 circles, mark out with washable powder paint or line paint using a dotted/ broken line. Once painted on the ground all twine and pegs can be removed.

4. **Mark out the goal** on circle (A) (*see fig 2.7*). Peg out with twine the parallel arcs0 that run 20cm anticlockwise around the dotted goal (A) and into the actual centre of the labyrinth. Then, starting from the lower left hand arc of the goal (A) peg out the parallel arcs of the inner wall that runs anticlockwise to the centre of circle (D). Note that you are pegging the first line 80cms from the goal wall and then a parallel line 20cms out from this. The middle wall begins life at the centre of circle (B). Mark out the line 80cms from the inner wall and its partner 20cms from this. The middle wall arcs anti-clockwise around the inner wall to wrap itself round the lower half of circle (D) and the top right-hand quarter of circle (C). Refer closely to the diagram. The out wall begins life at the true centre of the labyrinth, passing around the lower left-hand quadrant of circle (B) and arcing anticlockwise around the middle wall before ending in the centre of circle (C).

5. **Paint onto the grass.** Once you are satisfied with the design as laid out in pegs and twine it can be painted directly onto the grass. Note that, even when dry, washable powder paint ends up on clothes. We warn parents, letting them know it is completely washable. So far, no complaints! When the design is painted down, all string and pegs can be removed. The labyrinth walls are now cut into the ground by removing the turf to a spade's width between the 20cm painted lines. The lozenge shaped centre is dug out too. We use older students to physically cut the turf into neat 20cm squares, which are loosened but not removed. The turf squares are then carefully lifted by younger students and stacked neatly. It is a nice idea to re-utilize the turf to construct a feature, such as a turf 'seat' or bench. It is also the best turf to use if repairs have to be carried out to bare patches/ mistakes on the labyrinth itself.

6. With rubber buckets and plastic trowels, the youngest students then dig out the ground in the wall to a depth of 12- 15cms. The resulting trench is then backfilled with some soil conditioner. We have carried out this aspect of the work with children as young as four.

7. **Peg down the weed barrier into the wall trench.** It is best to cut the weed barrier to double the width of the trench (40cms) so that the edges can be turned in to prevent fraying and improve neatness. In a secondary school context, the entire process can be carried out by students. Younger children find this tricky. The pegs are hammered through the fabric into the side of the trench at a 45 degree angle. Children can be supported in this by making holes through the weed barrier to take the pegs with a sharp tool such as a pair of scissors. Coach hammering techniques first. With plastic pegs the head must be struck square on or the peg simply bends. Use short, sharp taps with the mallet. Pegging out the membrane can take 4 hours or longer, working with a group of 4 to 6.

8. **Plant the living willow wall.** We like to ensure that every student in the school is involved in planting. The willow design we use provides for strength in the early growing stages. The willow withies are planted in hoops (the withy will grow roots at both ends, thus speeding establishment). The holes are punctured through the weed barrier and 15cms into the ground with metal or wooden spike in the sequence – 40cms – 10cms – 10cms - 10cm – 40cms – 10cms – 10cms – 10cms – 40cms and so on (refer to fig 2.7). If the ground is hard and stony an adult uses a steel spike and a lump hammer. The willow sticks are very carefully bent to form a 60cm hoop with a 20cm overlap between hoops. In the middle of the overlap - hence the 3 holes - an upright willow stick is planted, which projects 60cms above ground when trimmed. The hoops of willow and the upright are then tied firmly together, where the hoops overlap the upright willow stick. It is important to use a sisal twine that will eventually rot away.

9. **Backfill with tree bark mulch.** The tree bark in the trench provides an attractive finish, keeps the weeds away, and is a great activity for your youngest children. Filling the trench with bark is accessible at 3 years of age, even if a lot of the bark ends up where you don't want it! In the case of 'living willow', a period of daily watering needs to follow, unless nature is doing the honours. Willow likes to be damp. The labyrinth will also need regular manicuring to prevent grass and

Fig 2.7　Making a Willow & Grass 3 Circuit Labyrinth

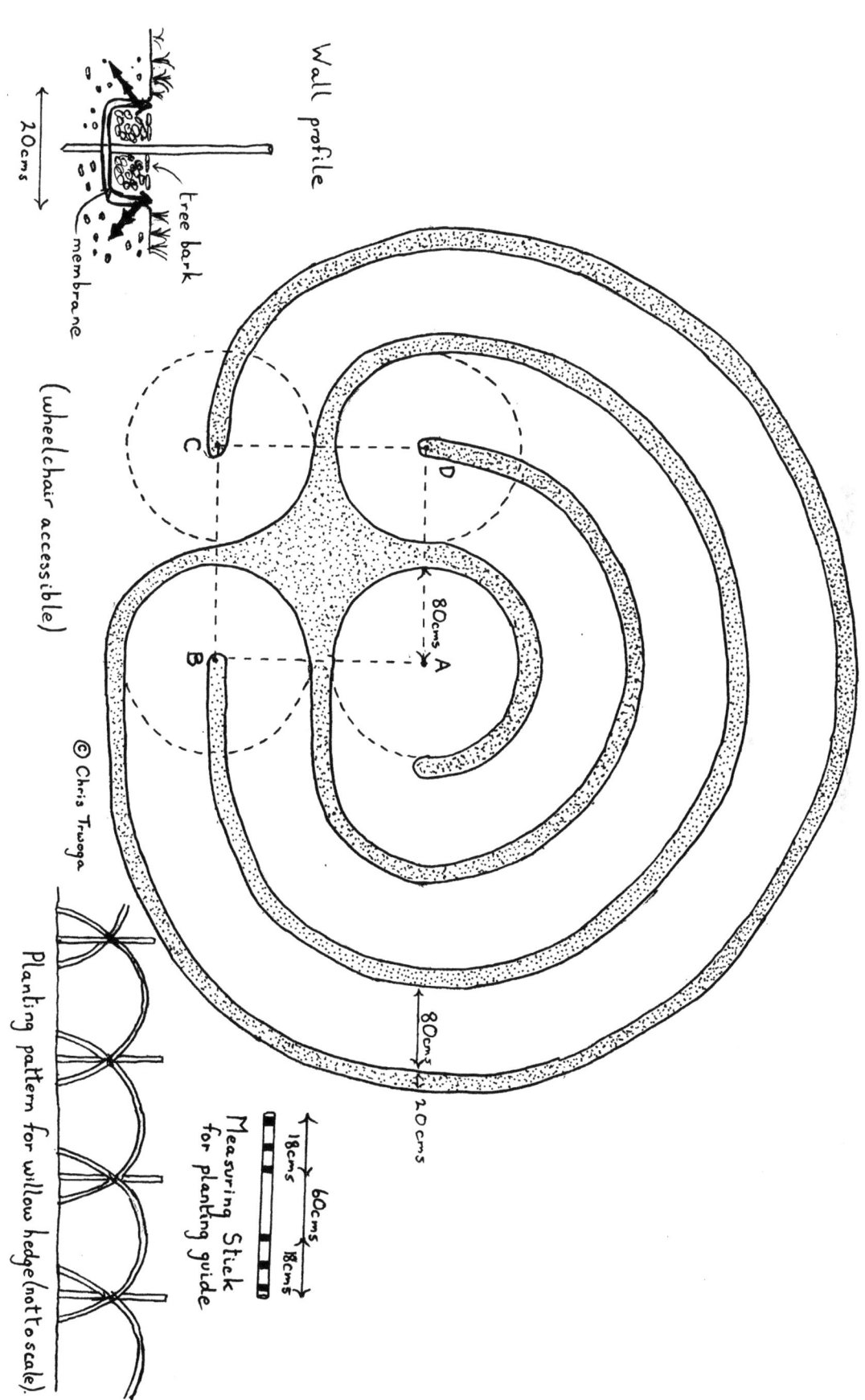

Wall profile

20cms

tree bark

membrane

(wheelchair accessible)

© Chris Truega

80cms A

80cms

20cms

C

D

B

Measuring Stick for planting guide

60cms

18cms

18cms

Planting pattern for willow hedge (not to scale).

weeds growing across the wall. Don't let your grounds people use strimmers for the first couple of years to avoid damage to the growing willow. Note that a tree bark mulch wall, without willow, will not last. Ground compression and weed growth **will** cause the wall to close in 12 to 18 months unless it is carefully maintained. If you don't want the maintenance issues that come with willow, you can go for a gravel alternative. The wall trench must still be protected with a weed barrier. When using gravel we use a creamy water-worn variety that provides a beautiful contrast with the grass and makes the design really stand out. We order in a 1 ton dumpy bag from a builder's merchants at around £100 delivered. Dorset gravel or similar can be half this price. The gravel needs to fill the trench and be pressed down firmly. This helps prevent the grass path being gradually compressed across the trench by foot fall.

Reflection. Making something that lives requires ongoing maintenance – otherwise it will die or grow wild and unsightly. What is the 'plus' side of making something that will live and grow?

2.8 Decorating the Labyrinth - Making Labyrinth Flags

Aim. To explore ways of celebrating the labyrinth or other community events.

In Brief. Students make flags, designed to reflect the theme of a celebration.

What you will need:

Flag sticks - pointed at one end to help push them into the ground. Hazel sticks or withies cut to 60cm lengths are best. Garden canes can also be used.

Rubber mallets (if ground is hard).

Ribbons and fabric scraps.
Plain fabric scraps. Plain paper can also be used

Felt tip pens, paints. Staple gun.

Method.

1. Choose a theme for your flags. You might, for example, celebrate diversity by painting the name of the place of origin of all the students in the school on different flags. Alternatively, the designs can reflect a religious festival, feature a labyrinth theme or be purely decorative.

2. Provide a square of plain fabric, or strips of fabric for each student. Explore ways of painting or decorating the fabric to reflect the theme.

3. Work outdoors in decorating the flags wherever possible. We set up a canopy and put out a tarpaulin and old rugs to sit on to make this a relaxed, informal activity.

4. Once the flags are decorated, they are attached to the stick with a couple of staples.

5. Students then can carry their flags in and out of the labyrinth in procession

6. before spacing themselves around the labyrinth and pushing or hammering into place.

Reflection. Think about the themes your flags celebrate – community, working together, giving, celebration. Think about the enjoyment your flags give to your group and to those who enjoy looking at them, even when you are not there. Discuss the different reasons why people use and display flags or bunting. Think about what your flag means to you.

2.9 Making a Fabric Labyrinth

Aim. To creatively explore labyrinths through sewing crafts.

In Brief. A 3 circuit classical labyrinth is sewn onto a large fabric square for use indoors. Consider doing this activity as a community project with every student in the school taking part.

What you will need:

1 piece of robust fabric 4.5m square for the base*	Lots of scrap fabric strips
As many pupils as possible!	Needles and thread for each student
Sewing pins, wide tipped felt-tip pens	Roll of twine, carpet / gatter tape

* The fabric should be as heavy as possible. Canvas is ideal. Good end of line curtain roll also works. Sew pieces of fabric together yourself to form the base (good sewing machine equired). Note, for another style of labyrinth make a scale drawing to determine base size. This method is for a standard 3 circuit 'cross and 4 dots' with a 50cm path.

Method:

1. If you haven't already done so, introduce your students to labyrinths and ensure they can draw them without reference to a diagram.

2. Produce a scale drawing of your labyrinth. You can do this yourself or as a group activity.

3. Lay out the fabric square on a flat, hard indoor surface. Tape down. Use the twine to lay out the "Cross and Four Dots" seed pattern on the fabric (see fig 2.1). Tack to the fabric with sewing pins or stitch.

4. Lay out the walls (see fig 2.1) with twine. Tack or pin down. This task can easily be carried out by young students; mistakes are easily remedied and they can decide when they are happy with the layout.

5. With felt-tip pens students carefully follow the twine and mark the design on to the cloth. Once the ink has dried remove the twine. It can now be worked on outdoors on a sunny day.

6. Pupils sew short strips of fabric – say 50cm long and 5cm wide - over the felt tip pattern. You may wish to create a particular pattern of colours or use fabric or ribbon of identical length; if so, colour code the pen design or mark into required lengths. If done by the whole school, pass the labyrinth from class to class for each pupil to sew a single strip. You can stitch down the strips through the middle, so that the edges are free and ragged, or stitch down all edges. Ensure they are securely sewn and the thread tied off to avoid pieces working loose. Students should be prepared to redo work that is untidy or loose and to ensure that the stitching does not gather or pull the fabric base.

7. When using, carefully stretch out the labyrinth and tape down the edges with coloured gaffer tape that blends with the design. Fabric labyrinths are fragile so they should only be used indoors by pupils in socks or bare feet.

Reflection. Celebrate the success of your project! Think about all those who worked on it. Use your labyrinth for *Quiet Time*. Walk it very slowly, think about all the good things that have happened to you in the week. Do you know someone who is troubled or has a problem; is there a simple way that you can help that person? Think of 3 things that make you happy. Enjoy thinking about those things as you walk round the labyrinth.

2.10 Making a Scavenger Labyrinth

Aim. To develop creativity by constructing a cost neutral labyrinth using 'found' materials. To Minimize adult involvement and encouarge independent thought and action.

In Brief. Students construct a 3 or 7 circuit classical labyrinth out of whatever natural forest floor or beach materials are at hand.

What you will need:

Suitable environment with ample natural material for students to scavenge. E.g. school grounds in Autumn, woodland, park or beach*	Timber right angles (see pic p71). 1m by 50cm and 1.5m by 75cm. Laminated labyrinth diagrams (figs 2.1 and 2.1a) if required.
The chosen site should be one where students can work safely with minimal adult oversight.	

Method.

1. Divide your class into groups of 6 to 8 students. Explain to the group that they are going to demonstrate their understanding of the labyrinth form by constructing a labyrinth out of materials they find – say, on the woodland floor. They will also be choosing a place to make their labyrinth that feels right for them – perhaps a locale with a special atmosphere.

2. Provide appropriate laminated diagrams (*see figs 2.1 and 2.1a*) and right angle measuring sticks for 50cm or 75cm paths.

3. Discuss the time that is available and whether they wish to construct a 3 or 7 circuit labyrinth, together with the appropriate width of path. The labyrinth should have a minimum path width of around 50cms and a maximum of 75cms to ensure that the labyrinth can be completed in the available time.

4. Check through discussion that they have understood what is being asked of them and begin the activity.

5. If in a woodland space they will need to clear the ground of existing debris and put it to one side. If materials are in short supply they do not necessarily need to construct a continuous wall but can use regularly spaced sticks, stones or other materials. On a beach, students can construct the walls by digging a shallow trench in the sand or by collecting cobbles and driftwood.

6. Let students use their labyrinth and those of the other groups. The activity can be extended by constructing labyrinths close to each other and connecting them with winding paths. Give the students time to enjoy the labyrinths in their own way.

Reflection. What were your thoughts as you walked your natural labyrinth for the first time? How do you feel about the people you worked with? How does it feel to make and use a labyrinth out of natural materials? What things did you think about in choosing the location for your labyrinth? Were you able to share your labyrinth with others?

3. THE POWER OF LABYRINTHS

PART 2. USING YOUR LABYRINTH

Wishing Tree, Sensory use of the Labyrinth, Experiencing the Labyrinth differently, Insights into Impermanence, Insights into Christian Pilgrimage, Theseus and the Minotaur, Understanding your Heart, Number and Labyrinths, Measuring the Labyrinth Path, Labyrinth Clock.

I have no idea how labyrinths work their magic – only that they do. I also know that they work their magic regardless of how they are used; hence our use of them for work and play as well as spirituality.

The labyrinth is regarded by many as a spiritual tool and traditionally it is used in a meditative way, walking the path slowly and silently. Some children want to use it this way when they are on their own. In groups, however, they are more likely to see its use as an extension of play. Barefoot is great. Running is great. Blindfold, walking backwards, large group huddle, how many can we squeeze in the middle, who can run it fastest are all ways of simply enjoying the space. 'Spiritual' should be joyful too. The important thing is that folk leave the labyrinth feeling better than when they went in.

The labyrinth can also be used for curriculum delivery. How do you measure the length of a spiral path? How do we calculate the number of withies we need to plant the labyrinth wall? What impact does heavy use have on the flora and fauna? How does running it affect our bodies? What is the history of labyrinths and how did people in the past use them? Where do we find labyrinths around the world? How do labyrinths feature in Art? What is their religious and cultural significance? What stories and legends are connected with labyrinths?

I would like to say there is no wrong way to use a labyrinth. With labyrinths made on grass, however, running *across* the labyrinth will degrade its visual impact and damage the walls. If the labyrinth path is always followed (make this your only rule) the design settles into the earth. On soft ground the footfall gradually moulds the earth as the path sinks deeper and the labyrinth assumes a sculpted shape

In free play children will tend to 'cheat' in labyrinths, using the path to get in but sometimes walking or running out any which way. Hence our preference for willow labyrinths, that over time develop a hedge-like wall. We recommend pruning tall enough to discourage children from jumping across the walls but not so high as to prevent children from seeing over the hedge and appreciating the labyrinth form.

Like anything else, if a labyrinth is neglected it will disappear over time. Nature sees to that. A gravel wall will narrow and sink and become grown over and the willow degrades to a jungle. The same, of course, applies to school gardens, Forest School areas, ponds and any other outdoor project. This is why it is so important to decide on a programme of activities and cross-curricular use before the build. Let each class have a walk round the labyrinth one morning a week instead of their 'wake and shake'. Use it once a week as a focus for Circle Time or other reflective activity. Consider its use for time-out for troubled youngsters. The more use it gets, the longer it will last.

The ideas set out below are designed for a number of curriculum areas. Hopefully they will serve to encourage you to use your labyrinth with your kids on a regular basis. They have been written with the idea that they can be adapted for children and young people of all ages.

3.1 Wishing Tree

Aim. To give insight into an ancient spiritual practice used around the globe – that of leaving a gift behind to create a lasting and memorable connection between the individual and the sacred landscape or space.

In Brief. Children walk the labyrinth with a strip or fabric then tie the cloth to a branch of a nearby tree or bush.

What you will need:

Access to a 3 or 7 circuit labyrinth.* Any form will do (see previous chapter for how to build different types).	A tree or bush with branches low enough for the child to tie the cloth to either near the labyrinth or at the end of the walk.***
Students bring in their own ribbon or strip of fabric from something they have owned.** The more colourful and varied the better.	
* Alternatively a special 'pilgrimage path' can be devised or you might use a favourite 'welly walk' or an attractive route through a green area	
** If not possible, buy a bag of colourful fabric strips from a scrap store.	
*** If no suitable tree is available, the ribbons can be tied to a fence.	

Method.

1. Before setting out on your 'pilgrimage' familiarize your students with the tradition. You might discuss the many different ways people make a wish or say a prayer. A prayer can be an action as well as words. In this instance the prayer or wish is communicated through a small scrap of cloth, which is made personal because they chose it and touched it.

2. Discuss how Christian pilgrims may leave something at the shrine to a saint or at a holy well. Think about Buddhist prayer flags, where the prayer continues to be spoken through the action of the wind. They can then think about their wish 'living on' in the special place where they leave it. It helps them think about and connect with the special place when they are no longer there.

3. The children then walk the labyrinth with their piece of fabric, thinking and reflecting about their wish as they do so. On leaving the labyrinth they take their strip of fabric to their chosen wishing tree or bush and gently tie it to suitable twigs/branches. Note: do not choose a tree/bush with thorns!

Reflection. Think about your wish or prayer. Was it for yourself or was it for someone else? When do we make wishes (blowing out candles on a birthday cake, dropping coins in a well, making a wish on a dandelion seed head, seeing a solitary magpie)? Prayers may take the form of a wish. We should always try to include the well-being of others in our wishes.

3.2 Sensory use of the Labyrinth

Aim. To allow students to enjoy the labyrinth in a variety of different ways. To encourage well-being through quiet, reflective activity and play.

In Brief. Children walk the labyrinth whilst focussing on different sensory experiences.

What you will need:

Access to a labyrinth.

Weather is immaterial as appreciating the elements, such as wind or rain, can be part of the activity.

Consider being opportunistic with this. For example, bringing your group out after the grass has been mown or after rain to focus on smells.

Method.

1. Explain to the class or group that they are going to walk in to the Labyrinth and collect experiences through their senses. Each time they walk the labyrinth they will focus on a different area of sensation.

2. *Touch* – Walk the labyrinth barefoot. Shift your concentration to your feet. What are the different experiences as you walk round? Tickly, wet, warm, cold, sticky, stony and so on.

3. *Smell* – Can you smell the grass? Does each season have a special smell – damp in autumn, fresh in spring, flowers and mown grass in summer? Try and remember a special smell connected with walking the labyrinth.

4. *Taste* – Eat something plain whilst you are walking the labyrinth, such as a small square of bread. Think about the taste. Think about the importance of food and how wonderful even plain food tastes when we are really hungry.

5. *Hearing* - Listen for bird sounds, the sound of wind and the sounds of everyday activity around you. Try to remember all the sounds. How many different birds could you hear?

Reflection. Sit the children around the labyrinth. Use a talking stick. Ask each member of the group to share some aspect of their sensory experience. Sensory experiences often bring back memories. Did it remind them of other things they had experienced? How can focussing on our senses help us relax and forget our troubles for a while?

3.3 Experiencing the Labyrinth Differently

Aim. To enable students to experience the labyrinth in a variety of fun ways. To develop communication and coordination skills in younger children.

In Brief. Students experience moving round the labyrinth in several different ways.

What you will need:

Access to a 3 circuit labyrinth with a minimum path width of 75cm or a 7 circuit labyrinth.

Blindfolds.

Method.

1. Remind children of the universal labyrinth rule that those coming into the labyrinth have 'right of way' relative to those coming out. If the paths are narrow (50cm or so) the person coming out of the labyrinth stops, steps into an adjoining path, and then steps back when the other person has passed. Stopping and thinking means you are less likely to step back into the wrong path and find you are going back the way you came!

2. *Walk*. Begin by quickly walking the labyrinth as a group with as many as can comfortably use the labyrinth. The teacher or leader observes the group to ensure that the labyrinth is being used with consideration for all participants.

3. *Run*. Next, the group runs the labyrinth, taking care not to bump into people. Over-taking can either be banned or achieved by jumping into an adjoining path and jumping back again after over-taking.

4. *Backwards*. Children enter the labyrinth facing backwards. This time, no over-taking is allowed. The important thing is to avoid contact with the walls and for the group to all walk at the same pace. The last person to arrive (there will usually be a line leading to the goal as only a few will fit in it) leads the group out facing forwards.

5. *Blindfolded*. The group is paired and one volunteer in each pair is blindfolded. The sighted person leads the blindfolded person by the hand or shoulder and gives verbal instructions to help them. Contact with the walls should be avoided where possible.

6. *Animals*. Younger children enjoy going round the labyrinth as rabbits, bears or waddling like ducks. With older children you can do 'free-walking' with the emphasis on developing a particularly silly walk.

Reflection. Which way of using the labyrinth did you enjoy the most? What things did you learn by running it as a group? Were you considerate? Were others considerate? What did it feel like to go round blindfold? Were you aware of using other senses, such as sound and touch more? Did you feel closer to your partner as a result of being blindfold? How does this help us think about people with disabilities?

3.4 Insights into Impermanence

Aim. To give children an insight into the relaxing and meditational power of doing a simple task to a high standard - to do something *mindfully*. To give them an opportunity to reflect on a Buddhist belief that 'nothing lasts'.

In Brief. Students walk to the centre of the labyrinth and burn a mandala that they have made.

What you will need:

A suitable, attractive metal container in which a small fire can be lit (a large biscuit tin will suffice). Sides at least 20cm high to prevent fuel being blown out of the container.	Two buckets of water and a fire blanket to hand. A small bag of kindling or gathered, dry sticks of finger thickness. A small piece of firelighter
Watercolours, pastels, crayons etc. Blank paper to draw mandalas or photocopies of examples for the students to colour in.	Pictoral examples of mandalas to show the group/class. E.g. sand mandalas from Tibet.

NB. Only do this activity if you are confident with managing a small fire.

Method.

1. Discuss Buddhist attitudes to human activity and the importance of understanding that nothing lasts. Discuss the purpose of mandalas, particularly sand mandalas. Sand mandalas are made by Buddhist monks using multi-coloured sands. They can take months to make and feature extremely elaborate designs. When they are finished they are simply swept away and the sand thrown into a river. Why make something only to destroy it? How can it possibly help us feel better about ourselves?

2. Provide the group with a photocopied picture of a mandala. Invite them to colour it in to the very best of their ability and to work quietly and thoughtfully. Give them plenty of time and treat it as an insight into working 'mindfully' as well as a kind of meditation.

3. When the allocated time is over bring the group to the labyrinth and light the small fire at the centre goal. Students walk to the centre of the labyrinth, a few at a time, reflecting on the work they have done. Once at the centre they crush their mandala into a tight ball and place it on the fire. Give clear instructions not to touch the fire or its container.

Reflection. What would normally happen to their art work (marked/put on display)? What happens to most of the things we make in the end? What happens to us? What does this exercise tell us about what Buddhists believe?

Why make something only to destroy it?

How can it possibly help us feel better about ourselves?

3.5 Insights in to Christian Pilgrimage

Aim. To give students an insight into the idea of pilgrimage as a 'journey of hope'. To use the labyrinth as Christians may have used labyrinths as a kind of 'little pilgrimage'.

In Brief. Students use the labyrinth as it might have been used in the Middle Ages – as a substitute for a pilgrimage to Rome of Jerusalem.

What you will need:

Access to a labyrinth. An attractive bowl.	Card, paper and safety pin to make a badge.
Coloured paper, pens, glue and scissors to make a decorative offering to leave in the labyrinth.	Pictures and text about pilgrimage to make a classroom display.

Method.

1. Introduce the group to labyrinths in church contexts. How might they relate to the idea of Christian Pilgrimage? What is pilgrimage? Discuss the reasons why people go on pilgrimage. Reflect on the importance of having an opportunity to escape from our daily worries for a while and having time to think about things that really matter. What are the really important things in our lives? What are pilgrims hoping to achieve through their pilgrimage? How can pilgrimage help to 'heal' us? What do people get out of going to places like Lourdes?

2. Get your students to make a pilgrimage badge out of card, paper and a safety pin. Such items were - and still are - worn by pilgrims (the scallop shell of the Santiago de Compostella pilgrimage is perhaps the most famous). Discuss how labyrinths were used as a kind of mini-pilgrimage, as a kind of 'time out' to think things through and pray for healing.

3. Students can now think of their own reason for making a pilgrimage.

   • What can the labyrinth represent for them?

   • What special place would they like to visit in their imagination?

   • What would they like to achieve?

   • What might they pray for?

4. Encourage them to think not only of their own needs, wishes and problems, but those of other people less fortunate than themselves. Ask them to write their private thoughts on a piece of coloured paper. When they have finished it is folded in half and glued together to keep the thoughts private. The folded paper can now be cut into a decorative shape, such as a flower. Students now walk the labyrinth, thinking about what they wrote.

5. Students then walk slowly - in pairs or small groups - to the centre of the labyrinth where they leave their written wish in an attractive bowl.

Reflection. Think about labyrinths as a pilgrimage for those who were physically unable or too poor to make a pilgrimage to Rome or Jerusalem. What makes a pilgrimage different from other journeys? How do journeys help us think differently about things? Why are holidays important for us?

Notes. *Pilgrimage was commonplace in the Middle Ages, as it still for Hindus, Muslims and many Christians. You went on pilgrimage for many reasons. It was, at its simplest, a kind of adventure in an age when people did not make long journeys without good practical reason. Even so, such journeys were a great challenge and very risky. A pilgrimage to Jerusalem might take three years overland.*

Some reasons why a Christian might go on pilgrimage were: the forgiveness of sins (pilgrimage was sometimes given as a penance), to increase your chances of going to heaven, to ask for healing for yourself or someone close to you, to pray and come closer to God, to put aside the material world. The most popular pilgrimage places are associated with the relics of famous saints and a reputation for miracles. During the Middle Ages labyrinths began to make their appearance in churches throughout Europe. Walking the labyrinth was regarded as a pilgrimage, with the goal representing Jerusalem. It was also a reminder of the journey of life, with the heavenly kingdom as the goal. The church labyrinth belongs to a time when the nave was generally free of furniture and offered a large public space where people could mingle freely. The most famous surviving medieval labyrinth is at Chartres Cathedral.

At the time of writing, the labyrinth is making a comeback in churches. Witness the labyrinth at Norwich Cathedral and at St. John's Parish Church, Glastonbury. In the USA they are very popular. Generally situated outside the church building, they offer an opportunity for people of every faith and none to experience sacred space.

Students digging the labyrinth at St John's churchyard, Glastonbury

3.6 Drama – Theseus and the Minotaur

Aim. To explore labyrinth mythology by presenting a drama about Theseus and the Minotaur in an outdoor labyrinth context.

In Brief. The play is rehearsed and presented to an audience, using the labyrinth and nearby green areas as the theatre.

What you will need:

Access to a labyrinth.	A few old rugs to sit on (with tarpaulin underneath on a damp day).
2 spears, 3 swords, 2 oars and 2 flags on sticks (Athens and Crete). We use wooden ones, plastic toy versions will also suffice.	Several white ponchos made of white sheet with braid belts to identify the Athenian children.
4 crowns made of gold card and plastic/cheap jewels.	Four school chairs are utilized for thrones for the kings and queens of Crete and Athens.
A card Minotaur mask.	a ball of wool or string to unravel as Theseus enters the labyrinth.
A temporary labyrinth can be built close to tree cover where available to provide shelter in sun or light rain.	

Method.

1. The story should be read and discussed prior to the rehearsal activity. Children can draw pictures of the different episodes of the Theseus story to help them learn the plot and visualize events.

2. Parts are then given out. We give each student a sticky label to help them identify who is playing what part.

3. The area around the labyrinth is identified according to location – the ground closest to the labyrinth is Crete, an area around ten metres away is Athens. Flags and thrones are used to identify which country is which.

4. In the rehearsal, the story is read out and children given the opportunity to improvise and develop their speeches and movements. Some practice time should be given to ensure those playing soldiers can stand smartly and engage in non-contact mock fights.

5. Once rehearsed the play is shown to an invited audience from another class. Given the lighthearted nature of the text we suggest a pantomime style presentation with encouragement to cheer the hero and boo the villain.

Reflection. Did you enjoy doing your play? Do you think the audience enjoyed it too? What did you like best about doing the play? Think about other things you do where you can enjoy yourself and help other people at the same time. Share and discuss your ideas.

NARRATOR'S SCRIPT - THESEUS & THE MINOTAUR

Characters

KING MINOS OF CRETE (sword, crown)

QUEEN MINA OF CRETE (crown)

ARIADNE, DAUGHTER OF KING MINOS (tiara, ball of wool)

MINOTAUR, (bull mask with horns),

CRETAN NAVY (2 children with oars),

CRETAN ARMY (2 children with swords)

KING OF ATHENS, THESEUS'S DAD (crown)

QUEEN OF ATHENS, THESEUS'S MUM (crown)

THESEUS (sword)

ATHENIAN SOLDIERS (2 children with spears)

ATHENIAN BOYS & ATHENIAN GIRLS (7 - 12 in simple white slips, tied at the waist with a piece of rope or braid)

Divide the acting space into 2 areas, one for Crete and one for Athens. The labyrinth is on the Cretan side of the area. Mark out each area with a flag for each.

The narrator tells the story and the children follow the acting directions. Children should be encouraged to improvise and develop the action.

"Once upon a time there lived a king named Minos (*Minos walks to centre of Acting Area and takes a bow*). King Minos lived on a lovely island called Crete. King Minos had a powerful navy (*Navy sails into acting area and takes a bow*). Minos loved his navy. (*He gives one of the 'ships' a little polish on the head*). Minos also had a beautiful daughter, called Ariadne, and a really big palace (*Ariadne enters, takes a bow. Minos kisses his daughter on the cheek*). Minos also had a strange and evil son, the Minotaur, who was half man and half bull. He was so dangerous they kept him in a labyrinth.

The Minotaur who is sat in a bull-like fashion to the centre of the labyrinth, stands up, shows his muscles, and makes suitable bull-like noises.

But the Minotaur wasn't clever enough to figure out how to get out of the labyrinth (*the Minotaur wanders backwards and forwards, scratching his head and looking puzzled*). Every now and then Minos liked to give the Minotaur a treat – a nice juicy child to eat. Of course, this made him a bit unpopular with his people. So he thought 'aha, I'll get those not so friendly people from Athens to give me some children to feed to my darling Minotaur. Every seven years they can send me seven boys and seven girls. King Minos did not like the people of Athens. In the past Athens had made war on him. Now the boot was on the other foot. On the other side of the Mediterranean sea from Crete was the kingdom of Athens. Athens had a king and a queen and they were very nice people (the king and queen of Athens take a bow). They had a son, Theseus (*Theseus takes a bow*). He was a brave and mighty warrior with big muscles (*Theseus flexes his muscles and poses*). He was also very handsome.

"Time to sail to Athens to collect the children." Says Minos. "My darling Minotaur must be getting hungry. Summon my army and navy."

The soldiers and the sailors, together with King Minos, got into their ship to sail for Athens. The sea was rather rough and King Minos was sick. The King of Athens and his army came to the beach to meet King Minos.

"I have come for fourteen children to feed to the Minotaur." *He said.*

"Not on your nelly." Replied the King of Athens. "You will have to fight me."

War breaks out and the two sides play fight each other. Soon all the Athenian soldiers are dead.

"Now you will give me the children," said Minos.

So the children were selected and brought to the boat and everyone was crying and making rather a lot of noise. Theseus came to his father.

"Let me go, Dad. I am a mighty hero with big muscles and all the girls like me. I'll sort out this Minotaur. With my trusty sword I'll turn him into mincemeat."

"No my darling son, I can't let you go. You mean all the world to me and your mum."

"Don't worry, Dad, the hero always wins in the story, remember?"

"Oh alright then. But your mum won't be pleased. She's done a roast for tonight."

So the poor children were forced into the boat and set sail for Crete, with the king of Athens crying into his hankie.

All the children get into a boat formation. With Minos at the helm and his guards behind him, the two oarsmen row them back to Crete.

When the ships approached Crete the queen and Ariadne came down to the beach to meet them. As the children were getting off the boat Ariadne caught sight of Theseus. She fell in love with him immediately.

"Oh he's so handsome," she said. "I think I love him. I can't let the horrible Minotaur eat him. He's too nice."

The children were led off to the prison where they were to spend the night crying and being generally miserable.

The children from Athens lie down and go to sleep. They sob every now and then because they know they will be eaten in the morning.

Late in the night the princess Ariadne wrote Prince Theseus a note and slipped it through the bars of the cell. (Ariadne sneaks over and leaves the letter by Theseus. Theseus wakes up and reads the letter).

Dear Theseus (*Ariadne wrote*)

I am a beautiful princess as you probably noticed the minute you saw me. I am also a very bored princess. Without my help, the Minotaur will surely gobble you up. I know a trick or two that will save your life. If I help you kill the monster, you must promise to take me away from this tiny island so that others can admire my beauty. If interested in this deal, meet me by the gate to the Labyrinth in one hour.

Yours very truly,
Princess Ariadne

In her hands, Ariadne carries a sword and a ball of string. She passes them to Theseus

"Tomorrow, when you and the children enter the Labyrinth, wait until the gate is closed, then tie the string to the door. Unroll it as you move through the labyrinth. That way, you can find your way back again. You know what to do with the sword."

"Don't forget, now," she cautioned Theseus. "You must take me with you so that all the people can marvel at my beauty. A deal is a deal."

The next morning, all the Athenian children, including Prince Theseus, were shoved into the labyrinth. Following Ariadne's directions, Theseus tied one end of the string to the entrance.

The children walk into the labyrinth, with Theseus in the lead. The wool is unravelled carefully as they walk to the centre.

It took him a while, but Theseus finally found his way to the centre. Using the sword Ariadne had given him, he fights the monstrous Minotaur. (*There is a fight between Theseus and the Minotaur. After a struggle Theseus stabs the Minotaur and it dies. All the children cheer and dance. They follow the string back out to the entrance to the labyrinth*).

Princess Ariadne was waiting. She opens the labyrinth door. Without anyone noticing, Prince Theseus and the children of Athens ran to their ship and sailed quietly away. Princess Ariadne sailed away with them.

The children and Ariadne climb into the ship and row themselves back towards Athens.

After that, everyone lived happily ever after, I think. Well, maybe Minos didn't when he discovered his pet Minotaur was mincemeat! (*Minos cries when he sees the dead Minotaur*).

THE END

3.7 Understanding Your Heart

Aim. To explore the impact on breathing and heart rate of running the labyrinth. To gain understanding of the impact of exercise on respiration.

In Brief. Younger children experience changes in heart rate / breathing after running the labyrinth. Older students use watches to record pulse / respiration rates to produce averages.

What you will need:

Access to a labyrinth.	
Younger children require no materials other than access to a labyrinth.	
Older students will need watches, clipboards and charts to record heart rates and respiration, possibly as part of a wider study.	Some data / charts on average breathing rates for their age group.

Method.

1. Discuss the impact of exercise on heart rate and breathing. Explore how this can show if we are fit or unfit. Discuss the units of measurement – heart beats per minute and breathing rate per minute.

2. **Younger students**: Ask them to put their hands on their chest to feel their heart beating. Ask them to think about their breathing. What is it like when they are relaxed?

3. They then run the labyrinth in small groups.

4. When they emerge from the labyrinth ask them to feel their heart again and think about their breathing.

    *   How has their heart and breathing rate changed?

    *   Has it changed a lot?

    *   Discuss the need for oxygen.

    *   Why do we need more oxygen when we run?

    *   How does our body meet that need?

5. **Older students**: Teach them how to take a pulse correctly using a watch.

6. Walk to the labyrinth and relax.

7. When students are rested they record each other's pulse rate (number of beats per minute). They then run the labyrinth (both in and out) and record their pulse rate immediately on stopping. Results are recorded on the clipboards and charts provided.

8. After resting for 1 minute the pulse is taken for a third time. This measures how rapidly the heart rate comes down from the peak reading.

9. The outcomes can be entered onto a database so that the range of fitness present in a group can be explored. Compare with online statistics for their age group.

Reflection. Explore the outcomes. What have you found out about your fitness? What kinds of things can we do to improve our fitness? Where is 'fitness' in the list of things that are important to you? Why do people often worry more about their appearance than their fitness?

3.8 Number And Labyrinths

Aim. To help younger children develop their counting skills.

In Brief. Children count the number of steps it takes to walk to the centre of the labyrinth using a simple counting system. Children learn to count paces.

What you will need:

Access to a labyrinth.

A method of keeping score. This can be a stroke of a coloured pen on a page for every 10 paces walked or a pebble dropped into a small bucket or box. Colour coding each pair of children can help avoid confusion.

Method.

1. Begin by having the group run the labyrinth path in and out.

2. Guess the number of steps they think they took. Record the guesses.

3. The group work in pairs, each pair with their own colour. One child from each of the pairs walks the labyrinth. When the 'walker' has walked 10 steps they shout 'green 10 steps' or 'red 10 steps' and the 'marker' records the score with a stroke on a piece of paper or by dropping a pebble into a small container.

4. Once the walk is complete the pebbles / strokes are counted and the distance walked in terms of steps calculated by adding a 'zero' to the number of pebbles counted. When all the pairs have paced the labyrinth the 'scores' can be compared. Are the scores similar or are there big differences?

Reflection. Is it a good idea to use counting steps to measure distances? When might it be useful? When do people use counting steps today (e.g. can I get my car into that space?) Why is counting steps not very good if you want to be accurate?

Notes. Pacing is used in poor visibility to work out distance travelled when micro-navigation is necessary, such as to locate a critical descent point off a mountain summit. N.b. A 'pace' is two steps, or strides, not one, with the pace counted when the right foot is forward. A pace for a child might thus be 1 metre and twice that for a tall adult. The traditional pace was five English feet, measured from the point at which the heel of one foot is raised to the point at which it is set down again after an intervening step by the other foot. Accurate pacing for navigational purposes requires the pacer to have compared their pacing against a known distance beforehand.

3.9 Using Pacing to measure the length of a Labyrinth Path

Aim. To develop skills in estimating and calculating distances by eye and by pacing.

In Brief. Students measure the labyrinth path accurately by counting paces and converting them to metres.

What you will need:

Access to a labyrinth. A 7 circuit rope labyrinth provides an ideal distance.	A clipboard and a score sheet 3.9 (*see opposite*) - *one per group*.
A rope of known length (15m is ideal) pegged out on the ground.	A 25m tape measure to confirm labyrinth path length at the end of the exercise.
A couple of calculators.	

Method.

1. Explain the function of pacing to the students. It was a valuable method to measure distance over rough terrain before the development of surveying tools. It is still taught as a navigation aid.

2. Explain how to pace. You count each time you step off on the same foot. A pace for an adult is around 1.5 metres.

3. Divide the class into teams of 4 to 6. Discuss and practice pacing – that is, a pace is from the raising of the heel of a foot to the point it is placed on the ground again (two comfortable strides).

4. Each student in a team paces the labyrinth. The number of paces made by each student are recorded. The individual scores are then added together and divided by the number of people in the group to get an average score. (e.g. 50 + 47 + 45 + 48 + 51 = 241 divided by 5 = 48.2 (If the team are all of a similar size the scores should not be too far out from each other. If one score is wildly out don't use it. It is likely a counting mistake has been made).

5. Each student now paces the measured 15 metre rope. The scores are recorded. Add all the scores for pacing together and divide by 5 to get the average for the group. (e.g. 8 + 8.5 + 9 + 11 + 9 = 45.5 divided by 5 = 9.1 paces.

6. Divide the average pace score for the labyrinth with the average pace score for the paces for the rope. e.g. 48.2 divided by 9.1 = 5.296

7. Now multiply 5.296 by the length of the paced rope (15 metres) to get the length of the labyrinth path. e.g 5.296 x 15 metres = 79.45 metres.

8. Measure the labyrinth path with a 25m tape and see who got the most accurate score.

Reflection. Repeating or duplicating experiments is always a good way to improve accuracy. Discuss the different uses for averages in producing useful information.

Note: This activity can make use of a labyrinth or any outdoor space. It could be used, for example, to measure the length of a school field. The activity as set out below is for older children. A whole class, divided into teams, can be involved.

3.9 Labyrinth Pacing Activity Score Sheet

1. WRITE DOWN THE NUMBER OF PACES IT TAKES TO WALK FROM THE MOUTH OF THE LABYRINTH TO THE GOAL.

a)   **NAME**   ....   **NO. OF PACES**   ....

b)   **NAME**   ....   **NO. OF PACES**   ....

c)   **NAME**   ....   **NO. OF PACES**   ....

d)   **NAME**   ....   **NO. OF PACES**   ....

2. NOW ADD YOUR ACTUAL PACES TOGETHER AND DIVIDE BY THE NUMBER OF PEOPLE IN YOUR GROUP. (a+b+c+d = x divided by 4 = y)

YOUR TEAM'S AVERAGE PACE SCORE FOR THE LABYRINTH WALK

IS......................

3. WRITE DOWN YOUR PACES FOR THE 15 METRE ROPE.

a)   **NAME**   ....   **NO. OF PACES**   ....

b)   **NAME**   ....   **NO. OF PACES**   ....

c)   **NAME**   ....   **NO. OF PACES**   ....

d)   **NAME**   ....   **NO. OF PACES**   ....

4. NOW ADD YOUR ACTUAL PACES AND DIVIDE BY THE NUMBER OF PEOPLE IN YOUR GROUP. (a+b+c+d = x divided by 4 = z)

YOUR AVERAGE PACES FOR THE 15 METRE ROPE IS ....

5. DIVIDE YOUR AVERAGE PACES FOR THE LABYRINTH BY YOUR AVERAGE PACES FOR THE 15 METRE ROPE. (y divided by z = zy)

....

6. LASTLY, MULTIPLY THE SCORE BY 15 TO FIND OUT HOW MANY METRES THE DISTANCE PACED IS. (zy x 20 = xyz)

....

3.10 Labyrinth Clock – Constructing a Sundial

Aim. To help younger children learn to tell the time. To enable students in general to relate time to the movement of the sun across the sky and seasonal variations.

In Brief. The labyrinth is converted into a sundial, using a gnomon, or shadow-stick, and observation of the sun's shadow.

What you will need:

Access to a labyrinth away from sources of sustained shadow such as buildings or heavily canopied trees.	A fairly clear sky to position the hour markers, although this can be done over a number of days if the weather fails.
A shadow-stick or gnomon of around 1.75 metres long and 8cm diameter. Depending on the season, the post may need to be shortened for a small labyrinth to keep the shadow within the circle.	Lengths of ribbon or brightly coloured twine. - (ckeck the length of shadow the day before you do the activity). A rubber mallet, steel tent pegs. PIctures of Sundials.

Method.

1. Discuss methods for telling the time before the advent of mechanical clocks (candles with markers, water clocks, hourglasses, sundials). Look at pictures and locations of sundials online or have examples printed out.

2. With older children, discuss how the movement of the sun across the sky changes as the seasons change – high in summer, low in winter and shifting from south to north and back again. In prehistoric times wooden posts or stone alignments would have been used to provide dates.

3. Students decorate the shadow stick or gnomon.

4. They then help to hammer it into the ground at the centre of the labyrinth. Alternatively, a section of turf can be removed and the post dug in. The gnomon needs to be secure as movement will render the clock less accurate.

5. Bring your group out so that they are present at the turning of the hour. Attach the ribbon to the post. Note precisely where the shadow falls and lay out the ribbon along the length of the shadow and secure with pegs. Continue through the day or days until your pattern of hours is complete.

6. If the sundial can be left in place for any length of time, continue to make regular observations (say at midday) to explore how the shadow lengthens or shortens and shifts as the season moves on. These very simple sundials are only accurate for a couple of weeks after construction. Older students may wish to research online for the methods used to lay out a seasonal sundial.

Reflection. Think about the differences between 'clock' time and natural time. In nature, days lengthen and then shorten as the seasons change and the months follow the phases of the moon. The Muslim calendar reflects the cycles of the moon. Here in the west we have become much less aware of the role of the sun and moon in determining our year. Observe the moon for a few evenings. Write down your thoughts or draw a picture each night of the changing phases. Think about how the phases of the moon mark the passage of time. Use your observations of sun and moon to create a painting or a poem in school.

4. FOREST SCHOOL – STARTING OUT

Sticky Paper Quests, Crowns for the Seasons, Willow Towers, Tree Bark Rubbings, String Journey, C lay Beasts, Soft Toy Town, Stone Age Bling, Bird Nests, Bug Hotels, Gypsy Trails, Blindfold Challenge, Camouflage Game, Magic Carpets, Bats and Owls.

Forest School has its roots in Scandinavia, with initiatives at kindergarten level reaching back into the 1950s. Support for the movement grew in the 1990s when research carried out in Sweden demonstrated that children who had regular Forest School were happier, better socialized, less likely to demonstrate stressful behaviours and had less time off sick than kids confined to urban environments. In the UK, Forest School came to Britain in the mid 1990s initially as a result of research carried out by nursery nurses from Bridgwater College in Somerset, who visited Denmark to find out how Forest School worked. Hence, the initial impetus was in Early Years and it is in this context it has thrived. At secondary level its growth has been less secure, and from our experience has been utilized largely as an interventionist strategy for troubled or disaffected youngsters. One aim of this book is to put before teachers the application of the Forest School philosophy to the entire curriculum, for youngsters of every age and ability.

The heart of the Forest School philosophy is about getting kids outdoors – ideally into a natural setting, such as woodland or an unkempt copse in the corner of the school field. Of equal importance to the Forest School philosophy is that kids experience the outdoors rain or shine. Delivering Forest School begins with getting the kids used to changing in and out of wellies and wet weather gear and not cancelling because of a bit of rain and mud.

Forest School is also about relationships. Changing the setting in which students act out their relationships with each other and their adult carers allows those relationships to be re-configured. Difficult kids become a whole lot less difficult because they can achieve, get the attention they need and have the space to break from the negative forces that tied them to their old patterns of behaviour. For this reason, Forest School training recommends small groups and a high adult to student ratio. Fairly easy to achieve in the nursery or early years context, but a tough call in a secondary school!

Forest School is distinguished by specific training. For example, the BTEC Level 3 Forest School Leader course provides academic study in educational philosophy and psychology, basic outdoor skills, quality assurance and health and safety training. The existence of the qualification has led many schools to believe that Forest School cannot be delivered unless they have staff with the appropriate piece of paper. Whilst we wholeheartedly commend the qualification (all our staff, including myself, are qualified Forest School leaders), it was, for us, only part of the journey in exploring accessible strategies for delivering the curriculum outdoors.

Perhaps the most important thing I learned from Forest School is to keep in sight the tension between teaching youngsters traditional skill sets and giving them open-ended tasks that allow them to develop their own way of doing things. Forest School teaches the importance of open-ended learning whilst ensuring there is plenty of challenge and built in progression.

We also like the fact that kids seem more prepared to risk failure in the more informal outdoor environment. Confidence comes from resilience. Entrepreneurship is founded on risk, and the strength to take the knocks and begin again. If I learnt one thing in my thirty years as a classroom practitioner it was that 'fear of failure' was the main reason why kids didn't try in the first place. Structure building with groups, where they are left to 'get on with it', with only health and safety interventions, allows the dynamic of individual and group responsibility to become transparent in a setting where risk and experiment is commended. And the amazing thing is, even at infant level, freedom and competition usually results in youngsters achieving far more than you or they expected.

There are three chapters for Forest School. The first chapter describes activities that can be delivered by adults with only modest practical experience in Forest School type activities. The activities are designed to be accessible to very young students and require relatively few tools and materials. The second chapter describes activities that presume that youngsters have progressed in their practical skills. The activities also assume greater experience on the part of the teacher in things like working with fire and sharp tools. The final Forest School chapter describes activities relating to setting up and maintaining a Forest School area.

FIFTEEN FOREST SCHOOL ACTIVITY IDEAS

4.1 Sticky Paper Quests

Aim. To develop observation skills. To introduce students to collecting and classification of found natural items such as leaves.

In Brief. Students use double-sided sticky tape attached to strips of card to collect and organize found materials.

What you will need:

Access to a wood, park or green area of the school grounds that provides appropriate 'finds', such as leaves, small mollusc shells etc.	One strip of card with attached double-sided sticky tape per student. We usually guillotine pieces of A4 card lengthways to produce 4 strips. *
In wet weather issue a large freezer bag or plastic carrier bag to keep the card dry.	

Method.

1. Choose a collecting challenge appropriate to your topic and age group. Some examples are:
    *   Find specific colours using a colour chart attached to the card.
    *   Collect leaves, nuts and seeds, or grasses and common flowers such as daisies, dandelion and clover (***it is very important not to let students pick unusual or non-abundant species and to educate them in the reasons for this***).
    *   Gather natural material according to shape, texture, size or typology, such as 'animal, vegetable, mineral'.
2. Discuss the Sticky Paper Quest objectives with your group. You might be studying identification and classification of autumn falls of seeds and nuts, for example, and pairing them up with the appropriate tree. Younger students might collect different types of leaves.
3. Take your group to the outdoor environment and distribute the cards. Encourage neatness and specify the minimum number of different samples you want them to find. In a welly walk, you might want them to collect samples in different locations or environments so that comparisons can be made. Encourage the group to think up imaginative ways to display their cards back in the classroom.

Reflection. See if you can identify each item on your card. If it is a seed, for example, do you know which plant or tree it came from? Choose one or two of your finds to share and discuss with your group. What things did you become more aware of as a result of focusing on these particular finds?

4.2 Crown for the Seasons

Aim. To explore the form and beauty of natural things. To use found natural items to make an artifact that can be worn.

In Brief. A decorative crown is made to reflect the seasons.

What you will need:

One strip of card around 6cm wide by 55cm long per student (long enough to go round the head and rest comfortably on the ears).	Stapler to clip the ends of the crown together. Safety scissors. Double-sided tape. Plastic bags or similar to keep the card dry.
Access to a wood, park or green area of the school that provides plenty of colourful leaf litter. Autumn is best. Have a canopy to sit under in wet weather.	

Method.

1. Begin by telling a story involving fairy kings and queens, perhaps with reference to 'A Midsummer Night's Dream' and the faery king and queen, Oberon and Titania.

   - What would they look like?
   - What would their crowns be made of?
   - Where do we see golden colours in nature?
   - What colours might the jewels be?
   - Where might we find the colours of jewels in nature?

2. Explain that they are all going to make a crown, perhaps to wear in a play or to help with writing a special story.

3. Issue a collecting bag and head out. Collect special leaves or other natural objects off the ground, such as feathers and down or mosses. Make sure they are a suitable size for the crown.

4. Think about design. You might want two of each leaf colour so that they can be paired.

5. Encourage careful and selective collection. Share the finding of particularly bright colours – reds, golds, greens. In autumn keep an eye open for winged seeds, such as Ash, Sycamore or Maple. Return to your activity area to make the crowns.

6. Issue the card strips at this stage if you haven't already done so.

7. Students lay the leaves and seeds out on the ground first. Encourage careful working to create shapes and patterns, or use of particular colours. Don't throw away surplus leaves, take them back for other uses. Once the crowns are complete they can be worn on the walk back to the transport or classroom. If it is raining carefully pack them in carrier bags (don't forget to write names on them). Back in class or the outdoor activity area, make a line out of the remaining leaves. Rearrange them by colour and shade, perhaps going from green to gold.

Reflection. What is more beautiful – a crown of gold or a crown of golden leaves? Why do leaves change their colour before going brown and brittle and falling off the tree? Try and think of a special meaning for each colour in your crown and share it with the group. For example, 'green is for spring', 'red is for sun'.

4.3 Tree Bark Rubbings

Aim. To explore the textures of tree surfaces and learn to identify trees by their bark.

In Brief. Students use art paper and crayons of different colours to make a montage of different tree barks.

What you will need:

Access to a variety of mature trees.	Sturdy paper that won't tear or crease too easily.
A relatively dry day.	Thick, stubby crayons.
A couple of rolls of masking tape to secure the paper to the tree.	

Method.

1. Explain to the group that trees can be identified in several ways – their leaves, their bark, their seeds and their overall shape and size.

2. Take them for a walk, ideally to a wood or copse.

3. Demonstrate the rubbing technique and encourage them to produce an image of even density to accurately reflect the bark texture. Attach a leaf and a seed, if available, to each rubbing.

4. Back at school, the bark rubbings can be made into a montage and the leaves or seeds glued to the rubbing in an attractive arrangement.

5. Finally, write the names of the trees on strips of paper and attach them to the appropriate parts of the montage.

Reflection. Consider how every tree has its own character. No two trees are alike, even trees of the same species, because light, water, nutrition and parentage all play a part in making them unique. In that sense they are like us.

Reflect on the value of being able to identify different tree types and being able to use trees as landmarks. Think about the beauty of trees and what they add to our landscape. Think about all the things that trees give us – their shade, timber for buildings and furniture, wood for our fires and a habitat for so many living things. And remember the oxygen we breathe and the carbon dioxide absorbed by trees; they are the lungs of the earth.

4.4 Willow Towers

Aim. To develop teamwork and problem-solving skills. To encourage risk-taking and innovation in competing with other teams.

In Brief. Students work in groups to construct towers out of willow sticks or similar materials.

What you will need: *(per group)*

A bundle of 16 or so withies, hazel sticks or garden canes of about 1 metre length and 8 or so sticks of 50cms length.	A ball of twine and a pair of safety scissors, half a dozen steel tent pegs and a rubber mallet. *
* If your group are too young to tie knots provide rolls of masking tape to join sticks.	

Method.

1. With younger groups begin with the tale of 'Jack and the Beanstalk' and the challenge of making a tower tall enough to get to the giant's house in the clouds. Each group must try and make their tower taller than anyone else's to be sure of getting the goose that lays the golden egg!

2. In practical terms, explain that the tower must be free standing.

3. With an inexperienced group demonstrate the basic construction techniques, such as tying or taping sticks together, using the mallet and stake to make holes in the ground to take the sticks, tying sticks together to form tripods and using guy ropes.

4. Explain that this is a timed challenge (we usually allow 15 to 25 minutes depending on age and ability), that they are competing with other groups and their structure must be stable enough to stand unaided for at least sixty seconds.

5. Older students might be encouraged to consider pre-fabricating sections of the structure on the ground and attaching them after the base is complete and to make taller and more complex structures. A development on this activity, for example, is to make the tower able to carry a load in the form of a plastic bucket or jug full of water.

6. On completion, the towers are checked for stability and the winner declared.

Reflection. Share what you learned about making your structure stronger. What techniques did you use to give your structure stability? How well did you work as a team? What were the issues you had to resolve in coming to a decision about your structure? In what other contexts could you use these skills?

4.5 String Journey

Aim. To encourage students to think about how found objects can symbolize or represent a locale. To encourage sequential recollection of a journey.

In Brief. Students collect small items in a non-damaging way from significant points on the journey and twist them into a length of string.

What you will need:

Access to a wood or park.

A ball of sisal twine, enough to provide a 50cm length per student.

Method.

1. Explain how some people collect small items, such as unusual bits of dried wood or driftwood, leaves, flowers and so on as souvenirs to remind them of a place they have visited. Such items might be placed in a bowl of pot pourri or pressed between the pages of a book. Their task will be to provide a memory of a journey they will make by collecting small, natural items on a piece of string.

2. Cut the string into 50cm lengths and tie a knot in both ends to keep the string from unravelling. Give each student a piece of string. Demonstrate how to insert an item into the string. The string is held at two points a few centimetres apart and twisted so that the strands separate and open out.

3. A found item, such as an interesting twig can now be inserted. The threads are then twisted back in the opposite direction to tighten them again. Any light, elongated object can be secured in this way, but short items, such as acorns and pebbles have a bad habit of slipping out!

4. At different points on your journey, on wood or welly walk ask students to collect an interesting item that will help them remember the location – something they can talk about afterwards. Aim to collect eight to ten items to produce an attractive collection.

5. When the walk is over the strings can be tied to a washing line in class or the branch of a tree. Discuss the collected items with the students, perhaps by asking them to share their favourite found item. Comments might include a description and a location:

   - "I found the leaf under a tree. It was windy. The sun was in the tree."
   - "After the tree there was a gate. It was a kissing gate. I found a feather."
   - "There was a road. I picked up some litter for my string."

Reflection. What are souvenirs? How do souvenirs help us to remember good things that have happened to us? Do we have to buy souvenirs? What about things we might find, such as a pretty shell or an unusual pebble?

4.6 Clay Beasts and an Animal Ark

Aim. To encourage students to explore relationship in form and shapes in natural materials. To develop skills in observation.

In Brief. Students collect natural items - feathers, small pine cones, tiny pebbles, leaves and twigs etc. - to assist in the creation of a small clay animal for inside or outside display.

What you will need:

Access to a wood or park.	Safety scissors for trimming leaves, feathers and twigs.
A bag of air-drying or natural clay, enough to give each student a golf ball sized chunk.	Small freezer bags to encourage gathering of items of an appropriate size.
A flat work surface, e.g. log stump, picnic table or trays to mould the clay on. (We take a bag of small, metal trays that also support carrying the work back to the classroom or transport).	

Method.

1. Begin by exploring form in found items – a small white pebble might look like an eye or a tooth, a twig like an insect leg. Does a pine cone remind you of any animal? Students might begin by looking for something specific – such as a curly twig or leaf stem that looks like a mouse tail.

2. Explain that the task is to make a small animal for a special ark, perhaps to decorate a window ledge back in class or a length of fallen tree trunk in a wood. Consider theming the work, perhaps the creatures will be insects, birds or woodland mammals. Perhaps they will be strange creatures that have come on a special ark from outer space. Talk about technique and how a small amount of clay will provide the base to attach the things they find to make their creature.

3. On the walk encourage the collection of items that are to scale – the creatures, after all, will be mouse sized when complete. Look for tiny, distinctive items such as snail shells (possible ears) and tiny, white twigs that might be trimmed to size for teeth. Look for feathers too.

4. Back at the activity area, issue the clay. Before starting the animal, demonstrate making shapes with the clay. The main skills are rolling between the palms to make balls of different sizes, and rolling between a surface and the hand to make a sausage shape. Demonstrate how a twig can be used to impress a design into the surface of the clay. Finally, ask each student to briefly talk about the animal they would like to make.

5. Encourage attention to detail. Does the creature have eyes, ears, nose and mouth? Does it have hair or feathers? What are its legs like? When the animals are made they can be grouped together to make an ark display.

Reflection. What kind of animal did you make? What did you use to make your animal? What did you like most about making your animal? Look at other people's animals. Which ones do you like best? What do you like about them?

4.7 Soft Toy Town

Aim. To encourage imaginative play. To develop group skills. To enable children to create their own play environment.

In Brief. Children make a little town of natural materials, such as sticks, small branches and leaves and populate it with their cuddly toys.

What you will need:

Each child needs to bring in a soft animal or character toy from home.	An ample store of medium length sticks, branches or brash of around 75cm to 1m in length. *

Branches do not need to be stripped of leaves and evergreen brash does just as well. The availability of mown grass, dead leaves, snail shells and pebbles all help.

Method.

1. Share names of animal characters they have seen on TV or read about in books. Where do they live? What do their homes look like? Do they have gardens? What kind of furniture do they have in their homes?

2. Introduce the activity. Students work in twos or threes to make a home for their soft toys. Together they will be making a little town with a road running through it. The houses will be made of sticks, branches, leaves and grass and might have gardens will pebble walls. It will need to be big enough to take the two or three animals in their group.

3. Explain how to work safely with sticks and branches. Always walk, never run! Watch where you are going! Be very careful not to catch anyone else with the sticks or branches.

4. In small groups they explore the area and choose the places where they want to build their houses. As this is a little town, they should be quite close to each other – even opposite sides of the same tree. Students leave their animals at their chosen location and carefully gather their materials together. Allow them to work without guidance for a while. If necessary, you might provide some further inspiration by suggesting furniture, such as tables or beds. If some finish earlier than others, they might begin work on a road or other features they might find in their little town.

5. Students should start to share their work and further play may develop naturally. If not, organize a tour of the town, with the children explaining who lives in each house and to describe the different rooms, furniture and garden.

Reflection. Share what you liked most about making your town. Did you like working together? What things did you find that you used to make your house? What would it be like to live in a wood?

4.8 Stone Age Bling

Aim. To help students develop confidence in the safe use of sharp tools.

In Brief. Elder is used to make simple necklaces and bracelets.

What you will need: (*per group of of 3-4 students*).

For elder beads: Several lengths of straight, mature elder branches, 2cm to 3cm thick. Enough to provide at least 15cm for each student. Potato peeler.
Mini hacksaw*. Log stump. Wool or sisal garden twine. **
A blunt ended steel tent peg. Safety scissors. Brace and 5mm wood bit.

For hardwood discs: Approx 1m of fresh hardwood pole with a diameter of 4 to 6cm. Robust gardening gloves Bow saw and saw horse *(see activity 6.7)* or grooved log stump.

*Students who have little or no experience of using saws may need one to one support in the first instance. **For safety reasons we advise the use of twine or wool that snaps easily.

Method.

1. Explain to the class that they are going to make jewellery out of a special wood called elder, identified with distinctive bark, leaves, flowers and berries. Demonstrate its properties by sawing a bead and pushing the pith out with the tent peg. ***Explain that the pith must be pushed out away from the face and body. Before inspecting the hole the steel peg must be put down.***

2. ***Sawing the elder beads.*** Distribute the elder in lengths of 30cm or more. Working in pairs students now begin to cut 4-6 beads each depending on time (less if working with younger students for the first time). One student supports the elder on the block whilst the other cuts. Ensure careful, unforced sawing, with a relaxed grip on the saw. The younger students often need help with sawing.   By gently holding and guiding the opposite end of the saw, it is possible to support them whilst enabling them to do the actual sawing.

3. ***Sawing hardwood discs.*** Depending on the maturity of your group, for students aged 7 +. Requires 1:2 supervision. The pole is firmly supported on a saw horse or grooved log stump. Students help each other by sawing together, each holding one side of the bow saw *pulling* it towards them (they are more likely to force and twist the blade in the *pushing* action). ***Students wear robust gardening gloves with the exception of the hand holding the saw.***

4. Once the beads / discs are cut, place on a log stump and drill the central hole with a brace and 5mm wood bit. Young students can help each other by having one student press down on the brace whilst the second rotates the handle.

5. Strip the bark by peeling with a fingernail or potato peeler (ensure gloves are worn on the hand holding the bead). Peel all, alternate or none at all, depending on individual taste.

6. Beads / discs are now strung with wool or soft twine. Again, younger students often struggle with this. Demonstrate how to thin the end of the twine or wool by wetting it. Also it helps to gently twist the thread as it is fed through the bead.

Reflection. Share thoughts and feelings about successfully finishing a piece of jewellery. Compare your necklace or bracelet with others. How are they all different? Why do you think no two pieces are the same, even though you have been doing the same task?

4. 9 Bird Nests

Aims. To explore the complexity of bird nests. To consider the different locations of nests. To make a bird's nest of their own.

In Brief. Students examine old nests, then make a nest with suitable found materials.

What you will need:

An old bird's nest. Access to a woodland or park with plenty of trees.
Plastic carrier bag for students to collect their materials in.

Method.

1. Discuss the nesting season, which runs from early March to late July, depending on the weather and the species. *Think about carrying out this activity during this period so nesting activity can be observed.* Explain that they are going to make thier own nest and place it outside.

2. Introduce the nest itself. What is it for? How are the chicks fed and reared? How soon can a chick leave the nest? What are the chicks fed on? Where do we find nests?

3. Explore the nest structure. Remember that a bird might take more than a fortnight to make a nest. A blackbird, for example, makes a cup of small twigs, grasses, straw and other plants. This is then carefully lined with mud. Finally, softer material, such as moss or fine grasses provide the lining.

4. Head out on a welly walk or woodland visit to scavenge nest materials. Get the group to think about the different things they will need – long grasses or fine twigs to make the cup. Mosses, mud or soft clay to line it. Remind them that different birds have different techniques.

5. In an activity area, such as a woodland clearing or school grounds, make the nests, either in pairs or singly. Take particular care to achieve a cupped shape at the start – eggs or chicks might otherwise fall from the nest. Remind the group that the inner layer needs to be soft.

6. Now think about where to put the nest. It has to be high enough to avoid the domestic cat and concealed from above to avoid magpies that love to feed on baby chicks. The group then locate their nests in places that they think will provide shelter and be hard for a predator to spot. Back in the classroom, find out about unusual nests, such as that built by the wren. Make a display of paintings or downloaded images of different types of nest and the birds that make them.

Reflection. What can we do in our gardens or around the school grounds to help nesting birds? Think about making insect habitats or putting out bird feeders. What do we like about birds? What pleasures do they bring us? What is the purpose of bird song? Which bird songs or calls can they identify?

4.10 Bats and Owls

Aims. To develop team communication skills.

In Brief. Students use animal noises (owl hoots and bat squeaks) to direct a blindfolded member of the team carrying water across a stretch of ground to a bucket.

What you will need:

A warm day! This is a wet activity.	
Two buckets and an identical, large car wash type sponge per team.	One good blindfold per team
A measuring jug or similar to fill each team's bucket with an identical amount of water and to identify the winner at the end of the competition.	

Method.

1. Divide the group into teams of four to six.
2. Explain the rules:

    *   Each team member will take it in turns to be blindfolded.
    *   The blindfolding is monitored to ensure no cheating.
    *   The blindfolded person is handed a sponge loaded with water by another team member.
    *   The team then guides the blindfolded student to a bucket, which is positioned about 20 metres away.
    *   The only guidance they can give is animal noises – bat squeaks or owl hoots, depending on the team.
    *   When one team member has transported their water to the bucket they remove the blindfold, return to base, and a second team member takes their place. When all team members have had a go the competition is over. The winners are the team with the most water in their bucket.

3. Note that, although this not a race against time, the fastest team is likely to win because less water is lost from the sponge.

Reflection. How difficult was it to give directions without being able to use words? Share the techniques you used to communicate specific directions. Explore how both bats, and humans, use sound to navigate where light is not available.

4.11 Bug Hotels

Aim. To create a habitat for bees and other insects. To explore insect environments and contribute towards the creation of a wildlife garden or area.

In Brief. Elder sticks are sawn to length, hollowed out and tied together to make an insect habitat. The habitats are hung on trees or shrubs.

What you will need:

Sufficient quantities of mature elder twigs (preferably sourced from your local hedgerows). Students can work on their own or in small groups - this determines quantity required. Each bug hotel requires approx 1.2m of straight elder twig 2-3cm in diameter. *	
Mini hacksaw. Log stump. A blunt ended steel tent peg. Safety scissors.	Wool or sisal garden twine. Brace and 5mm wood bit. Robust gardening gloves.
It helps if students are already familiar with elder from exercises such as bead-making (see 4.8).	

Method.

1. Discuss different types of insect habitats. Refer to the importance of rotting wood to many insects. Insects like woody environments and confined spaces. A woody tube is therefore an ideal environment. Students begin by carefully sawing their elder into equal lengths of about 10cm. Encourage neatness – straight cuts and checking the cut pieces against each other to ensure they are the same length.

2. Use the tent pegs to push the pith out of the elder. Ensure that the hand holding the stick is gloved and they are pushing the pith out away from themselves. Ensure they put the tent peg down before checking by eye that the tube is clear. Encourage the thorough removal of as much pith as possible.

3. Once the pieces are cleared of pith, tie a loop round the centre of one stick, leaving two lengths of about 20cms free. This will be used to hang the bug hotel from a branch. Now tie the bundle together firmly at both ends. Pass the twine round several times, pulling tightly all the time before tying off as neatly as possible.

4. Now hang the bug hotels discreetly in your nature area. Position in different environments, such as shady, damp and sunny to see what difference this makes. Check regularly for occupancy after a few weeks and make records of the different types of bugs you find and in which bug hotel.

Reflection. What other things can you do to encourage wildlife in your green space? Make a list of the things you can do around the average small garden to encourage insects. What additional wildlife might be attracted by an abundance of insects? What things might we do in our gardens that are bad for wildlife? Why are insects so important? Think of all the things they do that are a benefit to us.

Fig 4.11   Building a Bug Hotel

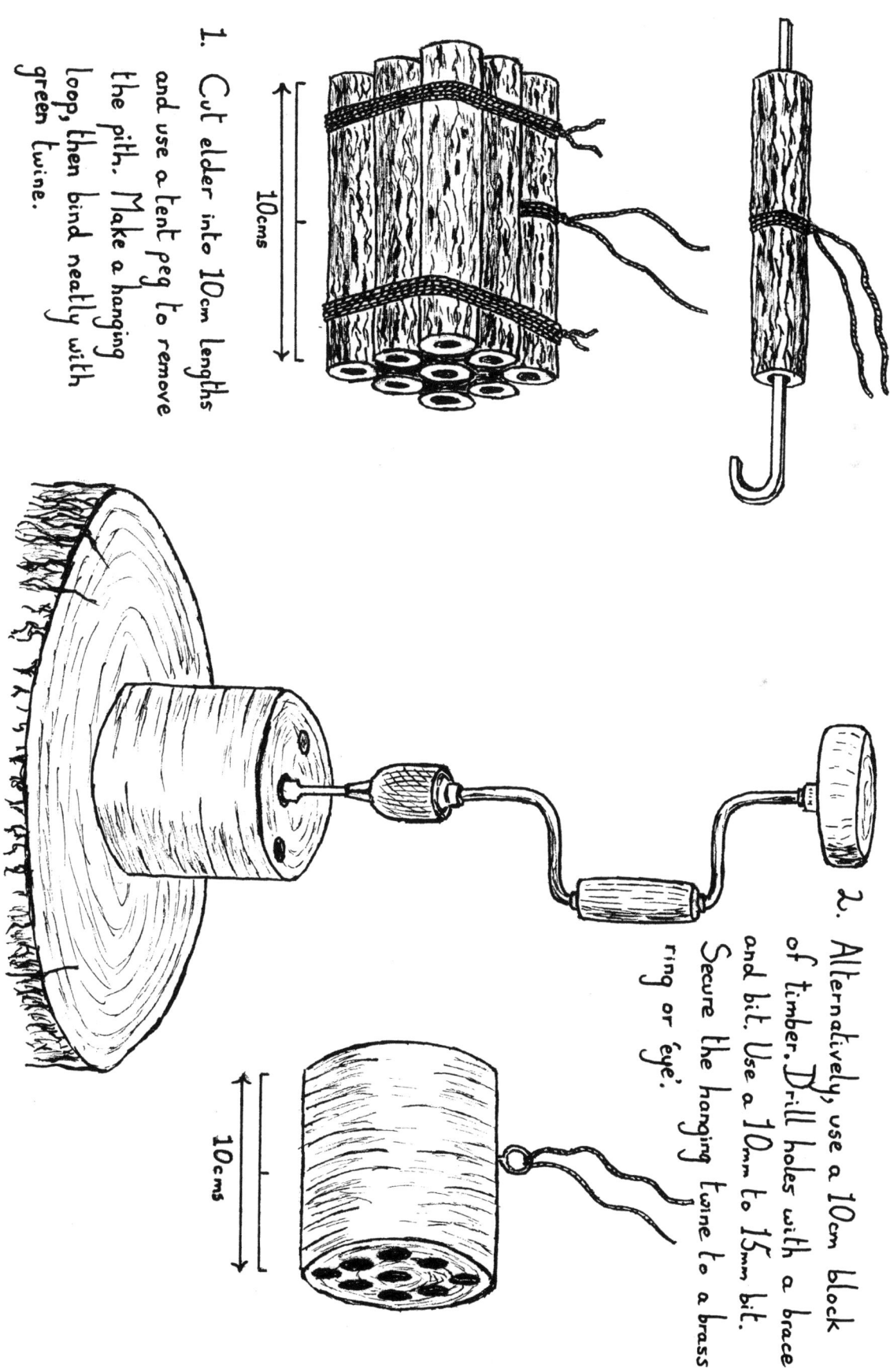

1. Cut elder into 10cm lengths and use a tent peg to remove the pith. Make a hanging loop, then bind neatly with green twine.

2. Alternatively, use a 10cm block of timber. Drill holes with a brace and bit. Use a 10mm to 15mm bit. Secure the hanging twine to a brass ring or 'eye'.

4.12 Gypsy Trails

Aim. To explore non-verbal methods of communication. To encourage observation and teamwork.

In Brief. Two to three separate trails are laid with coloured sticks through a wood. Each team has to locate the sticks and the concealed object at the end of the trail.

What you will need: *(if the whole class plays together)*

---

45 hazel sticks approx 25cm in length.
3 rolls of insulating tape each a different colour.

An environment that allows for twists, turns and concealment. Woodland is ideal, but school grounds with trees and outbuildings can do just as well. *

* The boundaries for the exercise should be clearly defined to ensure children do not get lost or stray to unsafe ground.

Method.

1. Prepare the sticks. Tape one end of each stick so that you have 15 yellow sticks, 15 blue sticks and 15 red sticks. One stick for each colour has 2 bands of coloured tape.

2. Start with the history of the game. Gypsies used to leave special trails across the countryside that other gypsies could recognize and follow. It might, for example, have been a stick in a grass verge with a bit of rag tied to it placed to indicate a road turning and the direction to travel.

3. Explain the rules. In the game, the 'runner' for each team will leave a carefully placed trail of sticks. The idea isn't to hide the sticks but to leave them where they can be easily seen when up close pointing the way to the next stick. They should follow paths and trails with the last stick placed at a prominent point. The winning team scores the most points as follows:

    •   one point for each ordinary stick returned
    •   four points for finding the last stick with two stripes
    •   four points for being the first team to bring the last stick back to base.

4. Brief the runners about ensuring sticks are clearly visible to make following the trail straightforward and that the coloured end of the stick is placed so as to point to the next stick.

5. Encourage the teams to think about tactics. How should they move as a group to give the maximum chance of finding all their sticks? The runners set off in opposite directions and are given several minutes to create the trail and then return. The runners then swap teams so they cannot help their own group find the sticks. Each group then follows its own colour trail.   The exercise is time limited and can end when the first team returns with their two striped stick or after 10 to 15 minutes if teams are struggling.

Reflection. How easy was it to find the sticks? Could you have used different tactics to make your search quicker or easier? Did you work as a team, with different people looking in different places? Travellers used sticks left at junctions of roads and trails to pass information to others. Think about and discuss the different methods of communication that use signs and symbols.

4.13 Blindfold Challenge

Aim. To develop verbal communication skills between students. To develop skills in giving specific directions.

In Brief. A blindfolded student follows an obstacle course, guided by the vocal instructions of a second student.

What you will need:

Rope at least 25m in length and 12mm in thickness.	Blindfolds.
Materials to create obstacles. These might be school games equipment such as cones or a tube to crawl through. Some woody obstacles, such as low branches are also useful, but avoid areas of spiky branches such as you might find with spruce. *	
* Also check the ground for hard trip hazards such as rocks. Logs should be positioned to present the rounded surface to legs.	

Method.

1. With this activity we often use older students to design and set out the obstacle course for younger students.

2. Lay a rope – anything from 25m to 50m, through an area with natural, but no hazardous obstacles. Secure to trees at hand height. Place obstacles along the trail, such as log stumps to step over, branches to duck below and play tunnels or tubes to crawl through. We have also done this activity on obstacle free school fields, using two ropes pegged to the ground in a zig-zag path with the challenge being to avoid contact with the rope. A sighted student guides the blindfolded student through the course with verbal instructions.

3. Explain that one person will be blindfolded. The blindfolded person will follow the rope trail, whilst their partner guides them through the trail, describing the route and any obstacles. The aim is to avoid contact with obstacles.

4. Three or four students can do the course together, each led through by their partner. When they have completed the course, the next group goes through. When all pairs are through the roles are reversed so that everyone has a chance to go through blindfolded.

Reflection. What did it feel like to be blindfolded? Did you feel you were using other senses, like touch, more? How easy was it to give directions and warn about obstacles? Did you feel that you got better as you went through? Reflect on how valuable a gift sight is. Think about those who have lost most or all of their sight and still manage to work and get about.

4.14 Camouflage Game

Aim. To develop skills in careful movement. To encourage cooperation in achieving a successful outcome.

In Brief. Students use available natural materials such as foliage and mud to disguise themselves and get as close as they can to the lookouts without being spotted.

What you will need:

A woodland space or piece of rough ground that provides plenty of opportunity for concealment.	
Old clothes or overalls for the students.	Mud to daub on faces. Foilage to place in hats or to attach to clothes.

Method.

1. Explain the rules and discuss tactics. The challenge is to get as close as they can to the target, usually a supervising adult, without being spotted. The winner is the student who gets the closest.

2. One or two adults position themselves about 100 metres from the start point and set up a lookout position.

3. Working in pairs the students camouflage themselves and attempt to sneak up to the lookout position without being seen.

4. Once spotted, the adult calls out their name.

5. Once 'out' the student returns to the start point being careful not to disrupt the movements of others.

6. The winners are the team that gets the closest without being spotted.

7. Suggest to the students that they keep an eye on the movements of other pairs. Who got spotted first? What mistakes did they make? Look at each other's faces and clothing. What stands out? What can they do to make themselves less easy to spot?

Reflection. Discuss who won. Why did they win? What made some people easier to spot? Were people quiet enough? What tactics can be used to move silently? Celebrate each other's camouflage. Who put in the most effort and whose camouflage do you think works the best for the environment?

4.14 Magic Carpets

Aim. To encourage team skills and co-operation. To provide a fun and exhausting activity that is also a great spectator sport.

In Brief. Teams race each other across a field by jumping a carpet across it and without making direct contact with the ground.

What you will need:

Two or three tatty old rugs (preferably oriental) capable of holding four to six students apiece. Alternatively, use old blankets.	
A relatively flat field - 30m course is ample.	Cones or flags to mark the start and finish of the course.

Method.

1. Divide the group into teams of four to six, depending on rug size.
2. Explain the rules:
   - The winners are the first team to travel across the field on their magic carpet without anyone's feet touching the ground.
   - One way of doing this - although we suggest not providing a methodology so that it is also a problem-solving exercise - is for two students to hold up the front of the rug and to pull the rug forward as the entire team jump together.
   - We have also witnessed teams swiveling the rugs across fields and even bizarre attempts to roll across, Cleopatra style. You may wish to use a point system to allow teams to continue if someone falls off the magic carpet.
3. Away you go!!

Reflection. This activity cannot be accomplished without fully coordinated teamwork. Was your team managed successfully? How was this achieved?

5. FOREST SCHOOL – INTERMEDIATE

Fire-lighting, Toasting Forks, Charcoal Pencils, Whistle, Wizard's Staff, Besom, Drop Spindle, Nature Weaving, Dream Catcher, Free Shelter.

Some of the activities in this chapter require the use of sharp tools such as knives, bow saws and bill hooks. If you are a Forest School Leader or a woodworker, you will be familiar with these tools. If your activities are to take place off-site, your educational authorities or school governors will expect you to hold a recognized qualification to run activities of this kind, such as a Forest School Leader Certificate. The real basis for the safe management of these activities, however, is experience and competence. The prevention of accidents is about understanding and applying safety rules consistently and without exception. Such rules include not letting children carry sharp tools with the blades uncovered, wearing suitable clothing, including leather gardening gloves and hard hats as appropriate, and providing immediate and consistent supervision for all sharp tool and fire activities. Experience, vigilance and consistency are the basis of safe practice.

The function of a risk assessment is to disclose the hazards and articulate the measures necessary to reduce risk. If the risks cannot be managed then the activity has to be re-thought. Do I have the competences? Can I provide sufficient, trained supervision? The information contained in the risk assessment should be known to all and regularly reviewed to ensure that safety standards are maintained. We are often asked if it is necessary to 'risk assess' every outdoor activity. Our answer is always 'yes'! Not to cover your back, but because identifying the hazards of any activity ensures that everything is as it should be. Usually this boils down to having six things in place – communication of risk to all, competence and experience in the leaders, good planning, correct supervision ratios, having the right equipment for the job and a safe location in which to work. I put communication first because a risk assessment is worthless if it isn't shared with all those involved. That includes the students. Their participation in the identification of hazard and the reduction of risk is a vital part of the learning process.

What if the competences to run the activities aren't in the school?

Paying for someone to train as a Forest School Leader costs time and money, but one or two Forest School Leaders on the staff can pass on their competencies as well as managing a whole school initiative. The final message is to design your Outdoor Learning programme with your competencies and experience clearly in focus.

About the equipment. You will find reference in the text to 'safety knives'. Any woodworker will tell you that a safe knife is also a sharp knife. We use 'Opinel' safety knives, which we purchased for about £10 each. They have a rounded point, like a butter knife. We tend to introduce knives for whittling in year 5 or 6, depending on maturity, and use a quality potato peeler with younger children. Children need training and practice with a peeler too, and we insist that the hand holding the item being whittled is gloved. In training youngsters to use a bow saw, we begin with 1:1 supervision, with the child supporting one side of the bow saw handle and the adult the other. Students often continue with this method, supporting each other in a way reminiscent of the techniques used by our Victorian forbears when using large saws. The same principle applies to the use of the brace and bit. Small hands find these much easier to use and one child can apply weight to the brace pad whilst the other rotates the handle. It is slow moving, highly visible technique and therefore easy to supervise. And a final reminder not to let children carry tools even for a short distance with uncovered blades. Before getting up from their working position they must either put the tool down or, in the case of a safety knife, close the blade. Insist on the sheath being put on bow saw blades when they are not in use, even if it is only for a short period.

5.1 Fire Lighting

Aim. To teach children the principles of combustion and how to work with fire safely.

In Brief. Students experience every aspect of fire lighting and fire management.

What you will need:

A fire activity area (*see activity 6.1*). Two full buckets of water and a fire blanket. Bow saw and saw horse if cutting firewood.	Fire steel and balls of cotton.* Sufficient firewood and kindling - ideally gathered in your school activity area.

* Using fire steel has the advantage of not putting matches or lighters in young hands. 'Light My Fire' Firesteel (about £10 online) we find the most reliable. Practice setting light to teased out cotton balls with fire steel before demonstrating with children. One strike is usually sufficient, once practiced.

Method.

1. Introduce the students to fire safety. Explain that the fire area is 'out of bounds' if no adult is present. Access is made by walking round the perimeter, usually marked out by seating, and approaching your seat from the rear. A fire area should not be walked across, and students should be sat down at all times unless given permission to feed the fire.

2. Practice arriving and leaving the fire area before lighting. Ensure it is free of trip hazards and that firewood is either stored in the firepit or out of the fire area altogether. Bring the students into the fire area in the correct manner (round the perimeter until they are behind their seat).

3. Discuss what makes good firewood. Demonstrate with green (fresh cut), rotten and dry branches/twigs. Show how green wood bends while kindling breaks easily. Wood for burning is a lot lighter because the water has dried out of it. Rotten wood is no good as a fuel. Why?

4. Demonstrate the different sizes and lengths required (from kindling to large branches/logs) then set them off in pairs or small groups to gather. Ensure they are vigilant and carry longer, heavier pieces in pairs. Where neccesary, cut wood to length, typically around 30cm

5. Discuss fire building. This includes a highly combustible core of very fine dry twigs, dry, crumbly leaves and bone dry grasses. The 'waffle' is a basic method - use a log to lean kindling material against, keeping easy access to the core for lighting. Before lighting give students the experience of lighting a cotton ball. They come forward one at a time for this, the group observes from their seated position.

6. Place 3 or 4 teased out cotton balls in the kindling core. A student now uses the fire steel to light the cotton balls. If access to the core is difficult, light a ball and use a stick to gently push the burning cotton into the core of the fire. Once the fire is going, sit back and enjoy! Once the fire session is over, dismiss the students in the correct manner – they turn round and leave directly. Don't put out a fire with students in proximity. Carefully soak the embers, avoiding dousing any stones, and cover with a layer of dirt. Don't leave a fire without putting it out!

Reflection. Discuss the uses of fire, such as warming houses, heating water and cooking food. Find out how many children still have open fires at home. Fires give a great deal of pleasure. Ask each student to share what they feel about the fire… "I like sitting round a fire because…." Ask the group "what are important things to remember about lighting a fire?"

5.2 Whittling a Toasting Fork and Making Toast

Aim. To introduce students to managing food hygiene and sharp tool activities safely. To train in the safe use of a fire for basic cooking. To introduce students to whittling.

In Brief. A toasting fork is made out of hazel and used to make toast. The toast is made over a fire, buttered and eaten.

What you will need: (N.B. Group leader requires a food hygiene certificate.)

A fire activity area and fire - *see activity 5.1.* A length of hazel (approx 50cm long and 1cm in diameter) - per student. **	Round-ended safety knives (one per student) or potato-peeler for younger children. Breadboard. Loaf of bread and butter/spread.*
Antiseptic wet-wipes / self-drying hand gel (non-alcoholic to avoid allergic reactions). Safety gloves for students. Secateurs (adult use only).	Loppers to cut selected branches (adult activity or 1:1 with students of secondary age). 2 mini hacksaws (wood-cutting blades). log stumps to saw on.
***(Only use hazel as it has antiseptic qualities).**	*(Use fresh and unopened produce only).*

Method.

1. Take students to your fire area and prepare the fire without lighting it. Explain the stages of the exercise and the emphasis on safe practice.

2. Take the group on a walk to find a source of sticks. Once located, students cut their selected stick one at a time. Secateurs, if required, are for adult use only.

3. Once you are back at the fire area, light the fire (*see activity 5.1*).

4. To make the fork, carefully saw a split in the end of the stick to a depth of 2cm. Students wear gloves for this in case of slips. A safety knife is then carefully inserted in the split (both hands gloved). Twist the blade and tease the split apart into two equal halves to a depth of 8 to 10 cm. Sit around the fire on your log benches or stumps ready for whittling.

5. Ensure that you have full and unbroken view all your students. If this is a first whittling session train in correct posture. Students sit upright, legs apart or tucked right in, and the peeling action is always away from the torso and legs. Discuss the serious danger of thigh lacerations, where major arteries are located. Children using potato peelers should also be trained in best practice. Use a glove on the hand supporting the stick when using peelers or knives

6. With safety knives or potato peelers whittle the split end of the stick to a rounded point. With the point shaped, the split is eased apart with fingers and a small piece of twig inserted and pushed deep into the split. This pushes the pointed ends of the stick apart to create the fork.

7. Before toasting, remind the group of fire accident procedures. Adults check students for loose clothing that could catch fire. Use the gel/wipes to ensure that all hands are clean. It is important that the fire has settled and the flames are low. Have no more than six students toasting together. They squat at a safe distance from the fire - minimum 1m - using extended arm and stick to reach the fire. Once done butter the toast and enjoy!

Reflection. Discuss all the steps taken to keep the activity safe – sharp tool use, fire safety and food hygiene. Share what the group enjoyed the most.

5.3 Charcoal Pencils

Aim. To introduce an ancient industrial process – the manufacture of charcoal - and allow students to understand the processes involved in converting ordinary wood to charcoal.

In Brief. Charcoal is made on a fire and used to make a pencil.

What you will need:

| A fire activity area and fire - *see activity 5.1.* | Fire gloves (teacher/adult only). |
| | 1 flat headed screwdriver (teacher/adult only). |

A metal container - with a lid that can be easily removed, such as a large cocoa tin. The lid **MUST HAVE HOLES DRILLED IN IT** (3 close together in the middle, approx 4mm diameter, is ideal). The holes are critical for safety as a fully sealed tin will explode! The lid sits firmly, but not so tight that it cannot be removed after cooling.

We work with a maximum of 12 students and have a second activity going; a class-sized group can be rotated between the two activities. Consider linking with an Art activity, such as Aboriginal painting.

Method.

1. Discuss the technological role of charcoal in history. Before the widespread use of coal, charcoal made possible the firing of ceramics and the smelting of metals. The technique was also used to refine coal for traditional smelters. In essence, it fueled the early Industrial Revolution. It is a clean fuel that burns at twice the temperature of wood. We have been making it for at least 5000 years! Also discuss how charcoal can be made sustainably – by coppicing trees for wood,

2. Discuss how charcoal is made – by burning wood in an oxygen starved environment. Water, volatile gases and other materials are driven out of the wood, leaving carbon behind.

3. Explain the best sizes of wood for making drawing charcoal. The branches should be about half a centimetre in thickness. The wood can be green or seasoned, but not brittle or rotten.

4. After students have gathered the wood place it in the metal container and put on the lid. The adult can then place the container carefully on the fire.

5. Have a second activity ready whilst the students wait for their charcoal. We often cut and whittle elder pencils at this stage (see the next activity for materials for working with elder).

6. The volatile gases coming out of the hole in the lid usually self ignite. If they don't, use a spill to ignite them. Discuss the useful by-products of charcoal, such as cleaning spirits, wood tar, and a variety of useful chemicals. Once the gases have stopped burning allow the charcoal to heat for a few minutes longer only and then remove from the fire. The charcoal and tin must be allowed to cool before attempting to remove the lid both for safety reasons and to ensure the charcoal does not ignite when removed from the tin. Once made, the charcoal sticks can be used as they are, or inserted in short pieces into the end of a sharpened piece of elder.

Reflection. Discuss how a material has been transformed by an industrial process – heating wood in an oxygen starved environment. How has the usefulness of the wood been affected or changed? Why does burning wood put less greenhouse gases than burning fossil fuels?

5.4 Wizard's Staff or Walking Stick

Aim. To develop sensitivity and awareness in the selection of woods. To develop safe whittling skills. To explore the ergonomics and functionality of walking sticks.

In Brief. Students find or select a suitable branch or stick and make a walking staff.

What you will need:

Any managed wood will provide sticks in abundance.	Provide a bow saw and log stump or saw horse to cut sticks to length.
Each student will need a safety knife to whittle the handle.	
To attach a decorative cord loop use a brace and bit to drill a hole through the staff and some attractive cord. To add decorative beads to the cord provide the kit to make beads (see activity 4.8). A few pieces of sandpaper of 60 to 80 grade will facilitate a nice smooth finish.	

Method.

1. Discuss sticks and staffs. What do we use them for? What did people use them for in the old days? Sticks used to be very personal things – everyone carried one a 100 years ago. They will be making their own personalized staff or stick.

2. First, the wizard must find that special piece of wood. The stick does not have to be completely straight. It needs to be a suitable length for staff, stick or wand and it needs to be a comfortable weight. If looking for sticks off the ground it can be green or seasoned but not dry and brittle. If a stick can be found with a projecting branch to make a finger fork or knob at the end, so much the better. Try bending the stick a little to make sure it is still flexible and not dry or brittle. Back at your work area, the first step is to remove any unwanted branches and to cut the stick to length. A good height for a staff is shoulder height for the actual hand grip. For a walking stick the maximum length is hip height.

3. The next stage is to shape the hand grip. This needs to be made smooth and comfortable to avoid blistering the skin on a long walk. Use a safety knife to carefully whittle away any projections. If the bark is to be removed use a knife or junior saw to cut a neat ring around the staff about 20cms from the top and then peel away the bark with the knife. The top of the staff can be whittled to provide a rounded end if this is desired.

4. A feature of some staffs and sticks is a hand loop. A hole is cut using the brace and bit and the hole edges reamed out with a knife and sandpaper to provide a smooth finish. A loop of cord is now fed through. I recommend tying by feeding the two ends of cord through a wooden bead before knotting to make an attractive toggle.

Reflection. Which aspect of the staff-making work did you enjoy the most? Compare staffs with the rest of your group. Think about the differences between individual staffs. What has brought those differences about? Why do you think staffs have been associated with magic?

Think of the dozens of ways a staff kept a walker safe (for example, in testing boggy ground).

5.5 Making a Whistle

Aim. To provide an opportunity to make small scale instrument that requires precision and attention to detail.

In Brief. A small whistle is made out of elder (*see fig. 5.4*).

What you will need:

12cm of good, straight elder per student.	Green twigs to make the fipple (students can gather these).
Log stumps for sawing on.	Blunt ended steel tent pegs.
Mini hacksaws fitted with wood cutting blades.	Safety knives for whittling.

Method.

1. Discuss how a simple penny whistle works. A thin stream of air is directed onto a wooden blade. This sets up a resonance within the whistle tube that creates the noise. Explain that the longer the tube, the deeper the note. The tone can be moderated by drilling finger holes in the tube.

2. Students support each other to cut their piece of elder to length. Ensure the elder is knot free. Use the safety knife to round off or "de-burr" the ends of the wood and make them as neat as possible.

3. Use the steel tent peg to thoroughly and carefully clear out all the pith. It is important not to gouge or otherwise deform the bore of the tube. The student should be satisfied that all the pith is out and there is a neat bore before carrying on.

4. With great care, cut out the wedge-shaped aperture (*see fig. 5.4*), Use both saw and knife for this. With the mini-hacksaw a 90 degree cut is made about 2cm from the end of the mouthpiece, extending half way through the tube. Use the safety knife to then carefully trim out the wedge. The wedge should be cut carefully and accurately so as to produce a neat, sharp edge onto which the column of air is directed. The quality of this edge will determine if the whistle works or not.

5. Now partially seal with a piece of dowel of the same thickness as the bore of the tube. This is known as the fipple. The student searches for twigs of a similar diameter to the hole in their tube. This is trimmed to the correct thickness (a good, tight fit) and tested for size by partial insertion into the tube. Now carefully trim off a neat, thin slither of wood from the top of the fipple or dowel. This will create the air gap through which the stream of air is blown onto the blade of the hole. Ensure the cut is flat and without rounded edges. Insert the fipple into the mouthpiece end of the elder tube, ensuring the air gap lines up perfectly with the blade of the hole. Check for a good, tight fit and a working air gap. Trim off any surplus fipple.

6. Once the whistle is complete and tested, the remaining bark can be trimmed off. With care, this can be done in a decorative manner.

Reflection. Discuss the success – or lack of – with your group. How many whistles worked? Think about all the things that go into being successful. Think about the things that contribute to failure. Making musical instruments is a highly skilled craft. Some musical instruments can take several months, even years to make. Why do some people love this kind of work?

Fig 5.5   Making a Whistle

Cross section

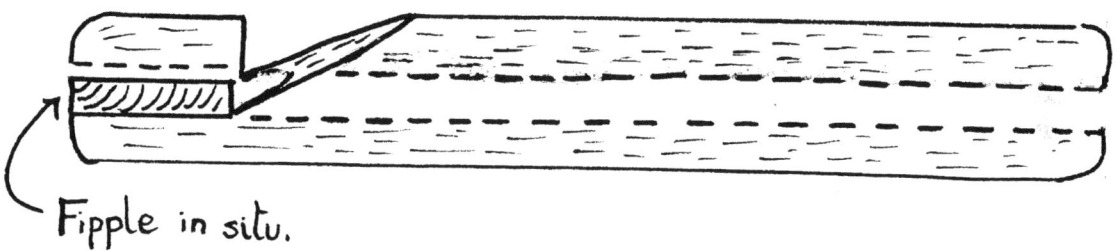

Fipple in situ.

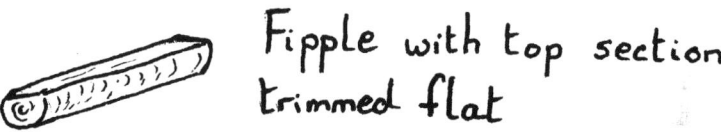

Fipple with top section
trimmed flat

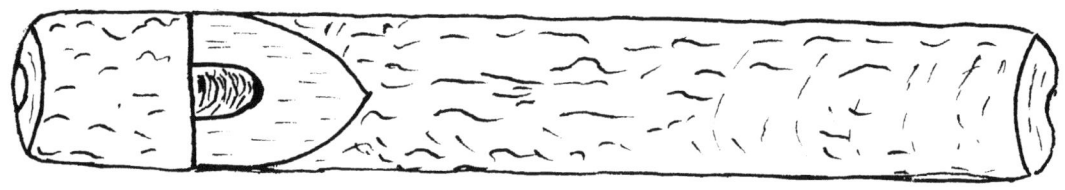

1:1 Scale   © Chris Trwoga

5.6 Besom

Aim. To make a useful tool out of natural materials and explore a traditional craft.

In Brief. A garden broom is made using brash and a suitable stick.

What you will need:

Enough sticks to make a broom handle for each student - typically 1.2m long and 4cm thick.* It doesn't have to be smooth or completely straight; ok to select on the grounds of visual appeal.	
Plenty of sisal string or garden twine. Bow saw and saw horse. Fresh brash or prunings for the broom head (60cm to 75cm long and thin enough to trim with scissors or secateurs)	Secateurs (adult use only) or loppers to trim brash. Safety scissors to cut thin brash. Gloves to prevent cuts and skin abrasion from handling the rough materials.

* Younger children can make smaller brooms with handles 75cm long and 3cm thick.

Method.

1. Discuss the role of broomsticks or besoms in fairy tales and in actual use. Do any of them have a besom at home ? What are the practical uses of besoms?

2. Students source a suitable broom handle - usually from a woodland walk.

3. Collect material for the broom head. Again, this can be gathered in a wood or brought in by parents or staff after a pruning session at home, or collected over time and stored.

4. Sort the brash. Hedge trimmings, for example, need to be sorted to size and thickness. Students use a gloved hand to pull away leaves. With cedar brash, the greenery is left in place.

5. Cut the broom handle to size with the bow saw and saw horse.

6. Bind the broom material to the handle. The string is first part unravelled from the bale or ball. Students work together with one turning the shaft of the broom and the second holding the string. A good method is to wrap the free end of the string round a stick to help the student holding the string to maintain the tension.

7. The broom material is attached to the shaft in small bundles, such that the broom head is built up in layers. Each bundle should be secure in itself. The tension in the string must be maintained at all times or the head will gradually loosen. When the broom head is the desired thickness tie off the string. The next step is to wrap more string tightly round the bundle, pulling it all tightly to the shaft.

8. With the broom material secure, the brash can be trimmed to an even length with safety scissors.

Reflection. In many countries people still make their own brooms to clean the house and yard and simply burn them when they wear out. Make a list of all the different tools we now use to keep our houses and gardens clean and tidy. Is using power tools, such as petrol powered leaf blowers, a good or a bad thing?

5. 7 Making a Drop Spindle and Spinning Yarn

Aim. To give an insight into traditional methods of making clothing. To teach students the basic technique of spinning yarn.

In Brief. A traditional spindle is made out of a hazel stick and a disc or spindle whorl cut from hardwood (*see fig. 5.7*).

What you will need:

A supply of carded or raw wool.* 1kg is enough for several small groups. Raw wool can also be bought in large quantities as insulation material.	Spindles - this is a 25cm length of hazel or willow per student. 1cm diameter. Mini-hacksaw to cuyt the spindle notches.
A brace and 1cm bit to drill the hole through the spindle whorl to take the spindle. Saw horse & bow saw. Safety knives for whittling.	A branch of hardwood 6cm to 8cm in diameter to cut the whorl or weight. 1 metre should provide for 25 students. **

* Raw wool needs to be put in an appropriate fabric bag and washed to remove lanolin, dirt and bugs and generally make the wool pleasant to handle. If you cannot obtain raw wool, a large bag of cotton wool can be used in the same way. ** Infants can make their spindle whorl out of air-drying clay.

Method.

1. Discuss clothing manufacture with the group. This has four distinct stages, spinning the thread, dyeing, weaving into cloth, cutting and sewing. Spinning and weaving was done at home until the invention of machines - even by wealthy women.

1. Make the Drop Spindle. Demonstrate the process to the students and construct in stages. Start with the whorl - this allows students to choose a spindle that will fit. Use a sawhorse and a bow saw to carefully cut a 2cm thickness disc from your hardwood branch. Use a brace and a 1cm wood bit to drill a hole through the disc, make sure it is central.

2. Select a piece of hazel or willow of 1cm diameter. It must be a tight fit through the hole. Pare down to fit. Pare away any edges at both ends of the spindle to produce a nice chamfered finish. The spindle shaft sits with about 5cm above the whorl and the remainder below.

3. Now cut or saw a notch at the end of the spindle (see 5.7) and a second notch into the edge of the spindle whorl. using a mini-hacksaw. Twist the whorl on the shaft until the two notches are on opposite sides.

4. Loosely tease the wool out into lengths. Using just the fingers, spin a short length of about 15cm. This is called the leader yarn and enables the students to get a clear grasp of the spinning process. Tie it to the notch at the top of the spindle.

5. Now attach the unspun length of wool to the leader yarn by spinning the fibres together. Once a sufficient length is spun, remove from the notch and wrap round the long end of the spindle. Pass through the notch in the whorl and hook underneath the notch at the top of the spindle.

6. Continue teasing out the yard and spinning thread until the desired length is obtained.

Reflection. Spinning yarn has become a popular pastime again. Why do you think people enjoy spinning their own yarn? Practice makes perfect. Did you have the patience to keep trying spinning until you got it right? What did you think about your staying power? How could you improve on the making of your spindle?

Fig 5.7 Drop Spindle and Spinning Yarn

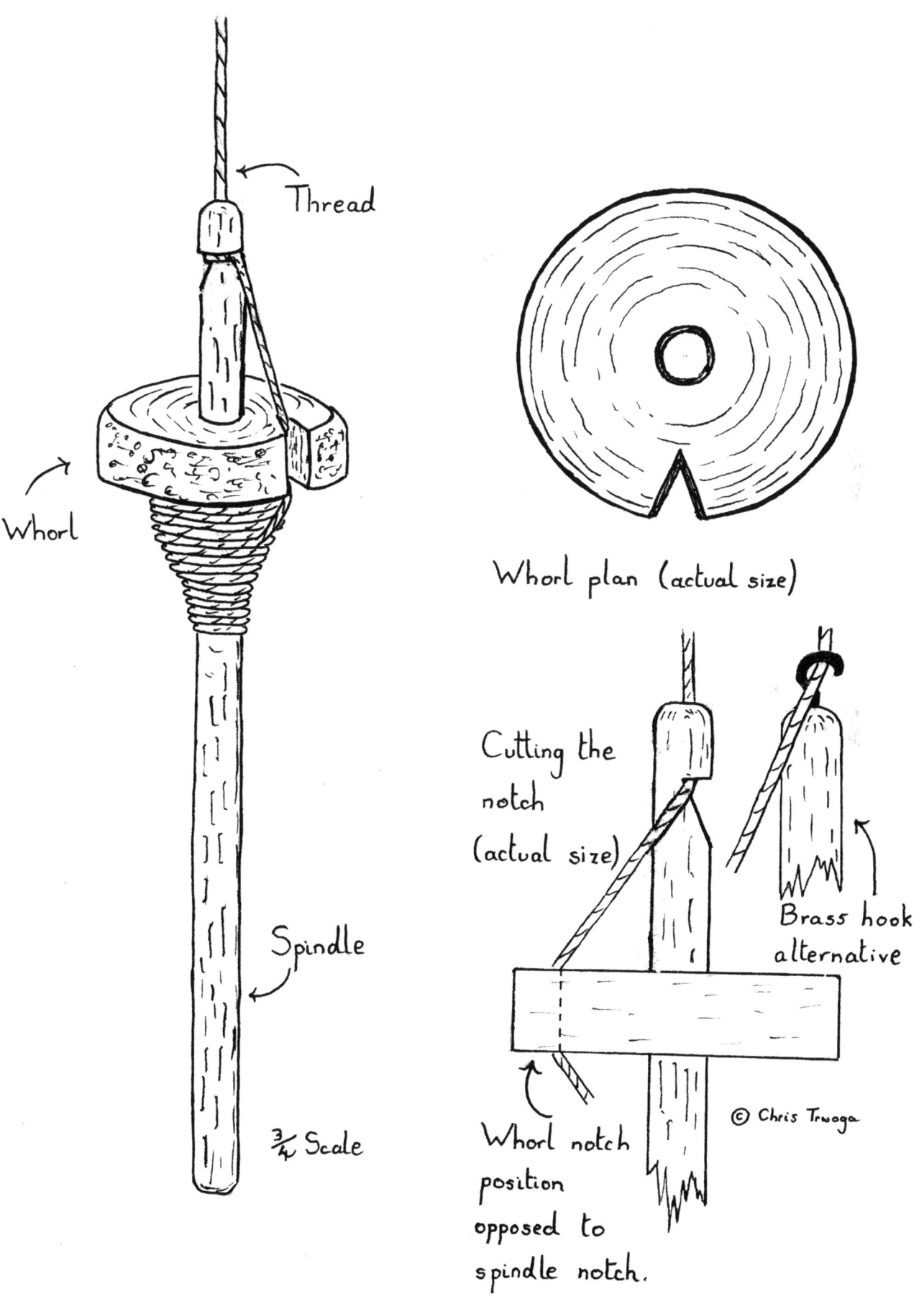

Thread

Whorl

Spindle

¾ Scale

Whorl plan (actual size)

Cutting the notch (actual size)

Brass hook alternative

Whorl notch position opposed to spindle notch.

© Chris Trwoga

5.8 Weaving with Natural Materials

Aim. To enable students to learn the basic weaving process.

In Brief. A simple wooden frame is made and woven with wools and natural materials, such as grasses (*see fig 5.8*).

What you will need:

Four sticks per student to make a frame of around 30cm sq. Hazel or willow is ideal but any relatively straight wood will suffice.	A variety of different coloured wools. Better still, students can spin their own lengths of wool (see previous activity)!
One mini hacksaw with a wood blade per 4 students.	Several log stumps for sawing on.
Several pairs of safety scissors for trimming the wools, grasses, stems etc..	

Method.

1. Introduce the basics of weaving. A loom is used to stretch the threads. The warp threads hang downwards and are kept stretched by being attached to a weighted bar. The weft threads are woven through alternate warp threads and tapped down into place. Share and discuss some loose woven items, such as pieces of sacking or muslin.

2. Begin by making the 'loom'. Using log stumps and mini-hacksaws measure and cut four sticks of 30cm length.

3. Once all the sticks are cut, tightly bind them together at the corners with coloured wools or twine to produce the frame (see fig 5.8). Encourage neatness and tight binding. The frame produced will not be rigid, but it should be sturdy.

4. Next, choose the wools for the warp. Tie these chosen threads to the top and bottom of the frame at approximately 3cm intervals. The warp should not be slack.

5. Now weave your grasses, stems and hand-spun wools into the warp. Demonstrate how the weft is woven in front of and behind alternate threads, with sequence reversed for each piece of weft material. Keep weaving until the work is complete.

Reflection. A long time ago, parents would make clothes for the family by spinning the thread, weaving the fabric and then sewing the garments together. How long do you think it would take you to make the clothes you are wearing? Some cloth is still woven by hand. On the island of Lewis, in Scotland, cloth is still dyed, spun and woven by hand.

Fig 5.8 Weaving with Natural Materials

30 cms

5.9 Dream Catcher

Aim. To make a decorative artifact utilizing a range of craft skills. To learn about a Native American tradition.

In Brief. A withy or similar is bent into a circle, a web made with wool or sisal twine and decorated with objects found in the wood or school grounds (*see fig. 5.9*).

What you will need:

Green withies or hazel of 1cm thickness or less and about 75cm to a metre in length. * Short stick/twig, approx 8cm in length per student.	Two large balls of red wool per class (red is the traditional colour for a dream catcher). Secateurs (adult use only) to withies to length. Cotton twine. Safety scissors
Withies can be left in water to keep them supple.	

Method.

1. Discuss the origin of dream catchers. Originally from the Native American Ojibwe Tribe, they were hung over a baby's sleeping place to ward off or "catch" nightmares. Nowadays, they are mostly decorative, often adorned with natural objects that are connected with happy memories.

2. Begin construction. Gently tease the withy into a circle. Warming the wood a little with hands, warm water or proximity to a fire will help soften the wood. The secret is to keep working the wood along its length, bending it a little at different points and working it slowly into a circle.

3. Once a circular form has been achieved, tie the two ends together with a neat binding so that the ends do not protrude. Both ends need to overlap by about 6cm. Alternatively, a tear shaped dream catcher frame can be made, which will leave the ends protruding outwards once tied.

4. Now issue each student with a small ball of wool of about 3m in length (more can be knotted to this later if necessary). Carefully wrap the wool around a short stick approx 8cm in length.

5. Begin weaving the web. Tie the wool to a single point on the hoop then wrap round to a further 7 or 8 points. At each point, wrap the wool round the hoop several times, then tie a simple neat knot (see fig 5.9 stage 1).

6. Now take the wool round again, looping through the existing web (see fig 5.9 stage 2). Pull gently each time you cross over/weave through. This will begin to create the web shape.

7. Pass the wool round for a third time, this time through the inner loops, again pulling gently each time you cross over. After passing the wool round several times, the web shape emerges.

8. Tie the wool off neatly in the centre.

9. Students now gather materials to hang from it. This might include larger feathers to hang below the hoop, small pine cones, mollusc shells or any other natural finds they feel drawn to.

Reflection. Share some of your dreams or nightmares with each other. Why is it that most children grow out of nightmares, or night terrors as they are sometimes called? Hang a couple of small things on your dream catcher that bring happy memories. Share your memories with a partner.

Fig 5.9 Dream Catcher

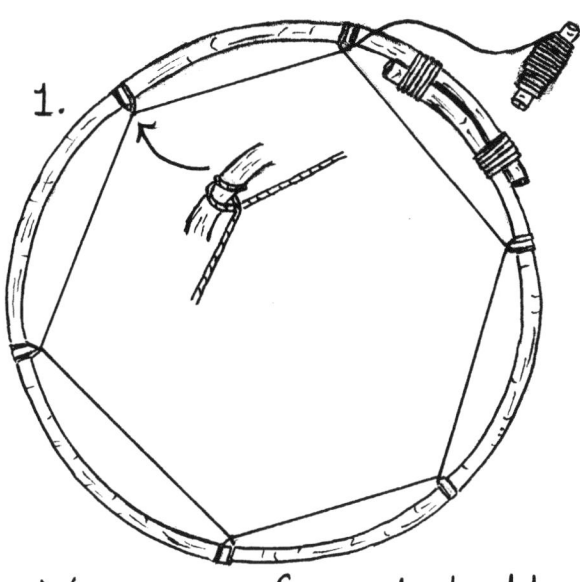

1.

Warm over a fire and steadily work into a hoop.

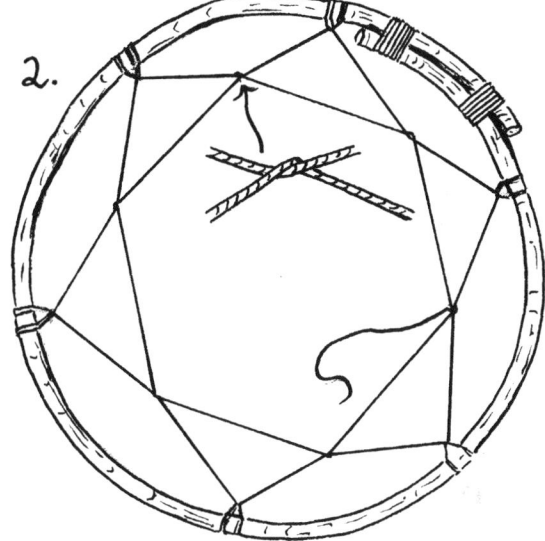

2.

Hook thread over the centre of each segment and gently pull.

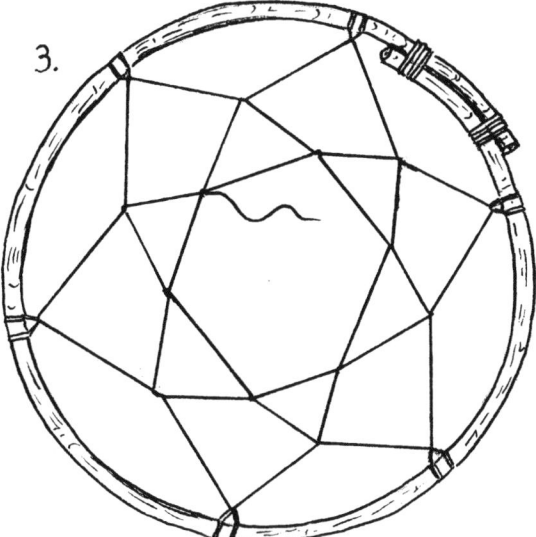

3.

Keep looping over the centre of each segment. Take care to pull evenly and not to miss segments

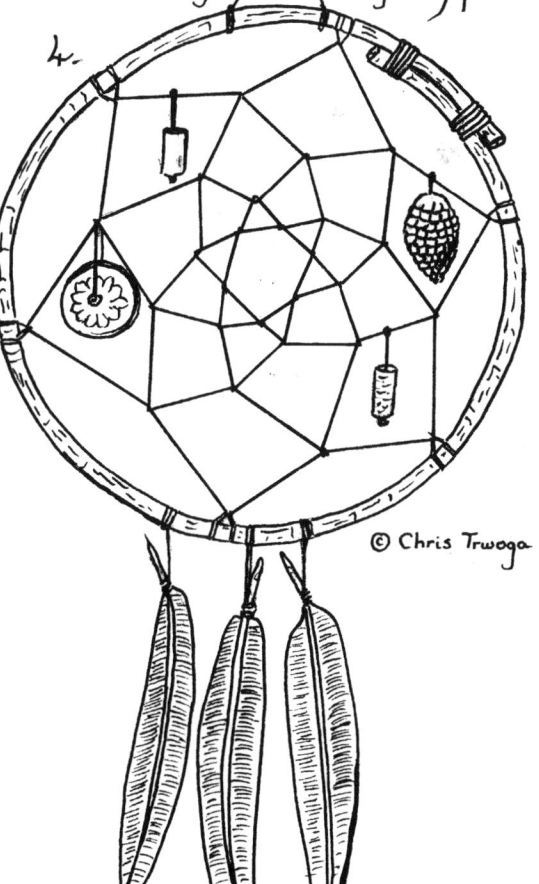

4.

© Chris Trwoga

5.10 Free Shelter

Aim. To develop problem solving skills in a group situation. To apply a variety of structure making skills in creating a viable overnight shelter.

In Brief. A group of four to six students make a shelter that will provide a dry shelter suitable for an overnight stay.

What you will need:

A suitable location. Woodland is ideal. School gounds are also fine.	
If in a wood, students can source thier own construction materials (see opposite). Tarpaulin and string.	If in school grounds you might provide a tarpaulin, a length of rope, ball of twine and a selection of poles, tent pegs and mallet.

Method.

1. The concept of a free shelter is that students decide where and how they are going to build their shelter. *Prior to this activity, the group should have had the opportunity to develop skills in the use of guy ropes and making structures with hazel poles or similar (see 6.1 and 6.2 in the Advanced Forest School chapter).*

2. Begin by discussing the challenge. Each group is to make an enclosed shelter that provides sleeping space for their group. The structure should be built to withstand wind and rain.

3. Discuss temporary shelter shapes – dome shaped benders, tipis, ridge pole tents, tunnels. The structure should provide for rain run-off and provide protection from the prevailing wind. Allow a specific length of time to complete the structure. Avoid interfering thereafter, even if a group is struggling or unable to agree on a design or a location. Simply remind them that the clock is ticking.

4. Remind them that such shelters may be built under pressure, with bad weather or night approaching. Once the structures are built call the groups together to share outcomes.

   - Is the location of the shelter well chosen and dry?
   - Does the structure provide adequate protection from rain?
   - Is there protection from the wind?
   - Does everyone in the group have space to sleep?
   - Where are the obvious weaknesses?
   - Discuss how the design, construction or location might be improved.

Reflection. Evaluate your work as a group. Did you pool ideas successfully or did one person dominate the design stage? Did you manage to use everyone's energies and was there good division of labour? Could you improve your teamwork? If so, how?

6. ADVANCED FOREST SHCOOL

SETTING UP AND EQUIPPING A FOREST SCHOOL ACTIVITY AREA

Fire activity area, Free-standing canopy, Bender (all-weather shelter), Mallet, Tent pegs, Cooking spatula, Saw-horse, Timber store, Kit rack, Pizza oven.

This collection of activities came about for two reasons. The first was to make it possible for students to take part in creating their own Forest School activity area. The second reason was to put a range of activities together that would enable students to advance their practical and team skills through more complex tasks. The activities were developed with students of primary and secondary age. In some instances, younger students might not be able carry out all aspects of the tasks in this section.

A Forest School area will typically provide for craft activities, timber processing and fire activities. Part of the work area needs to have a canopy so that work can continue in wet weather. Useful equipment to have includes log stumps for light sawing, a saw horse, benches, an earth oven and a covered rack to store bags and personal kit.

If your school is in an urban setting you may wonder where all the materials will come from. We recently supported a primary school in setting up a Forest School activity area and had expected to have to trailer in most of the timber. In the event, an appeal to parents brought in most of the wood we needed. Look in your local directory for tree surgeons and don't forget to talk to your own grounds maintenance people. If they have contracts in a number of schools they may be able to provide you with information about trees about to be felled or pruned in schools other than your own. Another useful contact is your local parks people. Always be specific about your needs. You don't want stuff 'donated' that's too heavy to move or little more than garden waste.

You will need a source of straight hazel poles of all thicknesses and lots of them. The best source for these, if you don't have access to a woodland source, is a fence-maker who makes hazel and willow hurdles. Typical prices for this kind of material are given in the introduction to the previous chapter. Getting in the materials is the hard bit. Once you have your big store of hazel poles anything seems possible!

Some of these activities will take many hours to complete. They constitute great team projects and it is worth considering assigning different tasks to different groups to allow for continuity, problem solving, and the satisfaction of seeing a job through. The great thing about outdoor facilities made with natural materials is they require constant maintenance and regular renewal. Keeping your area looking great can be an important part of your repertoire of Forest School activities and will give your students a sense of pride and ownership in the space.

6.1. Setting up a Fire Activity Area

Aim. To enable the group to identify the hazards associated with fire-use. To design and make a fire area that can be safely managed. To discuss and resolve issues associated with collecting and storage of firewood.

In Brief. Students make a fire pit, erect a canopy and make seating (*see fig 6.1*).

What you will need:

Seating - 4 logs approx 25cm in diameter 1 to 2m in length. *Stakes to secure seating* - 16 Hazel poles (or other suitable hardwood) 90cm in length, 4cm diameter.	*Fire pit barrier* - 4 logs approx 15cm diameter, two at 1m & two at 1.2m in length. 2 buckets full of water and a fire blanket. ***It is vital with all fire activities that you have the means to douse a fire immediately to hand.***
Canopy - large tarpaulin of 6 by 4m. 15m of 12mm rope. A ball of thick string. 12 heavy-duty wooden pegs (see the peg-making activity 6.5). If your canopy is to be permanent, use nylon 5mm cord for guy ropes.	Spades, plastic trowels (if working with infants), saw horse (see 6.7), bow saws, mallets (see 6.4) to drive in the stakes, and bill hooks to sharpen stakes. A lump hammer for stubborn ground (*adult use only*).
Whatever the age of your group, bear in mind that the lifting of heavy logs and stumps should be avoided. Logs are best rolled or dragged, and controlled with ropes and levers.	

Method.

1. Discuss the functions of the Forest School area with students. What is the best location in the available area? For example, are there two suitable trees to sling a canopy between? Consider time-scales for completing each task so that students do not have unrealistic expectations.

2. The group will already be familiar with lighting fires. Discuss the core safety rules – to keep the correct distance from the fire unless feeding it, not to walk across the fire area, to stand and sit at least 1.5m away from the fire. How will these safety aspects be built into the design?

3. **Make the fire pit.** First, decide on the precise location for the fire pit. If a canopy is to be slung over a rope between two trees it will be at the middle of a line running between them.

4. Dig a circular pit about 1m in diameter and 15cm deep. Let the group trample the ground to firm down the soil. Line the edge of the pit with large cobbles.

5. **Make the the timber surround**. Use saw horse and bow saw to cut two lengths of 15 – 20cm diameter log; two at 1m and two at 1.2 m (see fig 6.1). Make your square around the fire pit.

6. **Cut stakes** (see activity 6.5). Cut the hazel poles into lengths of about 90cm. Position the end of the wood on a log stump and use a bill hook and mallet to sharpen bothends to a point. This is a two-handed job, with one student supporting the stake at an angle on the block, whilst the second uses the bill hook and mallet to split away the waste. Younger students sometimes find it easier to do this 'three-handed' with one student supporting the stake, one holding the bill hook in position with both hands and the third using the mallet. This keeps all hands on tools and makes injury much less likely. Once the stake is sharpened at both ends it is sawn in two to make two stakes of between 45cm and 50cm length.

7. **Make the canopy.** If you are fortunate enough to have two convenient trees, the canopy is slung over a rope tied between them - see photo p147. If not, refer to activity 6.2 for how to make a free standing version. The line needs to be about 12mm thick or stronger and made as taut as possible. It also needs to be a good height above the fire – at least 3m at the apex.

8. **Make seating**. Seating should be arranged so that it is at least 1.25 m from the fire pit barrier. This gives room for an adult to walk around the fire whilst people are sat down. Green logs of 2m in length can easily weigh more than two hundredweight so don't allow students to attempt any kind of lift. Use ropes and several students to drag each log; then levers and a rolling action to place in position. The stakes securing the logs should be driven into the ground at an angle (*see fig 6.1*) so that they hug the sides of the log. You may need a lump hammer to do this (adult use only). An alternative seating design - raised on sturdy supports - is also shown in fig 6.1.

Reflection. The fire was once the centre and focus of every home or shelter. Why has this changed? Reflect on your feelings when sat round a fire, particularly on a cold day. Think of words to share those feelings with others. Why is the fireside a favourite place for telling stories? Some people say that if we still had open fires we wouldn't need televisions. What do you think?

Fig 6.1 Setting up a fire activity area

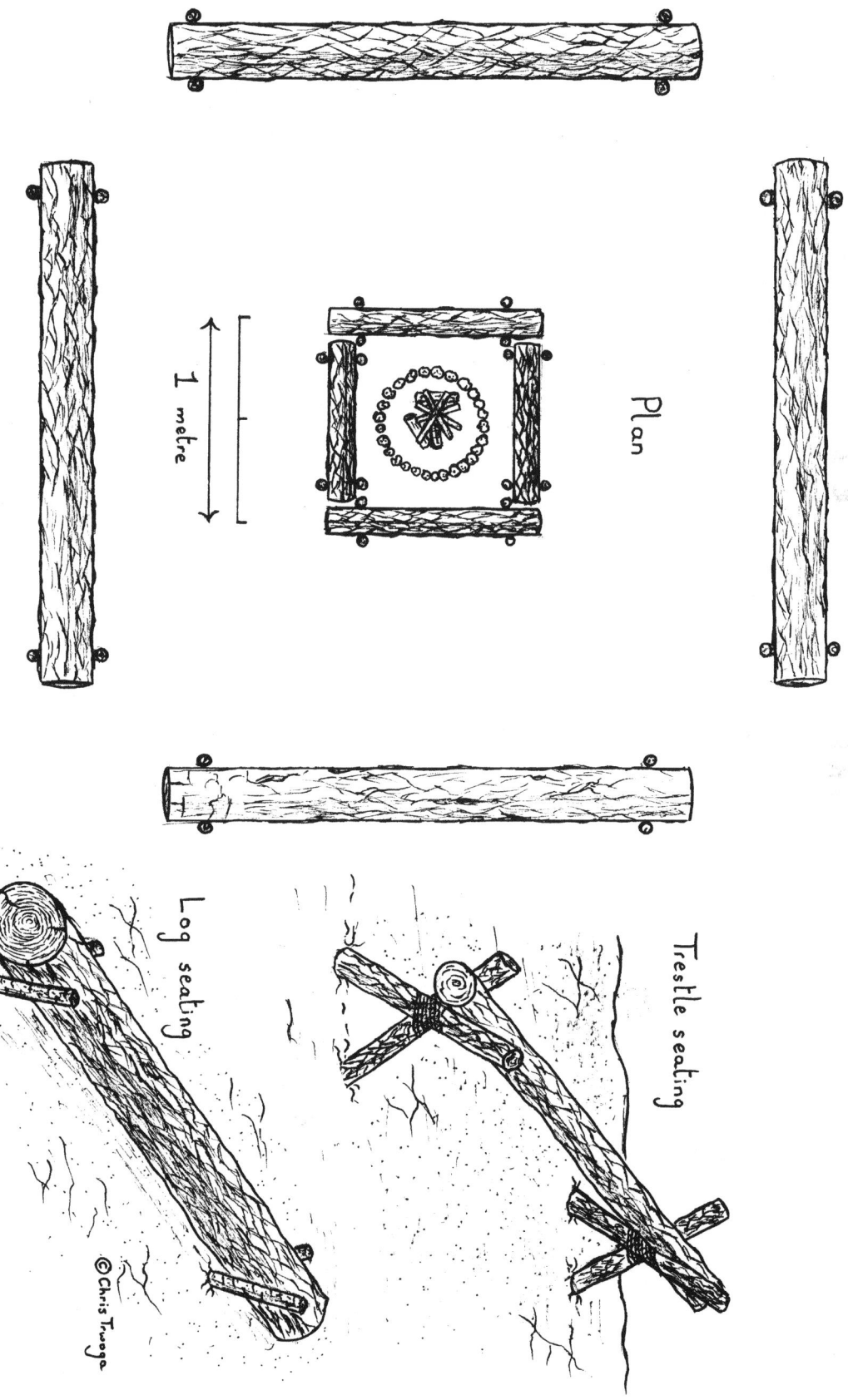

1 metre

Plan

Log seating

Trestle seating

©Chris Twigg

6.2. Making a free standing activity canopy

Aim. To develop skills in using guy ropes and poles to construct different forms of shelter.

In Brief. Students construct a free standing canopy, using hazel poles and tarpaulin (*see fig 6.2*).

What you will need:

Wooden tent pegs (*see activity 6.5*) - 20 per structure. *	A large tarpaulin, 4 x 6m or above.
1 pole around 4m and 4 poles of 2.5 m in length - all approx 4 to 6cm in diameter. Students can be provided with poles cut to length. If not, use a saw horse (see 6.7) and bow saw to cut in situ.	Two mallets (see 6.4). A bale of strong twine and safety scissors.

*Steel pegs can be used instead but these pull out of the ground very easily in windy conditions.

Method.

1. Reflect on what has already been learned from using guy ropes to build structures. Reflect on the functionality of the canopy as a space to sit and work.

2. Consider the site.
   - What is the direction of the prevailing wind?
   - What is the best direction to pitch the canopy to provide optimum shelter?

3. The technique set out below is only one solution. As a team-building exercise with older students it may be more valuable to let the group make these decisions.

4. Begin by making the 'goalpost' frame. The 4m pole is firmly lashed to the top of the 2.5m poles. The distance between the two uprights should be sufficient to take the width of the tarpaulin. Firmly attach three 3m guy ropes to the top of each 2.5m pole. With the structure held upright, peg the guy ropes out at 90 degrees to each other. Test for rigidity and add further guy ropes if necessary.

5. With the goal post in place, drape the tarpaulin over it and peg close to the ground at one end.

6. Next, tie a 2.5m pole to the two front corners of the tarpaulin using the 'string around a pebble' method (*see fig. 6.2*). Pull the poles upright and forward to stretch the canopy and make a veranda. Peg firmly upright and slightly tilted forward with the three guy ropes pegged down at 90 degrees to each other. Deal with any sagging in the canopy as this will lead to rain collecting.

Reflection. How long did your structure take to make? Reflect on your teamwork and discuss techniques to make the structure easier to erect and take down. Discuss how simpler and quicker structures might be made. Is the structure 'fit for the purpose'? If not, how can it be adapted to meet the needs of the group?

Fig 6.2 Making a free standing activity canopy

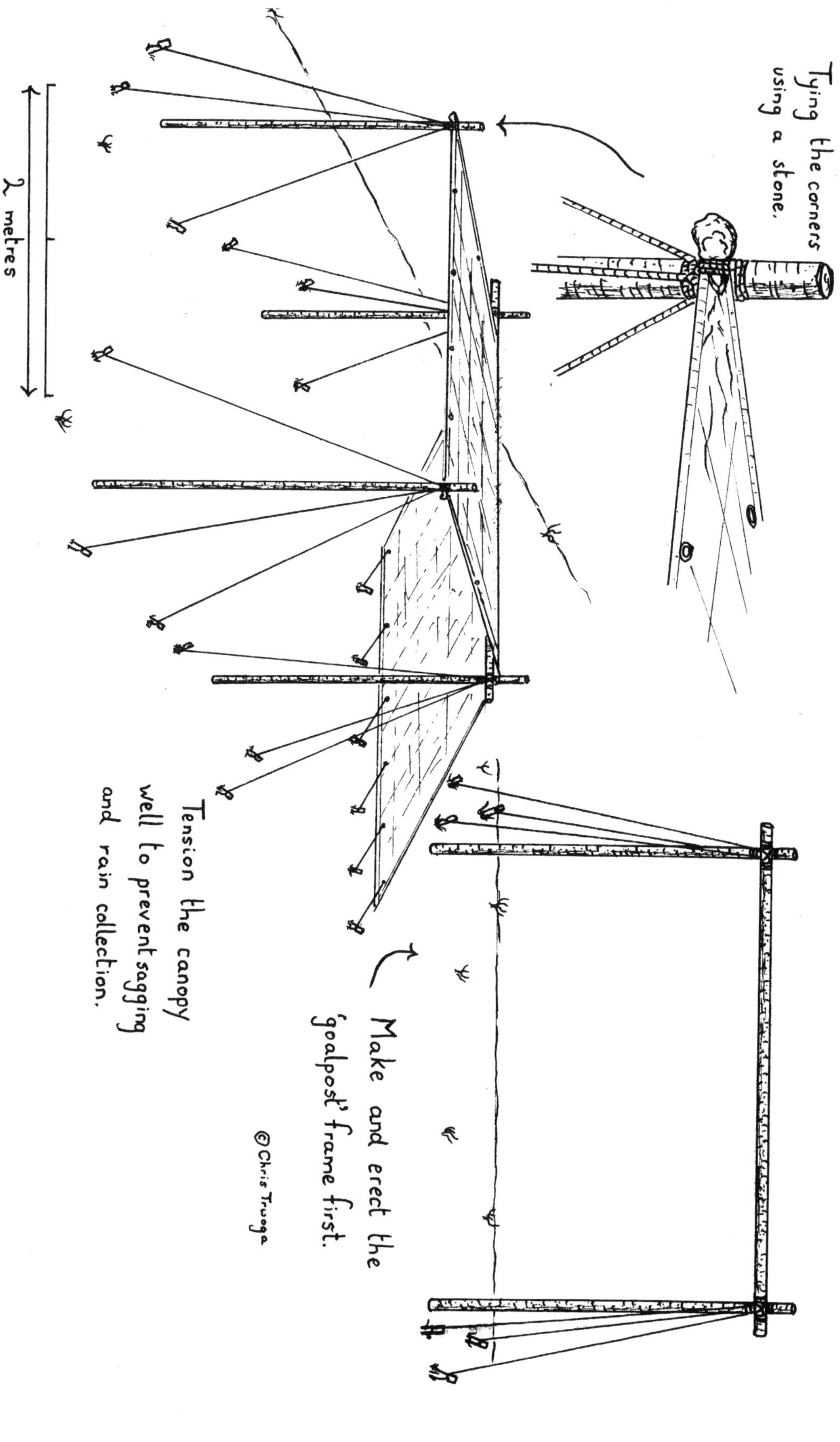

Tying the corners using a stone.

2 metres

Tension the canopy well to prevent sagging and rain collection.

Make and erect the 'goalpost' frame first.

© Chris Truога

145

6.3. Dome or "Bender" Shelter

Aim. To make a dome shelter using hazel and willow; to develop team skills / working practices realting to efficient construction. To gain insights into traditional itinerant lifeways.

In Brief. Students construct a dome out of long hazel poles, withies and tarpaulin.

What you will need:

For one bender: 11 hazel poles of 3m minimum length, average thickness of 3cm. * A large bundle of thin hazel poles, prunings or withies of 1 to 2cm thickness.	A couple of old tarpaulins. Tent pegs (see 6.5). Several large cobble stones. A bale of string.
A small bow saw and saw horse. Bill hook. Lump hammer and steel spike.	A couple of wooden stakes. A mallet (see 6.4). Safety scissors.
* If you want to build a decorative living willow structure, use thin, green withies.	

Method.

1. Discuss different forms of temporary shelter. When do people make use of temporary shelters (e.g. camping)? Discuss the different types of shelter used by travelling people. Discuss the dome as a structure. Where do we see the dome in use today as a shelter or roofing form? What makes the dome inherently stable?

2. Choose your construction site. Is the location level and well drained? Check the length of the poles and calculate the size and height of the dome. With 3m poles you should be able to achieve a 4m diameter bender.

3. Use a length of string tied to a peg to mark out the circle. Mark out the twelve holes as if marking out the twelve hours of a watch. The easiest way to do this is to divide your circle into 4 quarters and then divided each quarter into 3.

4. To make it easier to stick the poles in the ground sharpen the thicker ends on a log stump with your billhook. Use the stake and mallet to make holes at the 12 marked points. If the ground is stony or unyielding use a lump hammer and steel spike (*adults only*).

5. Set the 11 poles as firmly in the ground as possible, leaving the twelfth hole empty for the doorway. Two students bend the first opposing pair of poles together, being careful not to let them spring back. A third student ties the poles firmly together to form a hoop. Repeat the process with opposing pairs of poles until they are all tied together to form the dome.

6. To strengthen, weave a circle of withies around the dome about 50cm up from the ground and again about 1.5m. Remember to leave the gap for the entrance. Encourage neatness. When students are satisfied with the dome, throw over the tarpaulins. Tie down with string and weight round the rim with the stones. Use an old tarpaulin and rugs for the interior and enjoy!

7. You may want to remove the tarpaulin when you have finished with the activity. In an out-of-the-way corner of a wood or school grounds a bender frame can last a year.

Reflection. Benders can seem exciting places when they are crowded out with your mates. But what would it be like to live in a bender – as millions still do around the world today? Think through some of the hardships you might suffer. Think of a modern house. They may be dry and energy efficient, but in what ways can they encourage excessive consumption and waste?

Fig 6.3 Dome or Bender Shelter

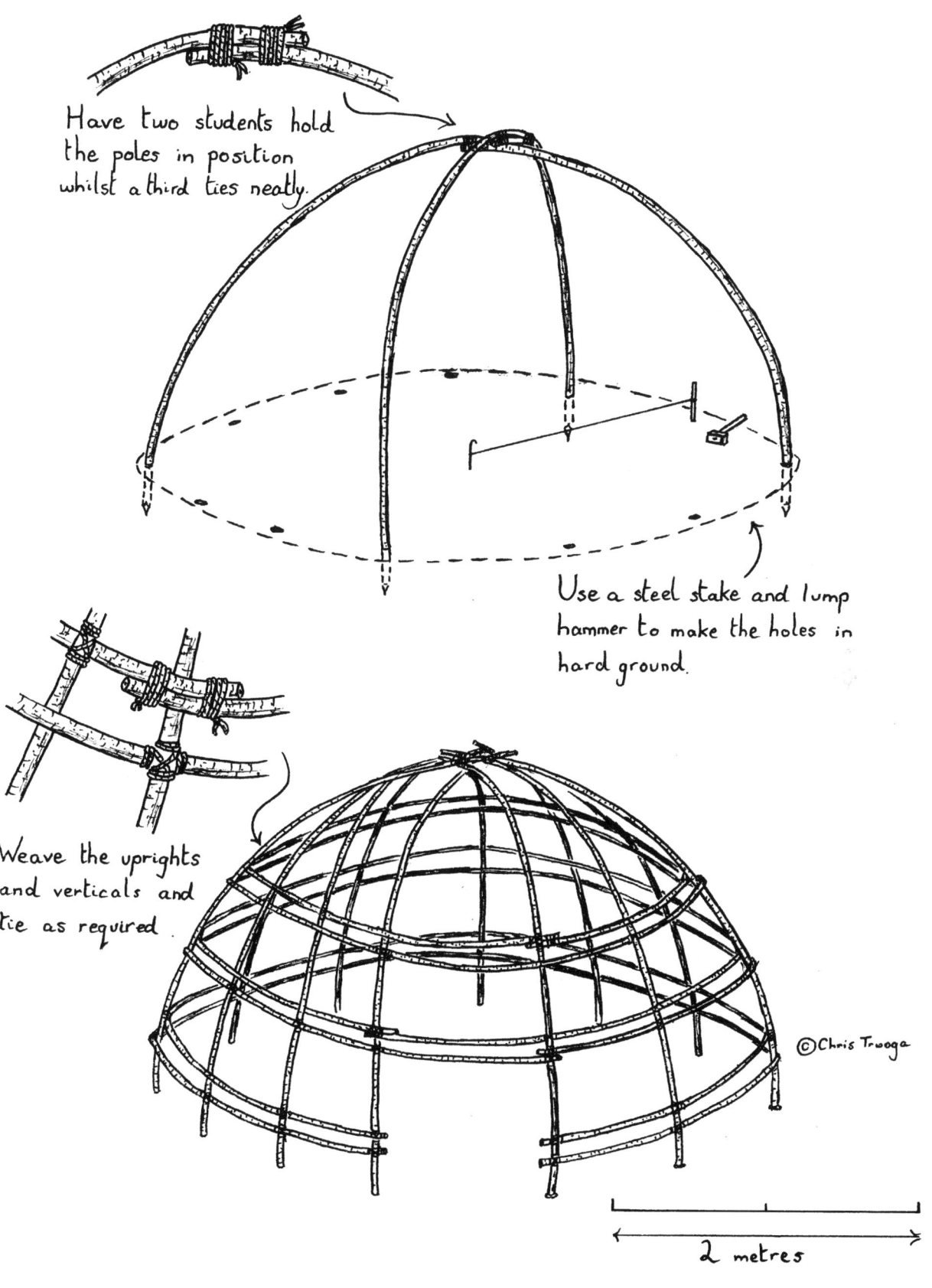

Have two students hold the poles in position whilst a third ties neatly.

Use a steel stake and lump hammer to make the holes in hard ground.

Weave the uprights and verticals and tie as required.

©Chris Twoga

2 metres

6.4. Making a Traditional Mallet

Aim. To manufacture a functional tool with a wide range of uses. To develop student skills in the safe use of bill hook and safety knife.

In Brief. Students make a one piece mallet (*see fig 6.4*).

What you will need:

Per student: A section of hardwood of about 10cm diameter and 30cm in length. A stout pair of leather gardening gloves per student.	Provide a bow saw, mallet, bill hook*, log stump, access to a saw horse and a piece of 60 grade sandpaper.
A maximum supervision ratio of one supervisor per 2 billhooks is recommended.	

Method.

1. Discuss the artisans who use the type of mallet they are making, for example sculptors and stonemasons. It is a serious tool with a wide range of applications. Demonstrate the splitting technique using billhook and mallet, with one student supporting the billhook, whilst the other strikes the centre of the blade with the mallet to drive it through the piece of timber.

2. Each student pair uses the bow saw and saw horse to cut their 30cm block of timber. Avoid sections with off shoots, as the wood will be knotty and hard to split. Using the saw horse, four saw cuts are made at the mid-point of the timber. The edges of the four saw cuts just touch, leaving a 5cm square of timber in the middle uncut. This requires care. If the cuts are made too close the piece should be discarded.

3. Choose which side of the working piece you want to make into the handle. Place the piece onto a log stump handle end up.

4. Students work in pairs to split out the handle. One student (wearing gloves on both hands) holds the bill hook in place in the direction of the cut to be made. The second student uses a mallet to drive the bill hook through the block of timber towards the saw cut. Encourage removing the wood in thin layers, working carefully towards the end of the saw cut and removing one quadrant of the block at a time. Insist on controlled strikes. The mallet should not be raised above shoulder height.

5. The outcome will be a square handle. Four fine cuts are now made at the the four corners of the handle to a depth of about half a centimetre. Carefully trim away the wood with the bill hook to produce an octagonal handle. You now have your rough piece. A safety knife is used to pare the handle into a comfortable, circular shape. The remaining bark can be pared off the mallet head with a knife and the handle finished off with sandpaper.

Reflection. You have now made a tool that can give good service. How do you feel about your work? In what ways was the job made easier by working as a pair? What do you plan to do with your mallet? For example, make a gift of it to someone or use it yourself. What other things could be made using the same technique?

Fig 6.4 Making a Traditional Mallet

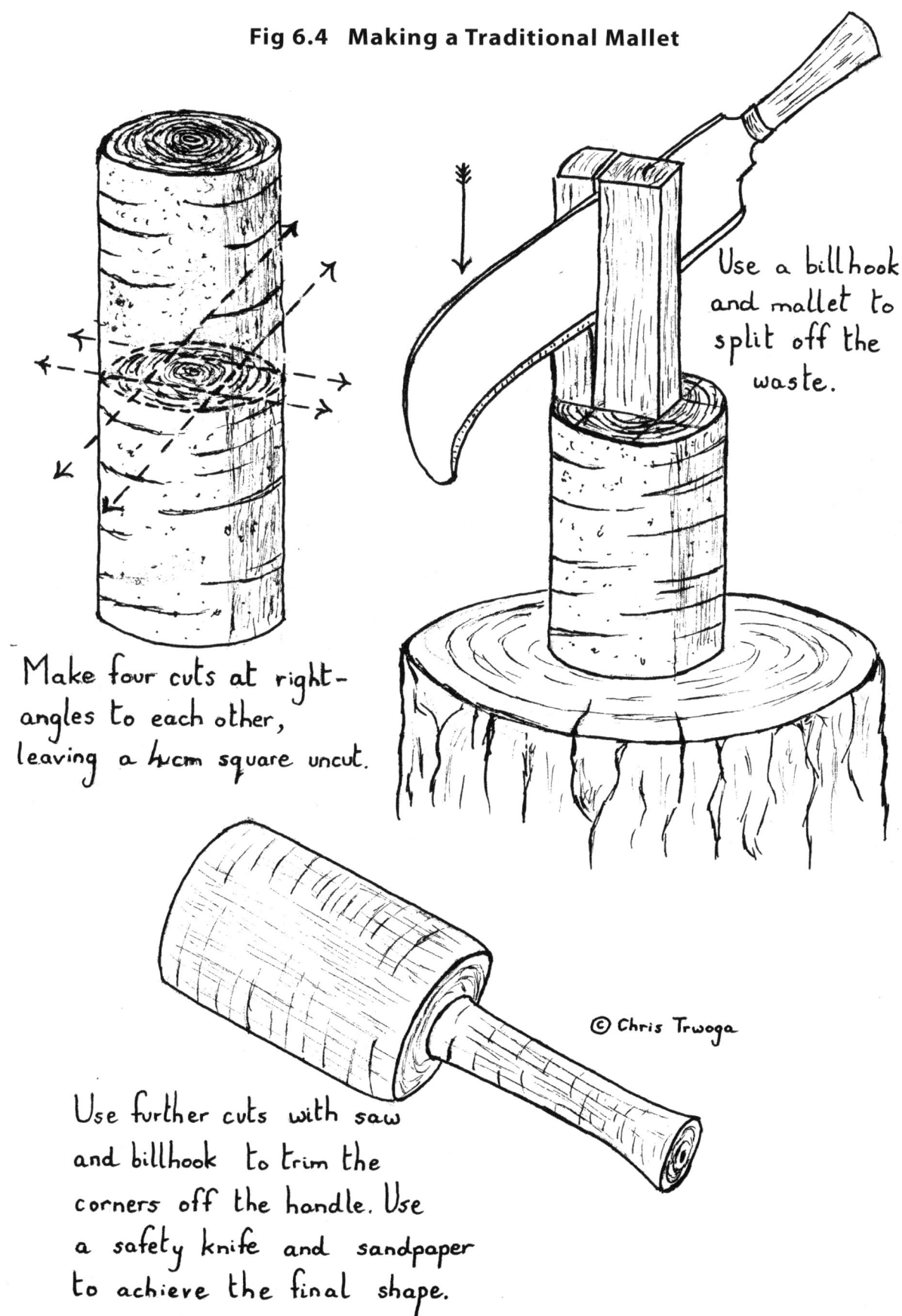

Make four cuts at right-
angles to each other,
leaving a 4cm square uncut.

Use a billhook
and mallet to
split off the
waste.

© Chris Trwoga

Use further cuts with saw
and billhook to trim the
corners off the handle. Use
a safety knife and sandpaper
to achieve the final shape.

6.5 Making Wooden Tent Pegs

Aim. To develop a systematic and rhythmic approach to the manufacture of multiple items.

In Brief. Students make tent pegs out of hazel poles or 2 x 1 sawn timber (*see fig 6.5*).

What you will need:

60cm of 4cm diameter hazel pole (or 2 x 1 sawn timber) per student. This will make 2 pegs.	Thick leather gardening gloves per student. One safety knife per two students. A bow saw, and access to a saw horse.

Method.

1. Talk about the usefulness of a good stock of tent pegs and stakes. Explain that the aims are efficient team working, with attention given to the safe working of the whole group.

2. Demonstrate the full procedure.

3. Ensure all hands are gloved. In this method students make two pegs together 'back to back'. Use a saw horse and bow saw to cut the sticks into 60cm lengths. One student steadies the wood whilst the second cuts. The cuts are made at a 45 degree angle to facilitate sharpening the tent pegs (*see fig 6.5*). Students take it in turns to do the sawing. Cut both ends of the wood at 45 degrees.

4. Mark the centre of the 60cm piece 5cm from the centre on both sides, cut the string notch to a depth of 1cm. Now cut in half to produce two 30cm pegs.

5. The student sits down to whittle the tent peg to shape. All paring must be made away from the body, with the legs apart or tucked in so that they are away from the direction of cut. Gently whittle away the string notch, working towards the saw cut from below. Encourage the removal of slivers rather than chunks. Work until a neat, smooth-surfaced notch has been achieved. Ensure the closure of the knife blade on completion of the task.

6. Next, sharpen the end of the peg by whittling the 45 degree cut. Work to achieve a curved, sabre-like appearance.

Reflection. Discuss how the different tools work – the knife as a paring tool and the billhook as a splitting tool. Why does splitting a piece of timber usually produce a stronger piece of timber? (Splitting means that the cut follows the grain – and the reason why a bill hook loses its advantage when used for hacking) People often enjoy 'whittling' sticks simply to pass the time. Why do you thick whittling can be so relaxing?

Fig 6.5   Making wooden tent pegs

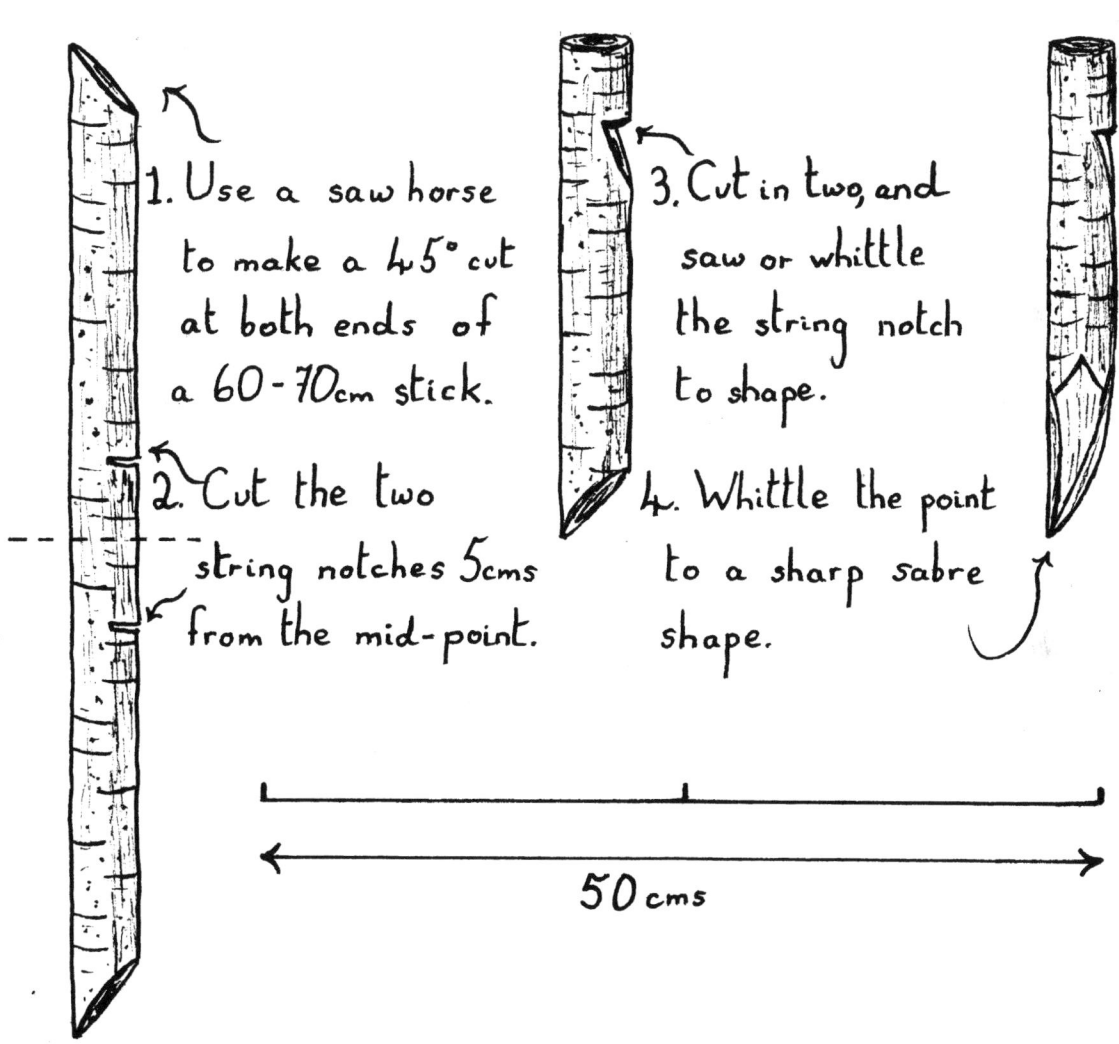

1. Use a saw horse to make a 45° cut at both ends of a 60-70cm stick.

2. Cut the two string notches 5cms from the mid-point.

3. Cut in two, and saw or whittle the string notch to shape.

4. Whittle the point to a sharp sabre shape.

50 cms

6.6 Spatula – Cooking Gear

Aim. To make a simple piece of cooking equipment. To encourage attention to form, functionality and detail in wood carving.

In Brief. Students use a bill hook, mallet and safety knife to make a cooking spatula.

What you will need:

For every three or four students: A relatively knot free block of timber, 30cm in length and 10cm diameter.	*Per 4 students:* A pencil, bill hook, wooden mallet (see 6.4), log stump and bow saw
Per student: A mini-hacksaw, safety knife, gloves and a piece of 60 grade sandpaper	*For the whole class:* One brace with 6mm wood bit. Access to a saw horse (se 6.7)

Method.

1. Provide an example of a spatula and discuss its various culinary uses.

2. Each group of three or four students cuts their block of timber from the tree limb. Ensure they avoid sections with branches or where a branch has been removed. Depending on the thickness of the wood and the straightness of the grain it may be possible to get four blanks out of a single piece of timber.

3. Use the pencil to mark out the smoothest end of the block with the number of cuts to be made. Each cut should produce a "blank" of between 6mms and 1cm thick. Place the block on a log stump and gently tap the bill hook through the block with the mallet. Do this in pairs with one student (gloved) supporting the billhook and a second using the mallet Keep tapping the bill hook down until the waste piece has completely split off. Check the cut for shape and knots.

4. Move on to the second cut. This will split out the first blank. Students take it in turns to split out a blank. Once all blanks are cut, each student can prepare their blank for carving by paring the flat surfaces with a knife to remove any unevenness.

5. Using the pencil, draw the shape of the spatula on the blank. Now use a log stump and mini-hacksaw to begin to cut out the shape, (see fig 6.6). Carefully use the billhook to make cuts along the grain that can't be reached with the hacksaw. In a seated position, now begin to pare out the desired shape. Students should be encouraged to take their time and remove thin parings. Attempting to take off too much wood will split the blank. It takes time to pare a spatula to shape and it is a good exercise for developing mindfulness or 'flow'. Warn that the care needs to increase as the work progresses to avoid damaging an almost completed piece.

6. Once the desired shape has been achieved, very carefully drill a hole through the handle. Do not go all the way through from one side, but drill until the bit just begins to show through then reverse and finish from the other side. This prevents the wood splitting.

7. Do any final paring and use the sand paper to finish. Encourage a patient approach and allow 20 to 30 minutes for thorough sanding.

Reflection. What does 'working with the grain' mean? How has working with the grain affected the shape and appearance of your piece? What will you use your spatula for? Did you enjoy the work? Did you find it relaxing?

Fig 6.6   Making a Spatula

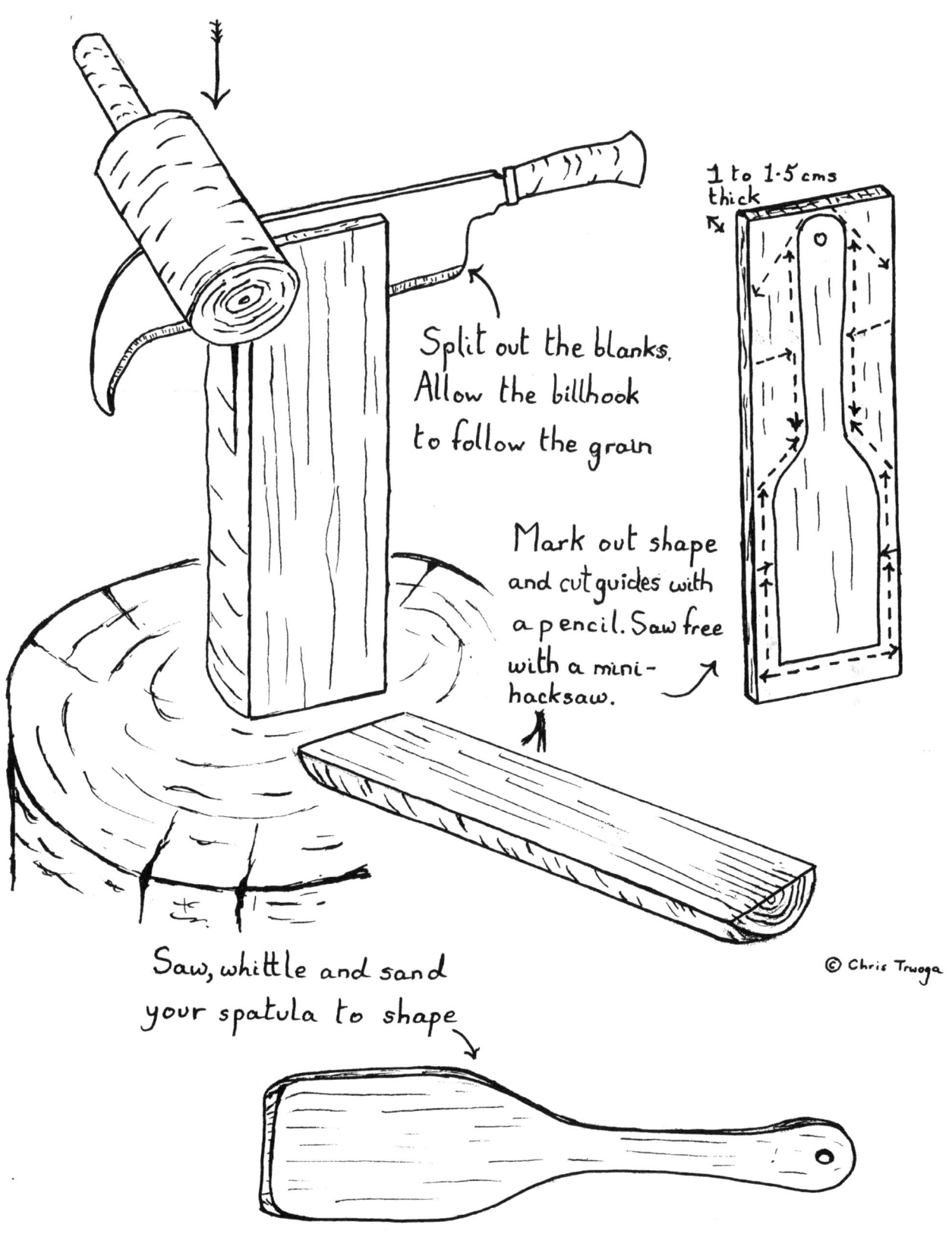

1 to 1.5 cms thick

Split out the blanks. Allow the billhook to follow the grain

Mark out shape and cut guides with a pencil. Saw free with a mini-hacksaw.

Saw, whittle and sand your spatula to shape

© Chris Truoga

6.7 Saw Horse

Aim. To develop simple jointing skills that have a wide range of applications.

In brief. Students work in a team to make a basic saw horse out of timber poles and reclaimed planking (*see fig 6.7*).

What you will need: *(per group making one frame)*

6m of fairly straight 10cm diameter timber pole (wet or part-seasoned is fine). 4 pieces of reclaimed 4 x 1 or 6 x 1 planking about 80cm in length.	1kg of 12cm oval nails. A bow saw, 2 bill hooks, 2 mallets, a hammer A brace with 4 mm wood bit. Safety glasses. Gaffer tape.

Method.

1. Explain that the saw horse is perhaps the most practical piece of outdoor carpentry equipment you can make. The basic form used is the 'X' frame (*see fig 6.7*).

2. Students begin by making three 'X' frames between them. Cut six 1m lengths out of the 10cm diameter timber. Put the two pieces of the 'X' together and mark out the joint in the centre of each piece with gaffer tape. Tape the area so that the wood to be removed is left exposed. Make saw cuts across the joint area at 2cm intervals. The cuts are made to a depth of 4cm or no more than a third of the way through the timber.

3. Now cut out the joint. Rest the timber against a staked log with a student stood, supporting it from the top and a second cutting from the front. It may be easier for younger students to do this 'three-handed'. One student supports the timber against the log from above and behind. A second holds the bill hook at an angle against the timber to be removed, whilst the third strikes the bill hook with the mallet. This is a safer method as all the students can be positioned such that they cannot be struck by either bill hook or mallet. ***All must wear thick leather gardening gloves. Don't let students use the bill hook like an axe. This risks serious injury and creates flying splinters. If you find the wood prone to producing flying splinters use safety glasses. Ensure the student holding the wood is stood behind the supporting log.***

4. When the two joints are cut, select the nailing points and drill starter holes in the timber to reduce the risk of splitting. Nail the two pieces together, two nails to the front and a nail to the rear. Check for rigidity. Check if nail points have gone through to the other side. If they have hammer them flat.

5. Two students support the three 'X' frames, whilst a third nails the stretcher to each 'X' frame. Drill starter holes in the reclaimed planking. The first pair of stretchers are positioned at the top of the 'legs' and the lower pair 10cm from the ground. Note that accurate nailing is important to ensure the wood does not split and there is good penetration into the 'X' frames. Check for protruding nails and hammer flat as necessary.

6. Ensure that the saw horse sits level and is steady in use. Trim the ends of the legs with a saw to level off if required.

Reflection. Try out your sawhorse. Does it do the business? How satisfied are you with the outcome? How many tasks required teamwork? Reflect on how well you worked as a team. Reflect on your enjoyment and satisfaction with this kind of task.

Fig 6.7   Making a Saw Horse

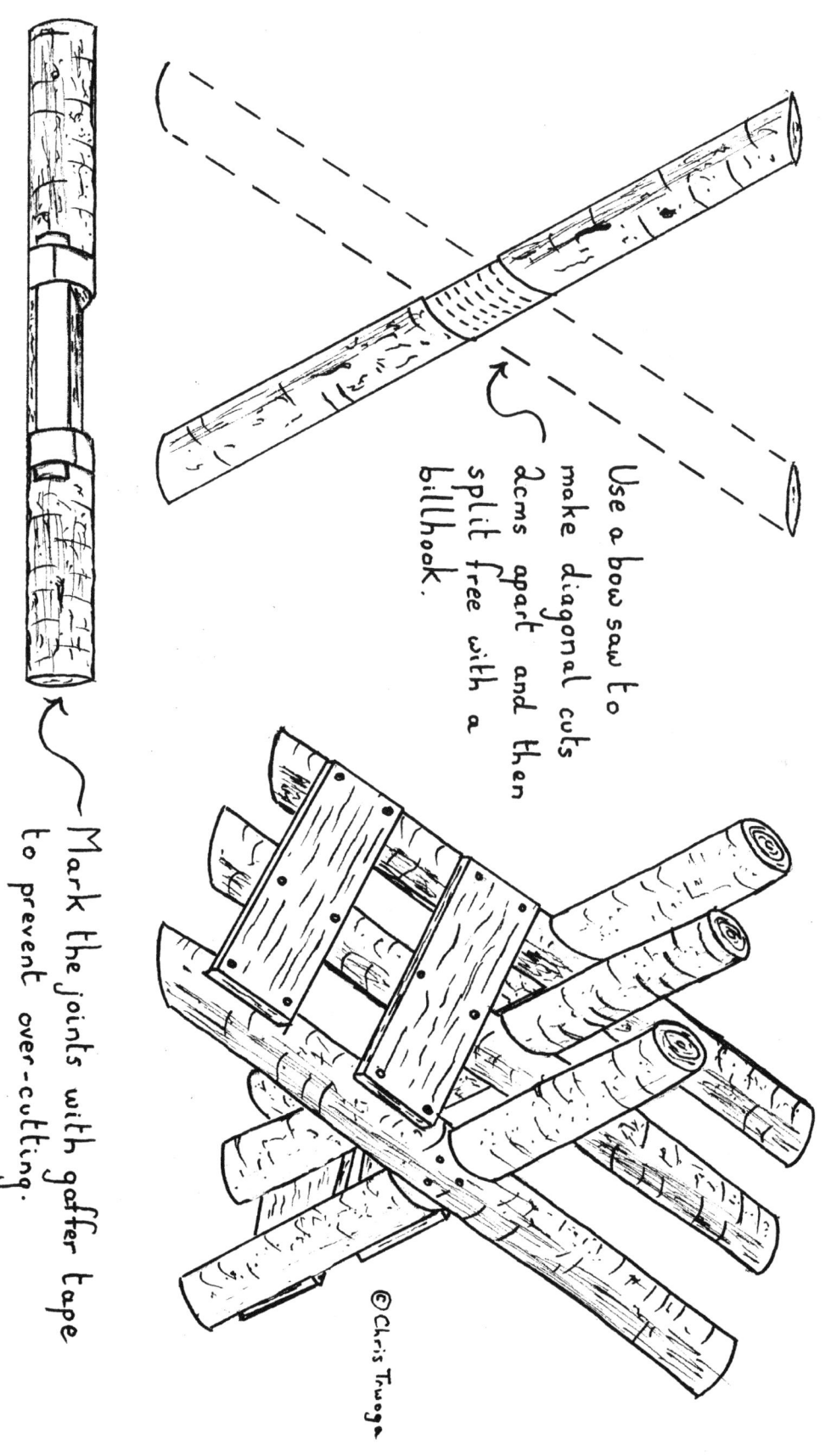

Use a bow saw to make diagonal cuts 2cms apart and then split free with a billhook.

Mark the joints with gaffer tape to prevent over-cutting.

© Chris Truога

6. 8   Making a Timber Store

Aim. To develop skills in structure building. To develop understanding of the forces involved in supporting a roof.

In Brief. Students construct a timber framed store with turf or brash covered roof.

What you will need:

30m of timber poles, around 8cm in diameter. Lots of thinner walling and roofing poles and branches of various lengths and thicknesses. A 300m bale of string, tarpaulin, and a covering material, such as evergreen brash, turf, tree bark or simply earth.	Saw horse, bow saw. Scissors. Spades to dig large post holes. Wooden stake and mallet for making small post holes. A short ladder.

Method.

1. Several sessions may be needed to complete the structure so it is important to use a working diagram. Work out the design with the students using a scale diagram (see fig 6.8).

2. Consider alternatives to the diagram provided if it does not meet your needs.

3. The first stage is to construct the main frame, which should be strong enough to be used for pull-ups by a 10 stone student. Make the front 'goalpost' frame. This frame is reinforced with diagonal struts so that it stands freely. Cut your front posts to the desired height, allowing for burying 30cms into the ground. Thus a two metre high structure requires 2.3 metre posts. Assuming the width is two metres, dig 40cm deep holes and fix the posts in the holes and tamp them in firmly with stones and earth.

4. Next, cut the crossbeam, allowing for excess to either side. Measure the distance between the two posts, say 2 metres, and add an extra 40cms. Cut the crossbeam and lash to the uprights as securely as possible. To strengthen the front frame, dig a 1.5 m long, 5cm thick pole into the ground about 75cm behind each upright. Bend the pole towards the upright and lash the two together. Check that the frame is sufficiently rigid. Repeat the process for the rear frame, using a much shorter upright. Remember to allow for the 30cm below ground in cutting the uprights. You can make a perfectly satisfactory shelter with a very low rear bar – no more than 20cm from the ground, to which the 'front to back' roof poles are lashed. A very short bar may not need bracing. Check that the structure is rigid when complete.

5. The next stage is to link the front and rear frames with a 'front to back' roof beam to both sides. These are lashed to the crossbeams. Again, measure the distance and allow at least a 25cm excess to both sides to facilitate lashing. Add more 'front to back' roof beams at 20cm intervals across the roof. Strengthen the two outside roof beams with posts mid-way along the wall. These should be 10cms thick and firmly dug in. Lash them firmly to the two outside roof beams. Strengthen with diagonal struts as necessary. Check all lashings are as tight as they can be. Using thin hazel poles as battens, tie them across the roof beams at intervals of 20cms. Check the strength and the rigidity of the whole frame.

6. Before continuing with the roof, make up the walls to either side using thin hazel poles or similar. These should be buried to a depth of about 15cms and lashed to the outside roof beams. Thin material such as old withies or brash can now be woven into these to create screening.

Fig 6.8   Making a Timber Store

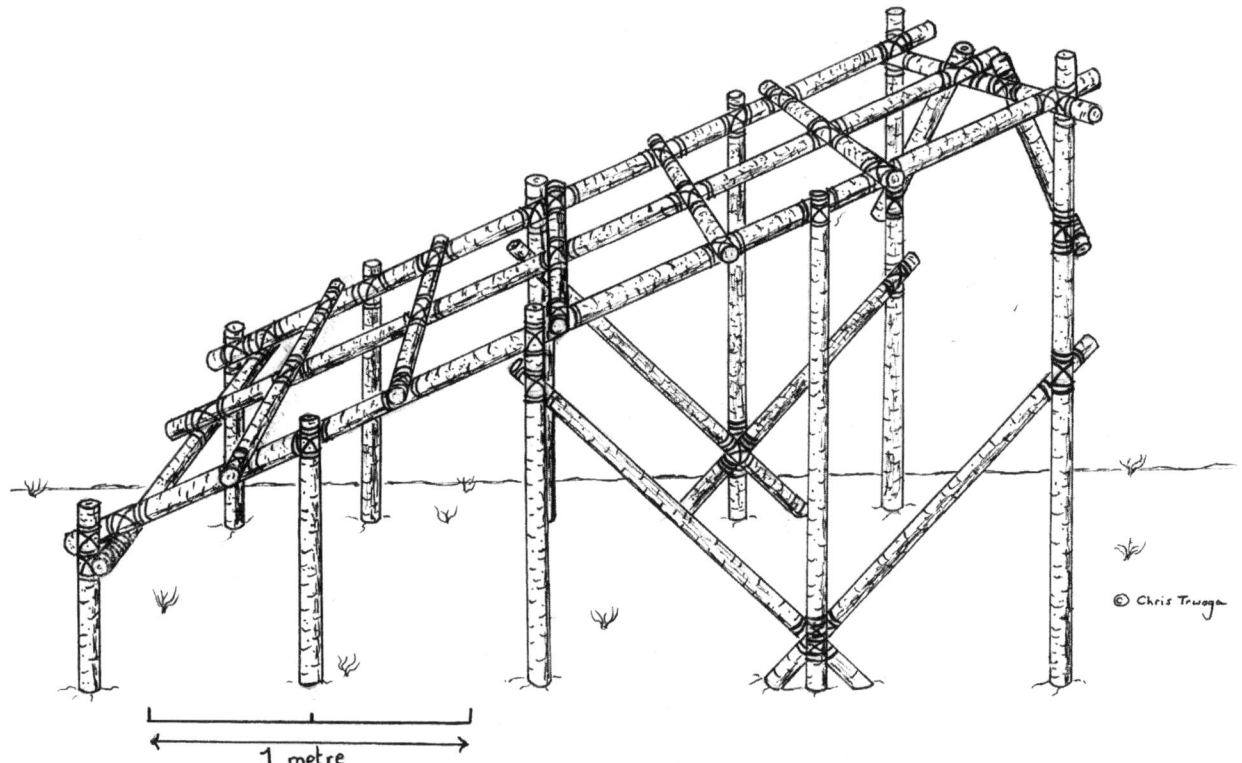

© Chris Trwoga

1 metre

7.   Now the woodwork is complete, the tarpaulin can be laid on the roof. This should be firmly tied to the battens around the edges. Tarpaulins are unsightly and short-lived in the sun – hence the need for a protective layer of turf or other natural covering. In the past I have bought turf from a D.I.Y. store if none was available from other sources. This won't stay green on a roof. Even dead, however, turf is a natural covering and looks good. If no turf is available think about brash – leafy branches of coniferous foliage, laid thickly in place and tied down. In making the roof, ensure that good practice in terms of safety is followed. There should always be someone supporting any ladder when a student ascends and the ladder must not be used as a work platform. They should never be more than half their height from the ground. Never allow students to climb on to the roof.

8.   Check the lashings periodically for rot and re-tie individual joints as necessary.

Reflection. You have just completed a major Forest School project. Share how you feel about the outcomes. You will have had to solve many different problems along the way. What have you learned in tackling these problems? Making a structure like this needs a lot of co-operation. Reflect on how decisions were made.

6.9   Making a Kit Shelf with Canopy

Aim. To develop group working skills, effective team management and division of labour. To develop and practice knot-tying skills.

In Brief. Students make a clothing and kit rack with poles, fixed between two adjacent trees, with all joints tied (see fig 6.9).

What you will need:

Two adjacent trees, between 2 and 3m apart with trunks of at least 20cm in diameter. 4 poles of at least 6cm diameter long enough to span them.	Several metres of thinner poles for shelving. Branches or poles of hazel or willow to make the rafters of the canopy.
Canopy - 200m bale of twine. Thatching material, such as evergreen brash or a bale of straw - green tarpulin can also be used.	A saw horse, bow saws. Scissors to cut string and trim straw.

Method.

1. Discuss the practical need for safe and visible storage of personal clothing and other kit. Not having a store point can lead to an untidy Forest School area.

2. Two groups can work on the rack and canopy separately. The rack has the appearance of a ladder and consists of two poles lashed around a metre high between two trees, with the 'rungs' lashed between them at 20cm intervals. The canopy is made using the same technique, but is tied to the tree at a slope.

3. First, measure the required length so that the poles pass the widest point of each trunk by about 25cm. Have your group cut a single pole first and check that the length is correct, then use it to measure the remaining poles. Once cut, lash firmly to the trunk with twine. Tie the top canopy "rack" to the trees so as to create a downward slope for rain run-off (see fig 6.6). **To avoid injury once the roof is on, it needs to be above head hieght.**

4. Now cut the rungs to size using a bow saw. The length of the rungs depends on the distance between the two poles. Measure the gap and add 30cm to create a 15cm overhang on both sides. Lash the shelf rungs to the *underside* of the poles (*see fig 6.9*). This means a plank can be rested between the poles to make a shelf.

5. Lash the canopy rungs on top of the poles, not the underside. The rungs are cut to project 25cm beyond the poles to make a wide canopy.

6. Once the canopy frame is complete consider the options for roofing material. A length of green tarpaulin or roofing felt can be tied or tacked to the poles. Alternatively, withies can be woven or tied to the rungs and a canopy made of turf or thatch. Thatching can be done with evergreen brash or straw. Tie the straw in bundles of around 8cm diameter and then lash to the rungs. The bundles need to be secured tightly against each other to resist rain.

Reflection. Discuss the practical skills you have developed and improved during this activity. How well did you work together as a team? What aspects of the work did you find most/ least satisfying? Can you identify why?

Fig 6.6   Making a Kit Shelf with Canopy

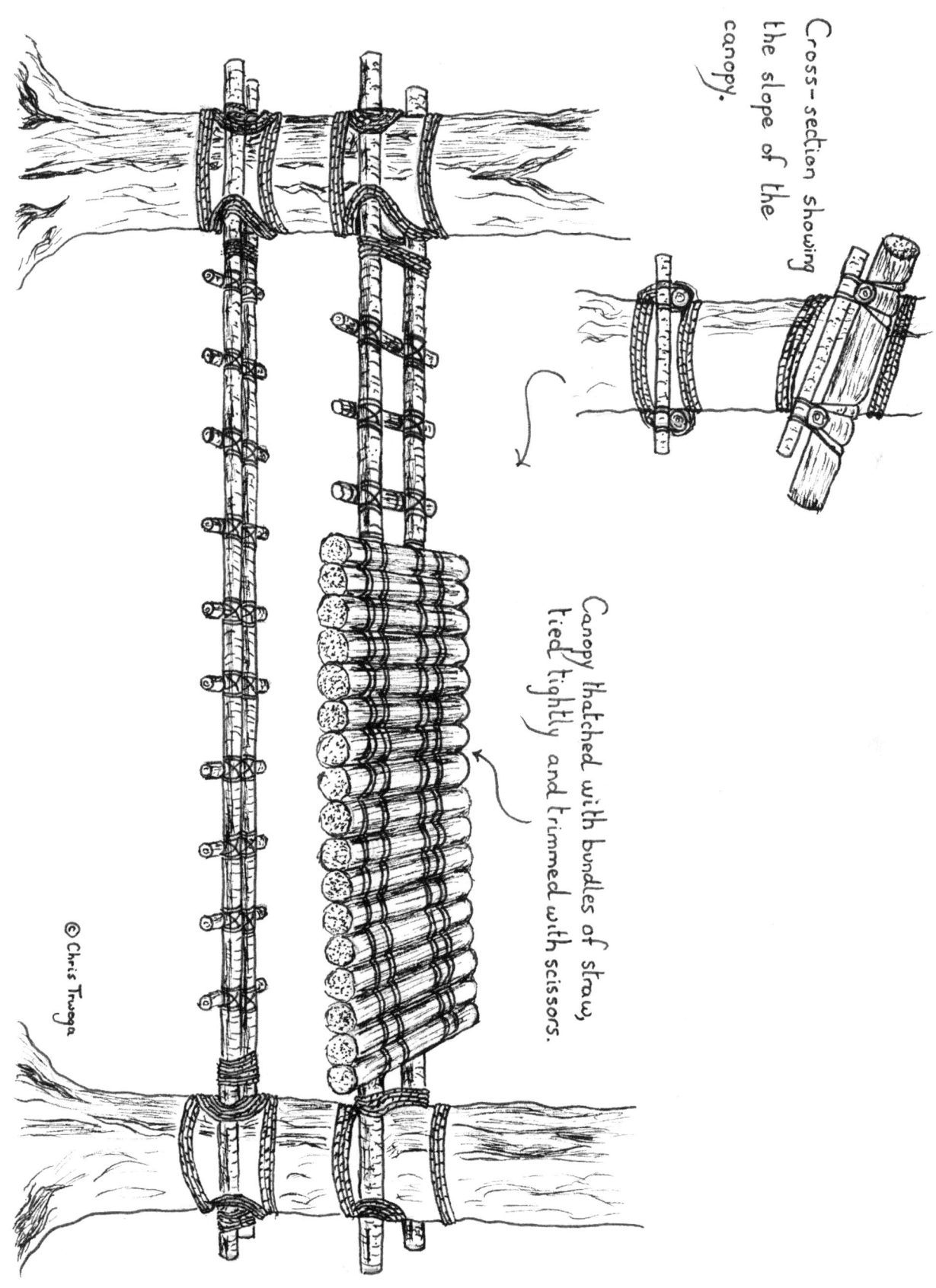

Cross-section showing the slope of the canopy.

Canopy thatched with bundles of straw, tied tightly and trimmed with scissors.

© Chris Truoga

159

6.10 Pizza Oven

Aim. To explore methods of heat conservation through the construction of an efficient oven. To understand how an enclosed fire works. To make an effective outdoor oven.

In Brief. Construct an oven using a traditional small steel dustbin (see also activity 10.9).

What you will need: (*use reclaimed materials where possible*).

A small steel dustbin with a lid and handle in good condition. A short section of iron or steel pipe a little over 1m in length and about 12cm in diameter.	20 good quality bricks. Clay to make cob (see activity 10.9). Materials to make some earth retaining hurdles about 40cm high.

Method.

1. Discuss oven technology. Consider the need for providing and retaining sustained heat.

2. Choose the site. The oven is best placed on a slight rise or slope so the door faces the prevailing wind - this improves draught and ensures that rainwater doesn't collect in the fire pit.

3. First, dig the fire pit. This should be 50cm wide, 1m long and 40cm deep. Tamp down the earth as firm as possible and line the back and sides with bricks up to the ground surface. Use a double layer at the back of the hole to create the flue and the platform to support the chimney.

4. Now rest the dustbin and chimney on the bricks so the whole structure sits square. If there is any space to the rear of the bricks fill this with clay or tamped down dirt.

5. Build a hurdling fence around the stove and the rear of the chimney (*see activity 10.3*). The fence should be about 30cm high and about 40cm from the wall of the oven. It will look neatest if made as one continuous fence, woven in situ. Reinforce the hurdling with stakes to resist the outward pressure of the earth or clay piled around the oven.

6. Now start to build a thick layer of clay, or tamped earth around the oven, starting with the chimney. Carefully fill the space between the chimney, the oven and the ground with clay to ensure that a good seal is created. With the same care, fill the gap between the oven and the ground to create an effective seal. The dustbin is now entirely covered with at least 15cm of clay. If working with clay or cob, work up the overall shape to make the surface as smooth and as decorative as you can. ***Note that clay or mud will disintegrate over time, whilst cob can be more lasting. Both will need regular replacement if not protected by a canopy.***

7. At this point, test the fire pit with some newspaper. Ensure the fire draws well, with smoke drawn out of the chimney. Make sure fuel can be safely added to the fire and ashes raked out. If unsuccessful, dig away more earth at the front of the oven to inprove air flow and access.

8. Make a canopy. The protective cover should sit a good 30cm above the oven and direct any rainwater clear of the oven and the firepit. An attractive technique is to use hurdling for the roof, resting on four posts. The hurdling is then covered in turves in the manner of a traditional crofter's roof. Once your oven is complete get on with making pizzas!

Reflection. Think about the meals in your life. Do you eat as a family? Do you eat with friends? Do you enjoy mealtimes? Does cooking food outdoors make it feel special? Has the oven made you think more about what goes into preparing and cooking food?

These ovens are remarkably efficient and can be constructed as part of a project relating to Food Technology, or as something the school can use for outdoor functions. They are a variation on a clay earth oven - see activity 10.9 - but are longer lasting and easier to construct.

The pizza oven is heated by a sub-surface fire; the heat is retained by the bricks underneath and the thick layer of cob or clay around it.

7. ART IN NATURE

Aboriginal Art, Scarecrow Sculpture, Rangoli Patterns, Corn Dolly, Tree Spirit Faces, Journey Mandalas, Nature Icon, Animal Cup, Painting with Plants, Stick Mobiles

"I believe a leaf of grass is no less than the journey-work of the stars."
Walt Whitman

Art provides a vehicle by which young people can negotiate and express their relationship with themselves, each other and the natural world in a way that is positive and constructive. It helps them to appreciate that there is nothing fixed in that relationship and we can use art to construct new meanings the better to cope with our experience of daily life.

Art outdoors is about utilizing the natural environment to inspire the creative process and mediate a student's experience of nature. You can begin by introducing the students to art that has been created in nature, particularly that of indigenous peoples. Very often, indigenous art has energy of colour and form that students can connect with and enjoy readily. They can identify how indigenous art makes explicit the connection the artist feels for the landscape.

The art of indigenous peoples has other qualities. It often serves a liminal function. Liminal means it sets a space apart from everydayness. It may express the presence of the gods, of ancestral spirits or a hidden entrance to the otherworld. The cave paintings of the Dordogne, the rock paintings of the shamans of the San peoples of Southern Africa and the carved menhirs of the European Neolithic are ways of signing gateways to new realities.

But the art of indigenous peoples does something else. It manifests the spirit of place. In Kilmartin Glen on the west coast of Scotland, for example, hundreds of rocky outcrops were carved in the Bronze Age with beautiful, magical symbols, the meaning of which is now lost to us. These carvings don't just transform a landscape visually. They reveal the meaning within a landscape as it is experienced by the artist.

Aboriginal Art is an outstanding contemporary example. Their haunting sinuous forms, constructed of vivid animals that merge into abstract landscapes embody the deep myths that tell how the animals of the Dreamtime made the land itself. Art, myth, and human connectivity with animals and landscape are manifested in a single creative form.

For a student, the making of Art in a natural environment can serve the same purpose. They can make art that connects them to natural space. It can give them a sense of place, identity and ownership within a landscape.

Any work you do outdoors needs to be designed with consideration to environmental impact. If something is to be taken away it should not degrade the living landscape. If something is to be added its longevity should be such as to disappear into the landscape in a relatively short period of time. It should be non-polluting, and unlikely to spoil the pleasure of others making use of the same space.

ART AND WELL-BEING

Art and 'Flow'. Art has perhaps the greatest capacity of all to achieve flow – the state of being so deeply engaged in a task that we are self-forgotten. Our consciousness is absorbed by and expressed in the task. Flow is also about attaining a sense of fulfillment – emerging from a task knowing that it manifests what is best in us. A sense of fulfillment needs deep engagement, an opportunity to learn and express new skills, and sufficient commitment in terms of time and energy to be truly proud of the outcomes.[1]

Art as Therapy. Art is used in some contexts to enable students to work through emotional trauma, as, for example, in war zones, where children are encouraged to draw and paint their experiences in order to manifest feelings that they struggle to put into words. For example, I have seen a collection of paintings from an Indian context, where students have charted the dramatic changes to their environment caused by the rapid urbanization and loss of the rural way of life that their villages have experienced.

Connecting with Self. Vivien Mountain describes Art as a 'safe place', where students can explore their identity and their relationship with place. In an article for the International Journal of Children's Spirituality, she describes her work with students based on a system of inquiry designed by the Melbourne Institute of Experiential and Creative Arts[2], involving the use of Art as a 'safe place' where self-awareness can be discussed and negotiated:

"As the engagement of listening and responding takes place, various levels of understanding and empathy are experienced. As the companioning engagement focuses on the creative art work a place of safety is entered where judgement and criticism of the person is suspended as understanding the art becomes the primary focus."[3]

Keywords and 'word clusters' were drawn from the pupil's work and analyzed to demonstrate the depth and integrity of pupil engagement. Mountain used Mandalas (*see activity 7.6*) and weaving and inter-connecting lines as a focus for discussion of self-awareness and self-connectedness.[4]

Art can be a powerful tool for healing as we use Art in Nature to encourage students to move away from highly judgemental and competitive media-based myths of self-worth towards one founded on self-realization through creativity.

Learning from Icons. The Icon is a spiritual art form that reflects a tradition going back to the Byzantine Empire and the time of Constantine the Great. Painted by monks, the images of saints are created using natural materials in a style and method that has changed little in nearly two thousand years. The artist uses the icon as a window to the Divine, rather than an art form in its own right. The natural materials used represent 'the spiritual, animal, vegetable and mineral'. The preparation of the panel, the mixing of the pigments and the use of special materials such as gold leaf connect the icon with all of nature.

The state of mind in which the icon is made is of the utmost importance. It is through the spirit of the artist that the spiritual is imbued into the icon. There is no attempt to innovate – that is to manifest the ego - simply to express the ancient forms meditatively and prayerfully. Unlike modern art, the personality of the artist is not important. It is not an expression of an individual creative act but of a communion, through form and nature, with the Divine. As such, it is medium through which an individual might connect with nature and the cosmos.

7.1 Aboriginal Art

Aim. To enable students to express their relationship with animals and landscape through aboriginal art forms. To explore the techniques of creating images with dots and lines.

In Brief. Students decorate a piece of tree bark or other natural material with Australian Aboriginal style artwork.

What you will need:

A natural object to paint, such as a large, smooth pebble, piece of slate, scrap of leather, tree bark (the smooth inner surface) an animal bone or piece of dead wood that has lost its bark. * PVA glue to bind paint. Powder paints or natural colours made from wood ash, soot etc..	Alternatively, students can cut a disk of timber, say 10cm in diameter. Pre-drill it so that the finished item can be made into a pendant or used as part of a display.

* These could be collected as part of the activity or gathered over time in preparation.

Method.

1. Seated round a fire, introduce students to Australian Aboriginal art. Read Aboriginal tales and talk about creatures like the *Rainbow Serpent*. Get them to experiment on paper with the distinctive dot and line style of painting animals, such as lizards or snakes and landscapes of hills and rivers. Discuss the *Dreamtime*. Reflect on your own local landscapes and animals.

2. Students choose their natural object. Think of function and material. It may become a personal ornament, sacred totem, throwing stick or a small shield; it could be wood, a smooth pebble, slate, tree bark (the smooth inner surface) or an animal bone - all great for painting.

3. Mix your colours with PVA glue. Make the paint smooth and thick. Get students to experiment with making their own painting implements. Dots can be applied simply with a flat-ended twig (*trimmed with a knife*) and different twigs can be used for different shaped dots. The application of dots needs practice! If a mistake is made, scrape away with a safety knife.

4. Students should be clear about the design before starting. Ideally, it has been worked out on paper. Designs that work well are the representation of simple animals, such as lizards or stylized representations of landscapes inspired from aboriginal artwork. Students should be given the opportunity to study how animal and landscape forms merge, such as 'snake' and 'river', to represent aspects of aboriginal mythology.

5. Once the work is finished allow a couple of hours for the PVA to harden off.

Reflection.   Authentic aboriginal art forms might be found in body painting, the decoration of rock shelters and simple, portable objects. Reflect on what the possessions of a nomadic Aborigine, living in the Australian Outback, might be. Aboriginal art often reflects the *Dreamtime*.   The stories often talk about how animals, humans and the landscape are closely related.   Aborigines feel they belong to the land and their ancestors are part of the landscape.   Do you feel especially attached to any part of the landscapes you know?   Find out about and discuss Uluru (Ayres Rock).

7.2 Scarecrow Sculpture

Aim. To connect with an old rural tradition that is both practical and creative.

In Brief. Students make a life-size free standing scarecrow.

What you will need:

A selection of sticks of different lengths. Plenty of sisal twine. A selection of old clothes, hessian sacking material and scrap fabrics or paints to make facial features.	It is useful to have a bow saw and saw horse to cut sticks to length. A couple of rubber mallets and hazel stakes. "Needle and thread" - large wool needles and green garden twine works well.
A bale of straw can be purchased for about £4 from a farm supplier, which will be enough for several scarecrows. Hessian sandbags can be ordered online for about £8 for ten.	

Method.

1. Introduce the theme by exploring stories that feature scarecrows and by discussing their traditional use. Discuss what scarecrows might have been made of and why only the oldest and tattiest clothing would have been used in the past. Find out the seasons when scarecrows were used. Think about how a scarecrow could be made to appear to 'move' to make it more effective. Explain how their scarecrow will be free-standing and a realistic height, as a traditional scarecrow would have to be. It is a scarecrow they are making and not a 'Guy' for a bonfire.

2. Students can work in teams of 4 to 6 and share the responsibility of finding or bringing in the materials. Insist clothing is kept to a sensible minimum (say 4 items per scarecrow) and the emphasis placed on using natural materials wherever possible. An example of this might be to make hands out of straw and faces sewn onto a bit of sacking

3. Discuss and demonstrate making techniques. Sisal twine is used to tie the poles together. Straw is used for stuffing and hair. Heads might be moulded from a roughly sewn hemp bag stuffed with straw and hands from sticks or straw tied to shape. Encourage efficient division of labour across the team.

4. Once the scarecrows are complete they can be set up where they can be usefully employed, such as the school garden. Or you can have a scarecrow competition around the school.

Reflection. Scarecrows still appear in rural gardens and fields. Recently, they have become a popular theme for village festivals. Scarecrow making is a seasonal activity, relating to the planting of seed crops and keeping flocks of crows from eating the seed before they had time to germinate. Share other popular activities that relate to the cycles of the arable year.

7.3 Rangoli Patterns

Aim. To explore a form of domestic art with a distinctive role in popular Hindu folk tradition. To learn about the role of rangoli patterns in Hindu life and spiritual practice.

In Brief. Students learn how to make Rangoli patterns (*see fig 7.3 for some simple designs*).

What you will need:

Powders, such as coloured rice flour, for a traditional approach. Coloured chalk sticks are easier to use and much less messy. Plain flour is fine for white designs. *	Paved areas where students can work safely or an area of beaten earth if using powders.

* Coloured Holi powders can be purchased online, but tend to be expensive in the UK.

Method.

1. Using pictures of rangoli patterns, discuss their use in Hindu culture and where you might expect to find them. Refer to the Hindu festivals when special rangoli patterns might be made. Rangoli patterns aren't just decorative – they are believed to bring luck and to protect the household from evil spirits. They are usually made in front of the main entrance to the house. They are found throughout India and often it is children who draw them. They wear out quickly and are refreshed or replaced on a daily basis. They can be simple or complicated. Explain what a threshold is. How many thresholds does the school have? There might also be other 'thresholds' such as the approach to a play area, in front of a gate.

2. Practice drawing rangoli patterns. Note how they begin with a grid of dots that support symmetry and planning. Study how they are often drawn with a single , uninterrupted line.

3. Students can then go outside and in a patch of playground use white or yellow chalk to practice the technique. Work in small groups or individually. A typical Rangoli pattern will be the size of a doormat. Once able to execute a reasonably neat and attractive Rangoli pattern students can decorate selected entrance areas of the school.

Reflection. Rangoli patterns are made for some Hindu festivals. Find out about the stories behind one of the festivals, such as Holi. The threshold or entrance to a house is regarded as a special place. It was traditional in many cultures not only to keep out unwanted human or animal visitors but against evil spirits and ghosts. Find out how the Chinese protected their thresholds and other traditional ways of guarding the threshold against evil. Maintaining a Rangoli pattern is a nice way of showing that you care about your house and environment. Even very poor people in India can do this because it costs very little. Think about the ways that we can all make our immediate environment more attractive.

Fig 7.3   Rangoli Patterns

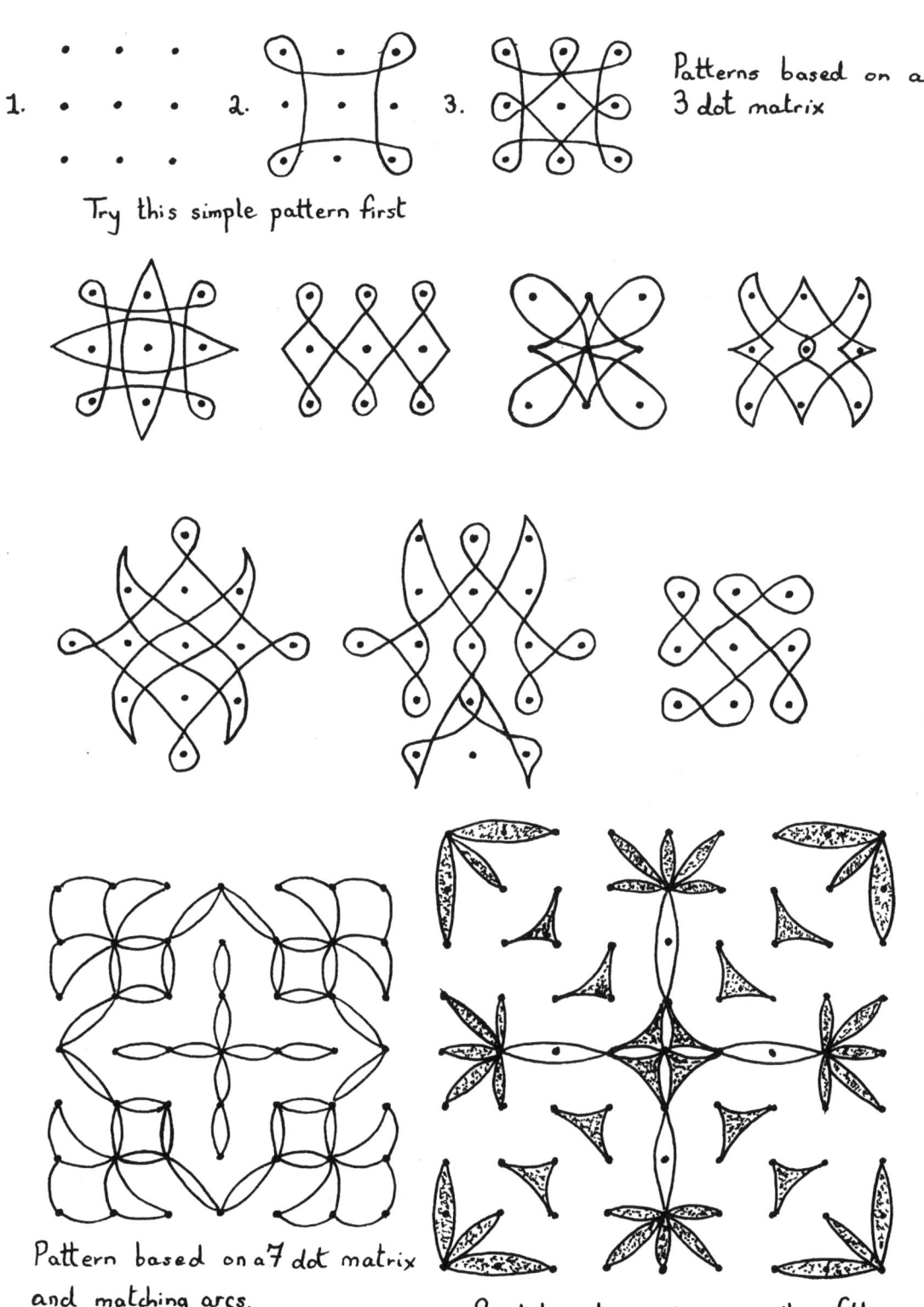

1.   2.   3.   Patterns based on a
3 dot matrix

Try this simple pattern first

Pattern based on a 7 dot matrix
and matching arcs.

9 dot matrix design with infill

7.4 Corn Dolly

Aim. To make a traditional artifact of natural materials associated with harvest time. To find out about harvest traditions and the role of the corn dolly.

In Brief. Students make a corn dolly out of straw or a similar natural material (*see fig. 7.4*).

What you will need:

A bale of straw (not hay) a place to store it. *	Different coloured wools. Safety scissors.
Found items such as small berries, nuts, daises etc. to decorate the dolly.	

* Thatching straw is best but is hard to get delivered in small quantities. A bale of straw should cost no more than £4 and will keep you in straw for a while.

Method.

1. With your group, study pictures of corn dollies or examples of the real thing. Find out about the traditions - who made corn dollies? (see notes below). Study the complexity of forms.

2. Take a section off the bale (bales break up into sections when the binding twine is cut) and tease apart on a tarpaulin. Students select approx 30 stalks for the body of the dolly - 35 cm in length - and then 20 stalks of about 20cm for the arms.

3. Begin by making the arms. Bind the stalks together at the 'wrists' with wool wrapped round several times for strength and neatness. The straw ends can then be trimmed and splayed slightly at the ends to form the hands.

4. Next bundle and tie the body. Tie it firstly at the hairline and the neck. Part the body bundle in the middle with a finger and slide in the arms beneath the neck to make a cross shape. Tie firmly at the waist to create the trunk and secure the arms. Remember to wrap the wool round several times for neatness and to make a distinctive waist. Trim the skirt base to form a flat surface so the dolly will stand upright. Trim the stalks above the hairline band and arrange to achieve the desired hairstyle.

5. Use small berries for eyes and nuts, grasses, leaves etc. to decorate. Use the pointed end of a thin stick to separate the stalks to insert the berry or flower stalk without damaging it.

Reflection. Discuss the significance of harvest time to a rural community. It is always a time of celebration, once safely gathered in. Harvests were considered a gift of nature gods in pagan tradition and a gift from God to Christians. Showing gratitude was always important. The Corn Dolly might be seen either as a gift to the earth or a gift to God (or both). Reflect on the importance of wheat in our lives and the uses made of every part of the plant.

Notes. In pagan belief, the corn dolly provided a refuge for the 'spirit' of the harvest once it was gathered in. Here the spirit could shelter, warm inside the house, during the harsh winter. On 'Plough Monday', when the ground was prepared for the planting of the next crop, the corn dolly was cast into the furrow so the spirit of the harvest could return to the earth. 'Plough Monday' is 'Twelfth Night', or the first Monday after the Epiphany. Christians adopted the practice, and in some parts of Britain it became the custom to fashion corn dollies in the form of a cross. The method described above is a hybrid of cross and female form.

Fig 7.4 Corn Dolly

1. Make the arms by tying neatly at the wrists.

2. Make the body by tying neatly at the crown, neck and waist.

3. Carefully part the body and push the arms through the middle.

4. Splay out the dress, hands and hair. Use small flowers on stalks to decorate the waist. Small berries on stalks are used for eyes and nose. Use scissors to tidy ends.

7.5 Tree Spirit Faces

Aim. To create a 'personality' for a tree. To reflect on how indigenous peoples think about all living things as having a personality or a soul. To practice clay moulding skills.

In Brief. Students make faces out of clay and other natural materials on the trunk of a tree.

What you will need:

A block of modelling clay. * A small quantity of water helps to smooth off the features.	A palette knife to split your clay block.**
** This activity can be done with a full class as this is the only tool needed.	
* Clay can be purchased from most educational suppliers and costs about £4 for 12 kilos. If the bags are firmly re-sealed the clay keeps indefinitely.	

Method.

1. Discuss the kinds of creatures you might find in fairy tale creatures in a wood, or the kind of face a tree might have. Share the idea of trees having a personality that might be expressed in a face. Think of Tolkien's 'Ents' or Tree People.

2. Students explore the trees in the available area and choose one that appeals to them. Discuss the personality of different trees:

    *   Would it be happy or sad, friendly or unfriendly?
    *   Think about the materials you might make a face out of.
    *   What could you use for eyes and ears?
    *   Will the mouth have teeth and what will they be made of?
    *   Give your face a name and a personality.
    *   What story would he or she tell of themselves if they could speak?

3. Students then gather a range of materials to make the face. Typically, the face will be small, say 15cm by 12cm, with leaves, nuts, small pebbles, grasses, moss – in fact whatever natural materials you can find – used to make the features. Three or four students can use the same tree if there aren't enough to go round. The faces are naturally short-lived with rain washing them off fairly quickly, so students need to understand that their work is temporary and will return to the earth.

4. Use natural tools, such as small sticks to smooth and shape the faces.

5. Allow time to visit and celebrate each other's work.

Reflection. Think about the pleasure we get from the trees around us. Think about the things that living trees give us, such as shelter from sun and wind and woodland to enjoy ourselves. Why is it important to look after trees? How old are the trees around you? Think about the age of trees. One of the longest living things on earth is a tree. Find out what the longest living tree species is called.

7.6 Journey Mandalas

Aim. To learn about mandalas and use the form to make a 'map' of a landscape and tell the story of a journey through that landscape.

In Brief. A mandala is made on a suitable area of clear beaten earth using found materials.

What you will need:

An opportunity to make a journey to inspire your students! This might be a welly walk, a walk through a wood or park or the school landscape, incorporating both natural and man-made features.	
A plastic carrier bag to gather materials from the ground - 1 per student.	A length of string which students use to define the edge of their mandala.

Method.

1. Introduce the students to mandalas with example images. Explain that they will be going for a walk and will experience certain things along the way. Their mandala will tell that story.

2. In groups (with a bag each) students collect natural (and non-natural if you wish) materials that represent the landscape through which they pass. At key points along the route, stop and reflect on what is special, memorable or distinctive. Is it a special view? Is it a distinctive smell? Is it especially quiet or noisy? What can they collect to represent this part of the story?

3. Construct the mandalas on a patch of bare ground. The frame in which it sits can be created with a circle of pebbles and decorated around the rim with leaves. With younger children, use a circle of string to define the area. The frame can also be made of grasses, leaves, twigs or thin branches. Different areas of the mandala can be coloured with grasses, moss, sticks, bits of bark or evergreen. They may even wish to use some man-made materials such as old litter. Encourage students to take time and make it as attractive and detailed as possible. Part of the spiritual value of mandalas lies in the care and 'mindfulness' that goes into their making.

4. Against this background the students can begin to add things that represent their journey. Greenery for a wood, stones to represent buildings and so on. Students should be able to explain what each part of their mandala represents. They can then indicate the special places on their mandala where events in their story took place using some of their special finds. Once complete students can be invited to re-tell the story of their journey, using the mandala.

Reflection. Mandalas are used to help us think about things. They help us to focus. Did your mandala help you to think about all the things you did in making it? Did it help you to remember your special journey? Did it help you see things differently?

Notes. A mandala is a pattern or a series of images, often represented in a circular or geometrical framework. It is used as a tool for meditation and reflection. Buddhism - and to a lesser degree Hinduism - make use of mandalas. They have their equivalent in Christianity in the use of devotional images, such as an icon, as an aid to reflection. A mandala can contain a great deal of information in pictorial or symbolic form and can be used to tell a story.

7.7 Nature Icon

Aim. To explore the role of icons in connecting the artist with Nature.

In Brief. A portable, framed image is created out of natural materials, guided by the principles of traditional icon making.

What you will need:

Dry weather! - rain will damage the work and make adhesives ineffective. Glue sticks. Safety scissors.	*Per student*: a piece of thick card A4 size, preferably coloured. Consider buying a bag of mount board off-cuts from a picture framer.
Gathered materials. These might include tiny mollusc shells, leaves of different colours, grasses, tiny stones, feathers, bits of bark, mosses, common flowers, twigs, seeds and tiny berries.	

Method.

1. Introduce students to icons. The traditional icon is painted by a religious person as a kind of meditation. They are made out of natural materials and help people to connect with nature and God. For example, icons are usually painted on wood covered with gesso. Eggs are used to bind the paint. Colours are made with materials, such as ground lapis lazuli for blue. Minerals also feature in the form of the precious metals, gold and silver. But the most important ingredient is the soul. The artist puts their spirit into the work, through which we may glimpse the Divine.

2. ***Make the frame.*** A frame of flowers, leaves, tiny mollusc shells etc. is glued to the board with a glue stick. Alternatively, the board can be edged with double-sided tape. The border might consist, for example, of small dried leaves or flower petals. This requires patience but it encourages students to focus and become absorbed in what they are doing.

3. ***Make the Icon.*** The form the icon takes should be meaningful to the student and not a matter of randomly sticking down the gathered materials. It may help for students to think of their design ahead of gathering the materials. Materials used to make the montage can reflect the season or the student's chosen theme. Remind them to use 'animal, vegetable and mineral'.

4. Use scissors to trim leaves and small twigs to size and shape. Consider how the shape of a leaf might be changed by trimming the edges. Consider composition. The materials might be arranged, for example, to represent a tree, flower or bird or it might be an abstract pattern.

5. When the icon is finished students can write a short poem or prose passage to describe their experiences. Younger students might use single words that sum up their experiences, such as colours, 'hot' or 'cold', 'bright' or 'dark', 'happy' or 'sad'.

Reflection. Icons are sacred objects. Encourage the students to treat their gathered items and their icons with respect. They reflect the world that sustains us, and, for students with a religious belief, the God who made the things they have gathered. Think about all the natural materials that have gone into making your icon. Share all the natural materials with a friend. What are the special finds in your picture? We are dependent on nature for everything. Even 'man-made' things are made from natural raw materials. Think about the things we do to look after nature. Think about the things we do that harm nature.

7.8 Special Animal Cup or Bowl

Aim. To explore forms that are both artwork and practical artifact.

In Brief. Students make a small clay vessel incorporating animal human design themes.

What you will need:

A bag of modelling clay.* A small quantity of water to smooth off the features.	A flat work surface. Log stumps are ideal. 2 or 3 baking trays to carry finished work.
Gathered materials. These might include tiny mollusc shells, leaves of different colours, grasses, tiny stones, feathers, bits of bark, mosses, common flowers, twigs, seeds and tiny berries etc.	
* Clay can be purchased from most educational suppliers and costs about £4 for 12 kilos. If the bags are firmly re-sealed the clay keeps indefinitely.	

Method.

1. Explore how animal forms occur in pottery vases, jars, bowls and other vessels in cultures past and present. Discuss why animals are a popular decoration, for example the luck and prosperity bearing status of the frog in Chinese culture. Explore popular animal forms that readily adapt to the shape of a bowl or cup – a frog with a bowl in the middle of its back, a lizard wrapping itself round a jar or featuring as the handle, a ewer with an animal's head for a spout with the mouth open for pouring. Also think of sea creatures such as fish, turtles and seals. Something that you might also consider is an Indian arti oil lamp.

2. Students now consider their own piece of pottery.

    • What function will it serve – bowl, cup, vase, dish?

    • What animal form will feature in the design?

3. The pot can be decorated too, and students can gather tiny stones or mollusc shells for decoration. Let the students experiment first with achieving the basic shape successfully and then rework the clay into their chosen animal design. Once complete, carefully decorate with the found items, paying special attention to the eyes of the animal.

Reflection. Share and celebrate the different designs. Discuss what they will be used for. What will they keep in their bowl?

7.9 Painting with Plants

Aim. To explore the colours that can be found in plants.

In Brief. Plants, berries, leaves and barks are tested for the colours they produce and used to create an artwork.

What you will need:

A firm surface to rest work on, such as an A4 board or clipboard.	Two pieces of heavy stock cartridge paper, one to collect a colour sample range and the second for their actual painting.
Access to a wood (school grounds or park are also ok) to gather natural materials. *	
Warn that some plant materials can be toxic so no hand to mouth contact once sampling has started. Check with students that they do not suffer from allergic reactions to plant materials.	

Method.

1. Discuss the sources of natural plant dyes. What plants are used to produce traditional dyes? A few examples are given below, a prep activity could be to research the subject in more detail.

   - Red, yellow and brown dyes can be extracted by boiling and mashing onion skins.
   - Carrots, alder bark - orange.
   - Roses with lemon juice - pink.
   - Boiled and mashed acorns, willow bark, Eucalyptus leaves - brown

   - Elderberries, iris, blackberry - purple.
   - Walnut husks - black.
   - Nettle and grass - green.
   - Willow leaves - yellow.

2. Divide the class into groups of 3 or 4 and issue with freezer bags, clipboards and a strip of cartridge paper to collect samples. A walk through a wood is the best environment, but parks and school grounds will also yield good results. Remind students only to pick flowers that are present in abundance. Working in groups of four, students search for dye sources. Plant materials are tested by rubbing them against the cartridge paper to see what colour they make. Once this is known, students make a note and place the sample in the freezer bag.

3. Once enough samples have been collected, return to the activity area to consider composition. One possible theme might be a study of light, shade and colour in the environment explored.

4. Experiment on scrap paper with different forms of application before starting the main artwork. Colours can be extracted using mashing and boiling and applied as a wash. Alternatively, colour can be applied directly by rubbing the plant against the surface of the paper.

Reflection. Consider how the materials affected your outcomes. How limiting was it to use only plant dyes to create your artwork? Did gathering the materials or the materials themselves prove the main inspiration? Did you find the process satisfying or frustrating? How much experimentation did you do? Which experimental outcome yielded the most satisfying results?

7.10 Stick Mobiles

Aim. To explore shape and form using short pieces of wood.

In Brief. Students gather twigs and sticks and tie them with coloured wools to produce a mobile for home, school or a favourite tree.

What you will need:

Small twigs and sticks - ideally, gather on a woodland walk. *Optional* - mollusc shells, pieces of bark, feathers, animal bone, pretty leafs etc.	
Mini hacksaws with wood cutting blades.	Scissors, green sisal garden twine or colourful wools.
If you are gathering from hedgerows take a pair of loppers (*adult use only*).	Brace and bit to drill items for hanging.
If a sufficient quantity of material isn't available in the school grounds, bring in bundles of sticks gathered from elsewhere. The wood can be green, dry or, best of all, weatherworn, wormed and characterful. If you can get to go to the beach with the kids, look for small, attractive driftwood.	

Method.

1. Begin by exploring the idea of mobiles – something that you hang up from a ceiling or the branch of a tree that looks great as it turns about. Think about the shapes you can make with bendy sticks and twigs – star shapes, loops, lozenges, crosses or a shape that looks a bit like a stick person. Geometrical shapes can be made, such as cubes or pyramids. Gather your sticks on a welly or woodland walk. You might also gather other things to decorate your mobile, such as mollusc shells, pieces of bark, feathers or animal bone.

2. Cut your sticks to the length you need them using a mini hacksaw. Try out the shape first on the ground. Now tie together as neatly as you can, wrapping the wool round several times and trimming the knot ends.

3. Your mobile can now be decorated with found items by hanging them from it using wool. Use your mobile to decorate a tree, your classroom or a room at home.

Reflection. Share and celebrate each other's work. Explore the items you have used to decorate your mobile. Where did you find them? How many different living things have provided the materials for your mobile? Think about a special place where you gathered one of the objects on your mobile. Try to take your mind and imagination back to that place when you enjoy your mobile.

8. STORY AND LANDSCAPE

Cuddly Toy Hunt, the Wizard's Spell, Reporting Imaginative Play, Story Stations, What Happened Here?, Story Cards, Nature Haikus, Shapes in the Landscape, Six Tales of Arthur, Treasure Quest.

"Day by day I float my paper boats, one by one by the running stream. In big black letters I write my name on them and the name of the village where I live. I hope that someone in some strange land will find them and know who I am."
Rabindranath Tagore

"Journeys and movement through the natural environment increase the active detection of novel play affordances: barriers to cross, trails to follow, stepping stones, changing surfaces, varying terrain, together with many natural features and elements that invite specific play activities along the way."
Martin Maudsley

Children's play is stimulated and shaped by the environment in which they find themselves. Toys are one stimulus, outdoor play equipment another. But the best stimulus of all is a less predictable, natural environment that is readily transformed by the young imagination. Each new feature or obstacle encountered has the potential to shift the story in a new direction. The adventure has the fluidity of real life.

In natural environments children become participants in an adventure where the boundaries between fact and fiction are blurred. After all, the den they build is real and the fallen tree a solid, physical obstacle. The sense of risk feels authentic. In a sense, the adventure is real – just as real as the adventures of grown-ups who climb mountains or cross desolate moorland in a storm.

Children enjoy opportunities to transform landscapes. A pile of branches can be made into a castle and then destroyed in some cataclysmic story event. In regular haunts, children will have their favourite dens and hiding places. The landscape becomes signed by the child's imagination and memory. Through play, natural locales acquire shape and significance in memory. The secret den is amplified in the imagination. It can be a place remembered, sometimes into adulthood and beyond.

In researching this chapter, I asked a group of eleven-year-olds who had experienced a number of woodland opportunities for free-play and roaming, to talk about their experiences. They were keen not only to talk about things they had seen and heard in the woodland space, but to take me to locations associated with particular experiences. One boy, for example, wanted to show me his hiding place from which he had observed deer and hare. They talked about the 'old camp', a location they had discovered, where there was evidence of the activities of a previous generation of school children. Already, the language of history and myth is at play, as fantasy and reality became woven into their accounts of what they had seen and heard in that spooky, atmospheric part of the wood.

As Jane Sahi explains in her book 'Education and Peace', imaginative play and shared storytelling is one of the best ways to compensate for the time children spend in front of computers and playing with their phones:

"The space by the seashore where children meet each other to share and explore is very different from the isolation of the virtual world of computer games and limited but expensive toys. Real play is being engaged with mind, body and heart which is a preparation for and participation in a fuller and creative life." [1]

Story-telling Outdoors

The main technique we use to weave story and the natural environment together is 'story trails'. This technique involves the re-enactment of the story in the landscape in which the events takes place. Children walk through the landscape as the tale unfolds. School grounds are one setting but a woodland environment is more powerful because of the unfamiliarity and greater uncertainties. Here trees, patches of glade or streams can be selected to feature in different parts of the narrative. Children are given parts to play in the drama, either assuming a role at a certain point in the adventure or given a role as the story begins. The real and the imaginary combine as fantasy is played out in real landscapes. It has the quality of imaginative play, structured into story.

Story-telling is, of course, a skill. Young children in particular, can lose the thread of a tale quickly without regular repetition and clear structure. Here are some tips to support your storytelling.

a) **Create the right environment.** Choose your location carefully and have a focus. A fire is an ideal setting for non-ambulatory storytelling.

b) **Encourage listening** through a circle activity that encourages children to listen to each other.

c) **Create a context**. Populate the landscape with 'history' - real or imaginary.

d) **Use physical props**. A child with a besom, for example, becomes a witch. A strange, twisted tree, covered in funghi, the place where she lives.

e) **Clearly sign the beginning of story**. Storytelling traditionally begins with a "Once upon a time...". The traditional openings, are "rituals" that serve as a signal that the teller was suspending "time and space" as we know it and transporting the audience to a world of imagination and play. They establish the audience's commitment to accept for the moment an imaginary world. Similar "rituals" also signal the end of the story and the return to reality.

f) **Map out the story** - The Beginning, which sets the stage and introduces the characters and conflict; the Body, in which the conflict builds up to the Climax; and the Resolution of the conflict. Observe how the action starts, how it accelerates, repetitions in actions and how and where the transitions occur. If simplifying or adapting a well-known story, do not alter the essential story line.

g) **Voice** - Make use of different voices for different characters. Use your voice to create the atmosphere or tension as the story progresses. Use gestures and facial expressions to add to the visualization of the story. Be aware of the volume and speed at which you speak. Dialogue slows a story's pace down, while narrating action speeds it up. Remember that Repetition and Exaggeration have always been basic elements of story telling.

h) **Keep their attention**: Many factors affect the attention of your listeners. A storyteller always needs to be sensitive to his audience and may need to regain attention at various points. Use volunteers from the audience to add voices. For example, creating the sounds and motion of the sea using the voice and hands of your entire audience.

Story Themes

Some story themes resonate with children – and for good reason. Carl Jung argued that certain archetypal themes are buried in the human psyche or unconscious. Some of the story archetypes are given below.

Ancestor Tales - The re-telling of events concerning significant ancestors. "Uncle Tom bought this field a long time ago. In those days it was full of rocks and stones and gave a very poor living. For years and years he worked to move the great stones so he could plough the field….. "

The Hero - The unknown hero appears to tackle a monster that is plaguing a community. Beowulf, for example, connects the hero with swamps, caves and ancient tombs that would have been a part of a known landscape.

The Once and Future King - Tales of heroes of old who will return at a time of crisis. Tales of Arthur's knights connect landscape with places where ancient battles were fought and where the mighty dead sleep, awaiting their call.

Abduction – Tales of faerie folk who entice people underground, link with holes, caves, door-shaped cavities in trees etc..

Landscape Legends - Tales of how strange rocks and stones, natural or placed by men, came to be where they are. Stone circles are revellers turned to stone for dancing with the devil at midnight, or a long line of hills might be a sleeping giant.

Talking and Shape-shifting Animals - Encounters with animals that have something important to tell, such as hares or seals. These animals might take human form under certain circumstances and vice-versa.

Story Themes continued...

A Lost Kingdom - Tales of a beautiful world that can no longer be accessed because of something we have done, but which can be glimpsed or visited by special people through magic.

Tales of Treasure - Rainbows and pots of gold, faerie hills containing buried treasure, lost palaces full of gold.

Faerie Gifts and Faerie Cups – that bring magical powers or cure ailments.

Encounters with Death -Vampires, ancient burial mounds, haunted woods and ancient ruins.

Underground folk disturbed by human action and intervention - Tales of the emergence of the little folk as a result of mining, cutting down trees etc. This features in the Beowulf tale.

Water Creature Legends - Tales of beasts or spirits that live in lakes and pools. Stories of human encounters when crossing water. Visits to underwater kingdoms.

Will-o'-the Wisp - Tales of strange sightings at night. Lights that were followed in the dark that led folk to a terrible end or a magical discovery.

8.1 Cuddly Toy Hunt, or the Teddy Bear's Picnic

Aim. To enable children to experience a simple, linear narrative in a woodland or other natural space.

In Brief. Children follow a trail or path populated with cuddly toys, in search of the teddy bear's picnic.

What you will need:

A collection of twenty or so cuddly toys.	Some plastic crockery for the picnic.
A suitable trail of between 200 and 400 metres - woodland is best, park or school grounds can also be used. The main thing is sufficient vegetation to part conceal the cuddly toys.	

Method.

1. Locate and set out your trail. Each cuddly toy should be positioned so that it is not immediately obvious where they are and some searching is required. Some, for example, could be positioned in low branches. A woodland environment, with winding paths, is ideal.

2. Brief the children that a letter has been received inviting them to the teddy bear's picnic. The only problem is that no address has been given. It can be a different theme if you wish. I have, for example, searched for 'the magic blue unicorn' – another cuddly toy.

3. As each cuddly toy is found the children are asked to identify the animal. They then ask the animal the question as a group, "Do you know the way to the teddy bear's picnic?" The children are asked to listen for a reply. Hopefully, an enterprising child will point the way. If not, teacher can suggest a route.

4. Eventually, the teddy bear's picnic is discovered. Sadly, the teddy bears have eaten all the food - although a box of uneaten treats might be discovered!

5. Children then gather in a circle to re-tell their adventure. They should work together to recollect the correct sequence of animals and any interesting or unusual event that happened.

6. Older children can provide simple written and illustrated accounts back in school.

Reflection. In what way is the story we have taken part in a 'real' story? In what way is the story not 'real'?

How did the hunt for the picnic make they feel about the wood or path? Did it make it more enjoyable?

Will you remember your adventure?

8.2 The Wizard's Spell

Aim. To enable young children to act out a magical event in a real landscape. To provide a simple narrative that children can reconstruct round the campfire or back in the classroom.

In Brief. The children are guided in a quest to find twelve magical objects to help the wizard cast a spell.

What you will need:

Eleven cuddly toys, ideally representing different animals. A wizard's staff. *12 magical object to concealed near or with the above.	Twelve laminated cards with a picture of the magical item and cuddly toy, i.e. 'Lily the Lamb' and a quartz crystal. Include large print text naming animal and object.

I use a bird's wing, bird's claw, sea shell, large quartz crystal, small oriental perfume bottle, goblet or chalice, ammonite, old brass doorknocker, large fancy golden spoon and an egg-shaped 'dragon stone'.

Method.

1. Conceal each of the toys and its magical object along a linear route through a wood or a route through the school grounds.

2. Number the cards, hole punch the sides and peg them in a circle. A class of twenty-four, can participate by two children sharing a card.

3. Bring the group into the circle of cards. Tell them a story about a wizard and his friends who live in the wood. The wizard says that if all the magical objects in the pictures can be found those who find them will be able to cast a spell and make a special wish!

4. Children are told that the objects must be located in the correct order - the order the are placed in the circle - and brought back one at a time. Get the students to pair up and stand behind a card. The object must be handed to these children to place on their card. If another child finds it he or she must hand it to the named child/children for that object. This makes every child feel they have a part to play.

5. The finding time for the objects will depend on how far along the linear route they are distributed. I have the group return to the circle as each object is found to maximize the physical exercise and remind the group of the next object to be found. The last object to be located is the wizard's staff. The group stand in the centre of the circle, each with a hand or finger on the staff. The wish is made and the spell cast with the words: "Iggery piggery poo, make my wish come true."

Reflection. Can we remember all the objects we found? Which were the hardest to find? Why was this? Do you know of other stories with wizards? Why is it good to make wishes? Do you make wishes for your friends or your family? What other things can we do to make a wish?

8.3 Reporting Imaginative Play

Aim. To encourage children to remember and share adventures from free-play. To enable children to talk in a way that differentiates between actual and imaginative experiences.

In Brief. Children are given free/imaginative play opportunities in a stimulating natural environment and share their experiences round a fire.

What you will need:

> A suitably stimulating location that is relatively natural in appearance and has natural materials that can become props in play.
>
> The environment should be one in which they feel safe and with which they already have some familiarity. Young children might want to take along a cuddly toy or other imaginative aid.

Method.

1. Walk your group to your chosen environment. Give the group twenty minutes free time to explore, find things, share their experiences with each other, to make simple tools and structures.

2. At the end of the play period they are brought together around the fire to share their experiences. Children can be asked about the children they played with and what they did in simple, factual terms.

3. The teacher can move on to open out the group experience by asking what the play was about, what did they see or find, who the shelter was for, and so on. In some instances, narratives will emerge, either of factual events or an underlying imaginative narrative. The group share these and reinforce them through ongoing recall and clarification of detail.

4. Back in school, the group can then draw or write about their experiences at the appropriate level.

Reflection. What do you remember best about your play?

What adventures did you have?

Did you see or hear things you did not expect?

Did others join in your story/play?

Think about the things you did you enjoyed the most?

What made those things special?

8.4 Story Stations

Aim. To facilitate the invention of a variety of characters and the construction of a narrative.

In Brief. A path is followed and items found that belong to a character. At each station a different student plays the character and develops the narrative.

What you will need:

A collection of items to represent different characters. For example, a pair of slippers and a walking stick might signify an old man, a broom and pointed hat a witch, a crown a king, sword and helmet for a knight, staff for a wizard, basket of wood for a woodcutter, and so on. Each character in the narrative is identified by these possessions. A single item – prop or costume – is often enough.

A woodland trail or school field. Depending on the time available you might want to set up ten stations. Adjust the length of route to suit the age of the children and the time available.

Method.

1. Introduce the students with a straightforward plot that is open to development. For example, it might be a search for a magic crystal that will defeat an evil wizard or a chest full of treasure. Explain that the group will come across a number of different characters along the way, where they may be asked to play a part.

2. When a story station is approached, students identify the items and decide who the character is who lives in the space. They take it in turns to assume the part of the character or characters. Begin by asking the group to identify the character the items belong to and what they might have to do with the story.

   - Are they the good guys or the bad guys?
   - Will they help?

3. A student then puts on the hat or other clothing and assumes the role. Other members of the group ask him or her questions relative to the narrative. For example, 'can you help find the magic crystal?' 'Would you like to join us on the quest?' The student playing the character provides the response, perhaps with a little support from the teacher to help the story along.

4. At the end of the quest, the group reconstructs the story. Later, as a class exercise, the story can be written down or illustrated with drawings.

Reflection. We had to decide what kind of person owned the things that we found. If you wanted someone to know what kind of person you are, what three items would you leave on the path?

8.5 What Happened Here?

Aim. To develop skills in deconstructing a narrative from found objects.

In Brief. Students interpret or 'read' a collection of personal items, such as a suitcase of belongings, in the way a detective might.

What you will need:

A collection of objects or personal belongings. These may be in a bag, old suitcase, satchel or wallet. It might include a few coins from a different country, something to indicate the owner's interests and lifestyle, such as cinema tickets, restaurant receipts or a plane ticket. There might be evidence of status or profession, such as a business card. There might also be clues as to age. Train tickets can give details of past journeys. Photos can give clues about relationships. There might also be receipts for the purchase of necessities, such as food or the payment of a utility bill.

Method.

1. Put together the 'incident scene' in portable form and set it out in a suitable location along a woodland path or corner of the school grounds.

2. Once the scene is established, students approach to deconstruct the finds. Questions include:

   - Can we deduce the kind of person the items belong to?
   - How did they get there (lost, stolen, hidden, thrown away etc..)?
   - How long ago did it happen?
   - What was the person doing?
   - Where were they going?
   - Where might they be now?

3. Once practiced, you can ask the students to put together their own incident scene(s) for a later date. With older students, discuss mise-en-scene and the careful placement of objects in cinema and stage settings to reflect meaning. Think, for example, about a hotel room, with empty whisky bottle on the floor, cheap suitcase containing a few crumpled clothes and a pile of discarded newspapers and magazines. What do these things connote?

4. The final stage might be to write an account of the day on which the person 'lost' the items or simply a day in their life. Alternatively, the finds can be treated as a 'crime scene' and a whole narrative constructed.

Reflection. Do possessions really tell others about the kind of person we really are? What can possessions tell people about our values? If you were to put together a collection of items to leave in a wood to reveal your character, what would they be?

8.6 Story Cards

Aim. To construct a narrative out of 'character' cards and 'challenges'.

In Brief. Students assume a role given to them on a character card and complete a challenge at the appropriate place on the narrative journey.

What you will need:

Laminted 'character cards' for the group. Here we use the Arthurian story but you can choose any theme or set of characters. In this instance the character cards are: *King Arthur, Queen Guinevere, Lancelot, Percival, Gawain, the Witch, Keeper of the Bridge of Doom, Merlin, the Lady of the Lake, Lord of the Castle of Mirrors, The Red Knight and the Grail King.*

Appropriate props for your story.
School grounds, wood or park, to mark out a route - approx 1/4 mile.

Method. *(using the Arthurian story as an example)*

1. Make the character cards and number them. The number relates to a location along the route where the student will complete a specific challenge. Place them along your chosen route.

2. Explain to the students that they are going on a quest to find the Holy Grail, a magic cup that will save the kingdom from doom and gloom. To achieve the Grail each knight or character participating in the quest must complete a challenge.

3. Issue the character cards and props so that students can get into their roles. King Arthur takes charge in leading the knights and other characters on their quest. The various characters can carry the items needed for the challenges if it is not possible to set out equipment in advance. At each station, the knight or character delivering the challenge is encouraged to get fully into character. The Quest Knights, for example, are encouraged to explain to the audience how wonderful they are and the mighty deeds they have done.

4. Challenges can be given to the group as a whole or addressed to individuals. Some can be topic related, such as a set of maths challenges and riddles cards. Others are simply fun. For example, throwing a rubber chicken into a bucket from 10 metres away, crossing a 'Bridge of Doom' blindfolded, knocking over a skittle with a kicked football, finding a concealed object, or making a simple shrubbery (refer to Monty Python!). The fun element is retained by keeping a mixture of physical challenges, riddles and questions.

5. To attain the grail, the chosen player must select the correct card as shuffled and held out by the Grail King. Use 4 cards, one with an image of a grail cup, the second a pork pie, the third a toothbrush and the fourth a sock (they might get two chances to pick the correct card!). At the end of the quest, students sit at the Round Table (in a circle) to relate their adventures.

6. Back in the classroom, invite students to write some bardic verses describing their adventure.

Reflection. Share your most memorable moment in the Quest with your group. What made the moment special? Did you succeed in the Quest? How important was it to succeed? How does it compare with, say, winning a game of football?

8. 7 Nature Haikus

"Winter by the pond
Ice hangs from a craggy tree.
Where did the frogs go?"

Dean, ArtHouse Children's Gallery

Aim. To explore haiku form as a medium to express sensory experience and feelings.

In Brief. Students enjoy a simple experience in a natural space and use it to write a haiku

What you will need:

> This is a straightforward exercise and requires nothing more than a stimulating environment and paper and pencil to record experiences!

Method.

1. Familiarise the group with haiku form. A traditional haiku is a simple poem of 3 lines with a 5 syllable, 7 syllable, 5 syllable structure. A haiku usually contains a word or phrase that symbolizes or implies the season. The other feature of Japanese haiku is the use of a word or punctuation that cuts or divides the stream of thought or consciousness – a kind of pause for reflection – that gives weight to the verse where you want it. The haiku should be self-contained, despite its shortness.

2. Prepare for the activity by considering how short phrases can capture an experience. Outside the classroom, practice with rainy or cold days. What words for example, communicate a cold, wet, grey day, as well as the emotions that go with such days? Try expressing a thought or feeling in just 5 syllables... "Autumn in my bones" or "Damp smell of autumn".

3. Take the group for a walk with pad and pencil to record their experiences. Encourage them to clear their minds of distracting thoughts and focus on sensation and feelings.

4. A good haiku will draw on close observation, on the little detail that communicates much more than a generalization ever can. Consider how a very simple sketch might help capture a moment, such as a raindrop dripping off a leaf or the brim of a hat.

5. Back in class or round a Forest School fire give time to carefully shape the haiku.

6. Now share the haikus. Give time for thought and reflection between the recitals. Write them up on coloured paper with a simple illustration and make a display.

Reflection. Very often we just don't see or hear what is going on around us, either because we are too busy, travelling too fast or listening to loud music. How does being still and listening to or observing nature help us?

8.8 Shapes in the Landscape

Aim. To explore shapes in the landscape as a stimulus for story and legend.

In Brief. Students create an artwork and a simple story inspired by shapes in the landscape.

What you will need:

Access to countryside, even from a distance.	A4 sheets of cartridge paper, clipboard, pencil and carrier bag to transport the work.

Method.

1. Share examples of landscape features that have inspired legends. Famous examples include the Devil's Causeway in Ireland, The Devil's Punch Bowl in Surrey or Arthur's Seat, near Edinburgh. This theme can also be linked to Art and artists such as Paul Nash who reduced landscapes to simple, bold forms that were nonetheless very evocative. Ancient monuments, such as stone circles and Iron Age forts also attract local legends that may have nothing to do with their actual origins. Ancient tombs in Wiltshire, for example, are described as 'Adam's Grave' or 'Giant's Grave' or 'Devil's Den'.

2. Begin by reading a story that connects landscape with human form (an exemplar about the Wrekin in Shropshire is attached to this activity). Aboriginal story can also be used to this end.

3. Discuss with the group if they are aware of landscapes they have visited or indeed trees or rocks with unusual shapes. There may be features in the local landscape that can be visited to provide inspiration, or a suitable vantage point from a local park of high area. We are fortunate in Glastonbury in having a very shapely collection of hills surrounded by flat moor, and an abundance of legend old and new. Where grand landscapes aren't available, look for the small – faces in trees and so on.

4. In a group, explore landscape shapes and discuss who or what they might be. Begin constructing story by getting students to describe the character they see in the landscape – male or female, old or young, sleeping or ready to pounce. Give time to draw in detail and explore how other aspects of the landscape might become part of the story. Make sketches that attenuate the human or animal forms. Begin to put together a story about how the person or animal came to be part of the landscape.

5. Back in the classroom, work up into colour sketches or painting and written accounts of the legend or myth that lies beneath the landscape.

Reflection Do you like thinking about the land as having a name and a history, just like you? If you were part of the land, what would you be? A rock, a tree, a mountain? Stories about landscapes were once an important part of folklore and popular culture. How do we talk about landscapes today? What has changed our attitudes and beliefs regarding landscape, particularly sacred landscape?

The Origin of the Wrekin

- Landscape Legend Exemplar

Long, long ago, in the days when there were giants in the land, two of them were turned out by the rest and forced to go and live by themselves, so they set to work to build themselves a hill to live in. In a very short time they had dug out the earth from the bed of the Severn, which runs in the trench they made to the present time, and with it they piled up the Wrekin, intending to make it their home.

Those bare patches on the turf, between the Bladderstone and the top of the hill, are the marks of their feet, where from that day to this the grass has never grown. But they had not been there long before they quarrelled, and one of them struck at the other with his spade, but failed to hit him, and the spade descending to the ground cleft the solid rock and made the "Needle's Eye."

Then they began to fight, and the giant with the spade (for they seem to have had only one between them -- perhaps that was what they quarrelled about!) was getting the best of it at first, but a raven flew up and pecked at his eyes, and the pain made him shed such a mighty tear that it hollowed out the little basin in the rock which we call the Raven's Bowl, or sometimes the Cuckoo's Cup, which has never been dry since, but is always full of water even in the hottest summers.

And now you may suppose that it was very easy for the other giant to master the one who had the spade, and when he had done so, he determined to put him where he could never trouble anyone again. So he very quickly built up the Ercall Hill beside the Wrekin, and imprisoned his fallen foe within it. There the poor blind giant remains until this day, and in the dead of night you may sometimes hear him groaning.

There is another and a better-known legend of this famous Wrekin:

Once upon a time there was a wicked old giant in Wales who, for some reason or other, had a very great spite against the Mayor of Shrewsbury and all his people, and he made up his mind to dam up the Severn, and by that means cause such a flood that the town would be drowned.

So off he set, carrying a spadeful of earth, and tramped along mile after mile trying to find the way to Shrewsbury. And how he missed it I cannot tell, but he must have gone wrong somewhere, for at last he got close to Wellington, and by that time he was puffing and blowing under his heavy load, and wishing he was at the end of his journey.

By and by there came a cobbler along the road with a sack of old boots and shoes on his back, for he lived at Wellington, and went once a fortnight to Shrewsbury to collect his customers' old boots and shoes, and take them home with him to mend.

And the giant called out to him. "I say," he said, "how far is it to Shrewsbury?"

"Shrewsbury?" said the cobbler; "what do you want at Shrewsbury?"

"Why," said the giant, "to fill up the Severn with this lump of earth I've got here. I've an old grudge against the mayor and the folks at Shrewsbury, and now I mean to drown them out, and get rid of them all at once."

"My word!" thought the cobbler. "This'll never do! I can't afford to lose my customers!" And he spoke up again. "Eh!" he said, "you'll never get to Shrewsbury -- not today nor tomorrow. Why look at me! I'm just come from Shrewsbury, and I've had time to wear out all these old boots and shoes on the road since I started." And he showed him his sack.

"Oh!" said the giant, with a great groan. " Then it's no use! I'm fairly tired out already, and I can't carry this load of mine any farther. I shall just drop it here and go back home."

So he dropped the earth on the ground just where he stood, and scraped his boots on the spade, and off he went home again to Wales, and nobody ever heard anything of him in Shropshire after.

But where he put down his load, there stands the Wrekin to this day; and even the earth that he scraped off his boots was such a pile that it made the little Ercall by the Wrekin's side.

8.9   Six Tales of Arthur

Aim. To develop narrative construction and improvisation skills. To facilitate imaginative play as part of rehearsal.

In Brief. Working outdoors, students role-play/ rehearse one of six stories from the adventures of King Arthur, before presenting the story to the rest of the group.

What you will need:

Story cards for the Arthurian Cycle - the 6 tales are provided on the following pages.
Access to an outdoor space - an historic venue, such as a castle, is ideal.*

Props - a typical list includes: 3-4 wooden swords, a couple of wooden spears, 3 crowns, a goblet, wizard's staff, witch's broom and a few bits of costume, such as cloaks. For sound effects, use coconut shells for galloping horses and a couple of toy trumpets for fanfares.

* Ensure ample space for the group to run around and have adventures like jousts and battles!

Method.

1. Print each tale on a separate card and laminate (see following pages).

1. Introduce the group to the stories before the actual day, but don't rehearse them (doing so makes it less likely that they will engage with the story as a theme for imaginative play). Introduce the idea of using a narrator to introduce characters and to provide a running commentary.

2. Head out to your outdoor location and divide the class into groups of 6 to 8 students. Give each group their individual story card. Encourage them to find their own space to rehearse, away from other groups. Explain how the action should move through the landscape and not be stuck to one place. A student from each group can act as narrator. Suggest to them that the drama begins with each character introducing themselves to the audience; i.e. "I am Arthur, king of the Britons."

3. Allow for plenty of rehearsal time so that students can get into their characters and enjoy the imaginative play. Visit each group to check on progress and gradually pull them towards getting ready to present their play.

4. The groups present their plays to each other at a single location. Find a spot with good acoustics and dry ground. Younger groups like a large performance area as their battle and jousting scenes often involve a lot of running around.

Reflection. Share what you enjoyed most about doing your plays outdoors – rehearsing, presenting or being an audience. Draw a picture of your character. Talk about it to your group. What was your role? Were you good or evil? What was your part in the action? Think about how well your group worked together. Are there things you could do better? Discuss them with your group.

1. Merlin & the Birth of King Arthur

Characters:

Uther Pendragon

Merlin

The Duke of Cornwall

Igraine

Sir Ector

Sir Kay

Soldiers

Uther Pendragon, King of Britain falls in love with Igraine, the wife of the Duke of Cornwall. He goes to Tintagel Castle to claim her.

The Duke of Cornwall is very angry about this and says he will no longer be loyal to Arthur. They declare war.

Uther tries to break into the castle. But the Duke's castle is too strong and Uther fails to take it.

Uther asks Merlin, the Wizard to help him. Merlin uses a spell to make him look like the Duke of Cornwall. But he says that Uther must grant him any wish he makes afterwards.

In the next battle the Duke of Cornwall is killed. Arthur says that Igraine must be his wife.

Uther and Igraine have a baby. Merlin appears and demands the baby. Uther and Igraine are very angry but there is nothing they can do. Merlin secretly gives the baby to Sir Ector to bring up as his own son.

Uther is ambushed and killed. Britain no longer has a king.

2. The Sword in the Stone

Characters:

Arthur

Sir Ector (Arthur's step-father)

Sir Kay (Sir Ector's son)

Sir Tristan

Sir Gareth

Sir Galahad

In a churchyard in London a stone magically appears. Stuck in the stone is a sword. There is a message that says whoever can pull the sword from the stone will be king. Every year afterwards there is a tournament on Easter Day to see who will win the right to try to pull the sword from the stone.

Sir Ector and his two sons, Arthur and Kay, go to the tournament. Arthur still thinks Sir Ector is his real father.

Sir Kay goes to joust. Arthur is his squire. Arthur carries Kay's sword and lance.

Sir Tristan has a joust with Sir Gareth. Sir Tristan wins.

Sir Tristan has a joust with Sir Galahad. Sir Galahad wins.

Now it is Sir Kay's turn to Joust with Sir Galahad. He asks Arthur for his sword and lance, but the sword is missing. He looks for the sword but can't find it. When no one is looking Arthur takes the sword from the stone and brings it to Sir Kay.

Everyone is shocked when they see Sir Kay with EXCALIBUR. They think he must be king. He admits it was Arthur who brought him the sword.
Arthur puts the sword back in the stone. Everyone tries to take it out but only Arthur can do it. Sir Ector announces that Arthur is the true son of Uther Pendragon, the last king. Arthur is declared king.

3. Arthur Defeats the Rebel Kings

Characters:

King Lot (rebel king)

King Urien (rebel king)

King Caradoc (rebel king)

King Arthur

Sir Kay

Sir Ector

Sir Galahad

King Lot, King Urien and King Caradoc don't want to follow king Arthur. They write him a letter telling him they are declaring war.

They get an army together to march on Sir Ector's castle where Arthur lives. (Caer Badon or Brent Knoll)

King Arthur talks to them but they won't listen. King Lot says he won't follow someone who isn't even a knight.

They attack the castle. There is a lot of fighting with arrows flying, and the rebel kings trying to break the door of the castle down.

Arthur fights King Lot and after a struggle defeats him. But he doesn't kill them. He forgives King Lot and the other rebel kings.

All the rebel kings kneel before Arthur and swear to be loyal.

They all go off together to fight the nasty invading Saxons.

4. Lancelot cheats on King Arthur

Characters:

King Arthur

Queen Guinevere

Sir Lancelot

Meleagaunt

King Bademagus

Elaine

King Arthur lives happily with Queen Guinevere at Camelot, walking round the garden admiring the flowers. When Arthur isn't looking the evil Meleagant kidnaps Guinevere and takes her to his dad's castle at Gorre.

His dad, King Bademagus, is very angry and tells Meleagant off for stealing Guinevere. But there isn't a lot he can do except wait for trouble.

Arthur asks Lancelot, his best knight, to rescue Guinevere. Lancelot is very happy because he secretly loves Guinevere. He sets off to find her.

He stays at the castle of the beautiful Elaine, who falls in love with him. They go to find Guinevere. They find a comb with strands of golden hair. Elaine says the comb is Guinevere's. Lancelot faints. Elaine realizes Lancelot loves Guinevere and goes home crying.

Lancelot rides on to the Castle of King Bademagus and his son Melegaunt. He has to cross a terrible bridge made of a huge sword. He cuts his hands, knees and feet.

Bademagus gives Lancelot ointment for his wounds. Lancelot demands Guinevere. Bademagus is a good king and gives Lancelot a horse and lance so that he can fight the evil Meleagant.

Lancelot and Meleagant fight, but the king stops the fight when he sees his son might be killed. Meleagant surrenders the queen.

Secretly that night, Lancelot meets Guinevere and they become lovers. He has betrayed his king and master.

5. The Quest for the Grail

Characters:

King Arthur

Sir Galahad

Sir Percival

Sir Lancelot

Sir Gawain

Lady with unicorn

The Grail King and an angel

The land falls into darkness. There is famine and disease. The king has lost his way. Arthur tells his knights that only by finding the Holy Grail can they save the land. The Quest Knights set off in search of the Grail Castle.

They come to the deadly Castle of Mirrors. They find 4 cups on a crystal table. They must choose the cup with the magic crystal or die.

Next they have to cross a Perilous Bridge. The bridge gets narrower as they cross. It is like walking a tight rope.

They meet a lady with a unicorn. She tries to persuade them to fight the evil Black Knight. Lancelot is tempted from the quest.

Galahad, Percival and Gawain take ship and visit seven islands. At last they come to the island of the Grail Castle.

Inside the castle is the Grail King. He is very sick. He has a wound in his thigh that smells a lot. They must ask him the right question. The first time they say nothing and the castle and king vanish.

The second time Percival asks the Grail King what is wrong with him and can he help at all? An angel enters the room carrying the cup. The Grail King drinks from it and give it to Percival. They have completed the quest.

6. The Death of Arthur

Characters:

King Arthur

Mordred (Arthur's evil son)

Sir Bedivere

Sir Lancelot

Morgana (Mordred's mother)

Meleagant (Mordred's knight)

The Black Knight (Mordred's knight)

Arthur has an evil son, Mordred, whose mother is the witch, Morgana. He is a nasty, evil character. He raises an army against his father.

Mordred comes to Camelot and demands that Arthur give him the crown.

Arthur says 'no'. Mordred declares war and goes off to prepare for battle.

Arthur rides out with his knights. With him are Lancelot and Bedivere.

A terrible battle is fought in which all the great knights of Arthur's court fall. Only Bedivere, Arthur and Mordred are left alive.

Arthur and Mordred meet on the battlefield and fight. Mordred runs Arthur through with his lance. Arthur kills Mordred with Excalibur.

Sir Bedivere is unhurt. Arthur tells him to throw Excalibur into the lake.

When he returns, Arthur asks him what he saw. Bedivere replies 'Just the ripples on the water.' Arthur knows he is lying and orders him again to throw the sword into the lake.

Bedivere can't do it and returns to Arthur. Arthur orders him to throw Excalibur into the lake for the last time. Bedivere does as he is told.

He returns to find Arthur being carried off in a boat to the magical Isle of Avalon.

8.10 Treasure Quest

Aim. To develop skills in narrative construction.

In. Brief. A story about buried treasure and a related map are deconstructed to enable the students to locate the treasure.

What you will need:

A letter - As in *'King Solomon's Mines'* or *'She'* by Ryder Haggard, a letter provides the clues to locate a hidden treasure. You will need to write such a letter! Perhaps it is from a student who came to the school long ago. ....

A treasure map - You will also need to decide what the 'treasure' is (perhaps a second letter that completes your story or resolves a mystery) and draw a simple map to help with its location.

Old box or chest of suitable size that begins life at the bottom of a classroom cupboard.

Method.

1. The activity begins with the 'discovery' of the box. Read the letter out to the group and study the map   An example of a suitable letter is given below.

   "To whoever finds this letter. A long time ago, I and my friends Jeremy and Susan came across an old chest in the loft of my house. The chest was very old. It looked empty except for an old army uniform from Victorian times. Then we saw, hidden under the uniform, a large envelope. We opened the envelope very carefully. Inside was a map. We recognized the map as being the school grounds (or wood/park etc) long before the school was built. It was the trees and the old houses nearby we recognized. There was an 'X' on the map but it did not say what it meant..... "

2. The letter goes on to describe the location of the mystery 'treasure' where the children found it or hid it once more to keep it safe. The letter and map should require that other clues are found to piece together all the evidence. The letter also refers to important features in the landscape that will be visited for clues.

3. The clues need to be given at two levels of detail. The first will guide them along a linear route and the second set will enable them to locate the treasure within a narrowly defined area. Typically, a small box might be hidden underneath a stone at the foot of a particular tree.

4. Once the treasure has been located, students relate the story of their adventure, either as an oral narrative or in words and pictures.

5. Students move on to create similar stories of their own, with hidden treasure. Younger children can draw narrative pictures and simple treasure maps. This should all be done in close connection with a landscape in order to practice and develop powers of landscape description.

Reflection. Are there things in your own family that have been passed down to you by great grandparents, or great great grandparents? What are they?
What do they tell you about their lives? Is it important to keep some things that have been passed down to you? Why?

9. SCIENCE OUTDOORS

Earthworm Populations, Insect Distribution Maps, Making Insect Habitats, Tree Health, Tug-of-War Maths, Playing Field Planetarium, Making a Giant Clock, Fairground Probabilities Challenge, Analyzing Earth & Stone, Trebuchet and Missile Trajectories, Ice and Insulation, Coordinates Game.

"maggie and milly and may
went down to the beach (to play one day)
and maggie discovered a shell that sang
so sweetly she couldn't remember her troubles, and
milly befriended a stranded star
whose rays five languid fingers were;
and molly was chased by a horrible thing
which raced sideways while blowing bubbles:and
may came home with a smooth round stone
as small as a world and as large as alone."

E.E.Cummings, 1977

There can be something hard about the teaching of Science – hard, that is, relative to the teaching of Music, Literature or Religion. Here we have (or so some of my Key Stage 4 students would have it) a world of facts. Facts are things you can bang on the table, trip over, or stick in a test tube, shake about and always get a known and predictable outcome. And in the dissection of scientific outcomes we come to the end of mystery, of wonder, of the great unknown. It is as if Darwin, as he made his notes on the rocky beaches of the Galapagos Islands, had stripped the universe naked and discovered it was all as simple as 1 + 1 = 2.

In classroom Science there is always the lurking danger that students will see the numbers and not the wonder. Here we have a law, a proposition, a formula that explains it all. I look up at the night sky (if I can see it through the fog of light pollution) and all I see are Prisoners of Gravity. Squeeze hydrogen atoms together hard and fast enough and you can blow up the world.

Being up close and personal with the real thing can take us beyond this. It's like comparing a diagram of a dissected human being with a living, breathing companion. A leaf might seem a simple organism – and yet look at under a microscope and it becomes a universe in itself.

The power of Nature to inspire students must never be underestimated and our teaching of Science should give them as much access to the world *out there* as possible. Science has a fundamental role to play in a child's spiritual development, for we cannot discover what we are without having a feeling, however innate, of our place in the Cosmos and the laws that bind us to all things.

Thus, a student sees the insect as a creature that has a world of its own and a life path that is ours and yet not ours. Dead on a dissecting board it is but a thing of parts. A tree growing has a lifespan that may reach back to the time of Elizabeth I, and can reveal to us the droughts and floods of each of its growing years. A ball, thrown through the air, will display the characteristics that hold the earth in its trajectory round the sun, and the galaxies that spin through time and space.

I have always been impressed with the way that children engaged in digging, will fuss and fret over the well-being of the worms they dig up, and mourn the worm split by the spade or trowel. And wonder more when I explain that, returned to earth, the head of the worm is capable of regenerating a new tail. And counting meticulously, they marvel at the millions, the City of Worms that inhabit the school playing field and want to discover how they live, breed and die.

Thus are scientists made.

Earthworm Notes:

Earthworms play a vital role in our well-being by breaking down and conditioning the soil.

Research suggests that an acre of farmland may contain between 250,000 and 1,750,000 worms, depending on the richness of the soil (Rothamsted Experimental Station statistics). The application of some chemical fertilizers to soil can lead to worm population collapse – hence the need for farmers to check worm populations.

Earthworms like pH levels between 6.5 to 7.5. Farmers will sometimes add earthworms to their land if the numbers have dropped below an acceptable level. Earthworm population sampling is carried out by most farmers as part of assessing the general health of their fields and to check that chemicals etc aren't impacting on the worm population. They are a vital component of soil health and therefore of our entire landscape.

9.1 Calculating Earthworm Populations

"It may be doubted whether there are many other animals which have played so important a part in the history of the world, as have these lowly organized creatures."
Charles Darwin, on earthworms.

Aim. To understand the importance of earthworms to soil fertility. To explore conditions that favour earthworm populations.

In Brief. Students calculate the number of worms in a given area of land by sampling.

What you will need:

Access to a piece of ground where several 25cm cubes of earth can be dug out and later replaced.

Per group: A ruler and steel pegs to mark out the sample area, a bottle of water, a spade, two or three plastic trowels, a plastic container or small bucket to put the earthworms in.
A clipboard and suitable chart to record the count and make notes with regard to soil condition.

Method.

1. Discuss the importance of earthworms to soil quality. Worms aerate the soil, improve drainage, break down organic materials, increase nitrogen and phosphate content, help mix and aggregate the soil and generally keep it in good condition.   They are most active in spring and autumn, so this is a good time to sample.

2. Divide into groups of four and issue each with their equipment. Choose locations that are dispersed and reflect different conditions – in a flowerbed or vegetable plot, under trees, in areas that get full sun and areas that are grassed etc.

3. Students mark out their cube of 25cm and dig out the turf and the soil beneath carefully so that it can be replaced; make as few cuts as possible with the spade to avoid damaging worms. Flex open the turf from the underside across its entire surface and extract the worms. Any lumps of earth can be carefully divided with the trowel and further broken up by hand. All worms are carefully removed and collected in a container. Count them and record numbers on the chart.

4. Describe the soil condition. Is it dry or damp? Is it stony? Is it well aerated or heavy clay? How deep is the humus layer? What is on the surface – grass, leaf mould, weeds, grass? If time allows, draw a scale soil profile to depict the different layers. Bring the groups together to compare results. Visit each other's sample sites to compare soil condition as well as worm numbers.

5. *Calculate the earthworm population*. Carefully return earthworms and soil into the hole. Replace and tamp down any turf. Multiply the worms in your $25cm^3$ by 16 to calculate the number per m². Now multiply that total by 10,000 to find out the earthworm population of a hectare. Optimum numbers are 10,000,000 per hectare or 62 earthworms per $25cm^3$.

Reflection. Compare the different sample areas. Were there significant differences? Can local conditions explain this? Looking at the averages, is your school earthworm population healthy? Discuss the role of other insect populations in maintaining the environment and supporting food production. Discuss the kinds of things we might do to the soil or growing crops that can have a serious impact on faunal populations. *See earthworm notes opposite.*

9.2 Snail Distribution Map

Aim. To develop skills in recording information accurately. To encourage scientific deduction at a level appropriate to the group.

In Brief. Students collect and record evidence of mollusc activity in different parts of the school grounds or outdoor area and produce a chart to reflect their findings.

What you will need:

A straightforward large map of the area to be studied. Make this yourself. Include buildings, trees, bushes and shrubs, grassed areas, buildings and paving. On the map, mark out sample areas of 5 metre squares, one for each group of 4 students. Copy A4 versions of the sample squares or get the students to map their own squares on location.	*Per group*: a clipboard, length of double-sided sticky tape stuck to a strip of card or alongside their A4 map, and a pencil. Gluestick. Double sided sticky tape. 4 steel tent pegs and brightly coloured twine to mark off the 5 metre square
A tape measure. Rubber mallet if the ground is hard.	

Method.

1. Discuss the role of snail populations as evidence of the type of vegetation in an area and its health. Archaeologists make use of snail shell samples (snail shells don't rot) to find out about the plants and trees growing in an area many thousands of years ago. Share possible ways of searching for and collecting snail shells, as well as recording any living snails they may find. What type of vegetation do they think might support the most snails?

2. Introduce the map and assign each group a 5 metre square. Walk the area with them so that they are familiar with how the map works. Check that the chosen area has a reasonable amount of the faunal remains you wish to sample. In some instances, such as in woodland debris, a certain amount of sifting of the leaves and decaying plant matter is necessary. In a school, encourage a careful search of flowerbeds, plant pots, underneath seating and other smooth surfaces, school pond surrounds and the surfaces of rotting wood.

3. Use the tape measure, steel tent pegs and twine to demarcate the 5 metre squares. If it is obvious that there is no snail activity, mark this square as 'empty' and assign another square.

4. Demonstrate the sampling – find a snail shell, stick it on the double-sided tape, number the sample, write the same number on the map where the shell was found. Where living snails are spotted the snail is given a number in sequence and additionally identified with an 'L' to indicate 'live'.

5. Discuss how to sample carefully. A patch of grass might need to be explored on hands and knees. A hedgerow might need care to avoid nettles. Allow the groups ten to twenty minutes to research their area. Check periodically that the location of finds is being accurately recorded. Once the time is over, get the groups together and compare finds.

6. Return to to the classroom and transfer the finds and information to the display map.

Reflection. Are the finds of snails spread out evenly? If not, in what kind of places are they clustered? There are many different species of snail. Are the different species grouped together or are they evenly spread out across all surveyed squares.

Look up 'snail species' online and use the available charts to identify your species of snail. Look at all the information and describe the kinds of places the snails appear to like. Find out about snail diets and how well the researched environments meet the dietary needs.

9.3 Making Insect Habitats

Aim. To examine the impact of human activity on insect populations. To enable students to compare the outcomes of a series of similar experiments. To encourage accurate recording of insect populations.

In Brief. Students create a series of insect habitats, with different materials that reflect human behaviour in the built environment.

What you will need: *(Per group of 4 to 6 students)*

A square metre plot of ground that can be left relatively undisturbed, e.g. an isolated corner of a school garden/grounds or a patch of woodland. Insect charts with pictures of common insects. Pencils and clipboards. Two plastic containers. Steel tent pegs and twine.	*Materials to create habitats.* Examples include: black bin bag weighted to the ground with stones, a pile of rotten wood, a pile of mown grass or pulled weeds, a pile of bricks or stones, a piece of corrugated iron, a pile of soggy newspapers and cardboard weighted with stones, a mix of man-made rubbish such as old plastic toys and pieces of MDF, a mixed pile of upturned plastic and clay plant pots stuffed with straw, a paving slab, and a log stump.

Method.

1. Begin by discussing the different insects you find in a garden. What types of habitats attract different insects, for example, woodlice on the undersides of log stumps?

2. Divide into groups. Through discussion let each group choose a habitat they would like to create. Give time to bring in or otherwise obtain the materials needed (see above for ideas).

3. Using steel pegs and twine, each group marks out and labels their one metre square of ground, It doesn't matter if they are close together or even adjoining. Complete a survey of any existing surface insect population (species found and their numbers) within the square metre, record the results. The groups now create their distinctive habitat. **Leave for two to three weeks.**

4. Return and carefully take apart the habitats. Examine all surfaces, such as the interior of pots and undersides of stones. Identify and transfer insects into one of the two plastic containers. Count by transfering to the other container before releasing. Record results on the charts.

5. Back in the classroom use the information gathered to make display charts comparing the different habitats. What was the overall increase in insect population in each habitat area, if any? Did the different types of habitat attract different insect populations? What types of habitat were the most successful in attracting insects?

Reflection. A healthy population of earthworms, beetles and other insects benefits a variety of birds, mammals, reptiles and amphibians, as well as plant life. Beetles, for example, can bring down the aphid populations and larger beetles, such as the Violet can help control slugs. Create a food chain chart that explores insects you might wish to encourage or discourage in your garden. Choose one insect to study. Explore the advantages and disadvantages or having the insect in the garden. What kind of habitat might you create to encourage or control the insect?

9.4 Tree Health

Aim. To encourage students to take a closer interest in trees. To develop an understanding of the life-cycle of a tree – young, mature and old. To develop skills to assess the life stage and health of a tree.

In Brief. Students make a special study of an individual tree and compare outcomes.

What you will need:

Access to a range of trees of varying age and species - copse or wooded corner of the school grounds is ideal. One tree per two students.	*Per 2 students:* An inclinometer (see fig 9.4) - made using: A5 card, A5 paper, scissors, glue stick, strong cotton thread, large metal washer, pencil. A 25m tape measure. Tree identification chart and clipboards.

Method.

1. Discuss the importance of trees in shaping our environment.

    * What is the role of the tree in producing oxygen and consuming carbon dioxide?
    * What part do trees play in improving our daily lives?
    * What are trees used for?
    * How long do trees live?
    * Do trees grow old?
    * How do we know they are old?
    * What happens to us when we get old?
    * Do the same things happen to trees?
    * If we want to measure the height of a tree, how can we do it?

2. Discuss how we can use the equilateral triangle to measure height. Draw the method on the board (*see fig 9.4*). If you walk away from a tree until you are looking at the top of the crown at an angle of 45 degrees then the height of the tree is the same as your distance from it. Alternatively, trigonometry can be used to calculate the height of the tree using a combination of angle to the tree top and distance from it.

3. *Make an inclinometer.* Provide each pair of students with an A5 piece of card, a piece of thin A5 paper, 30 cm length of string and a metal washer or similar with a weight of 8 to 10 grams. They will also need scissors and glue sticks. Using a ruler and protractor, begin by drawing a line 2cms from the top of the card. From this line carefully mark out the 90 degree and the 45 degree angles in pencil. Go over them neatly in felt tip to make the lines easy to see.

4. Wrap the A5 paper round a pencil to make a tube and glue the edge. Do this as neatly as possible. Glue or tape the tube to the card protractor along the top edge. Ensure that it is fixed accurately so as to make a 90 degree angle with the line drawn down the centre of the card. To attach the plumb line, make a neat hole with a compass point where the top line and the ninety degree line meet. Pass the thread through the hole and tape down on the far side. Lastly, attach the weight to make the plumb line.

5. *Measure the height of a tree.* Explain how to use the inclinometer. Keep walking away from the tree until you think you are as far away as it is high. Look at the tree through the tube on the inclinometer, whilst the partner checks that the plumb line is at 45 degrees. Adjust your position backwards or forwards until the tube lines up accurately with the highest point of the tree. You and your partner now measure the distance from where you are standing to the tree with the tape measure. Lastly, add the distance of the inclinometer when it is held up to your eye from the ground.

6. Things to discuss and note down when you and your partner are analyzing your chosen tree.

   a. What species of tree is it?

   b. Does it look young, middle-aged, or old to you?

   c. Measure and record the girth of the tree by passing the tape round it.

   d. Measure and record the height of the tree with your inclinometer and tape measure.

   e. Look for and record any damage, such as dead limbs and evidence of limbs that have broken off. How much pruning of big limbs has the tree had (look for old stumps on the trunk). Record your findings.

   f. Look for and record signs of decay – large trunk wounds or cavities, fungal growth on the bark, dead branches, evidence of wood boring insects, heavy ivy growth, patches where the bark has fallen off, exposing the bare wood.

   g. How healthy are the leaves? Are the leaves being eaten by anything? Are there lots of leaves or does it look a bit threadbare compared with similar trees nearby?

   h. Look at the size, shape and health of the crown (all the branches with leaves.) Has the tree got a healthy crown or does it look thin compared with other trees? Is the crown evenly distributed. Make notes of your findings.

7. When you have recorded your assessment decide if your tree is young, mature or old, healthy or unhealthy. Lots of fungal growth and dead branches means it is probably diseased. Do this by looking at your findings and comparing then with trees nearby of the same species.

Reflection. Trees die when they become heavily diseased or when new annual growth become too thin to sustain the tree, typically less than 5mm. As a tree gets bigger and older, the rings get thinner. In what ways are trees like us when it comes to ageing?

Why does our blood circulation deteriorate? Discuss trees that live a very long time – there are yews in British churchyards that are more than a thousand years old. Some olive trees in the Middle East are known to date back to the time of Christ. Sequoias can live 5000 years.

The average urban tree, however, is lucky to live 75 years. What kinds of things cause urban trees to die, or be cut down before their time? Remember that many of them will not be in their natural environment. Some simply grow too big for the space assigned to them. Explore the role of solids, liquids and gases in the life of the tree.

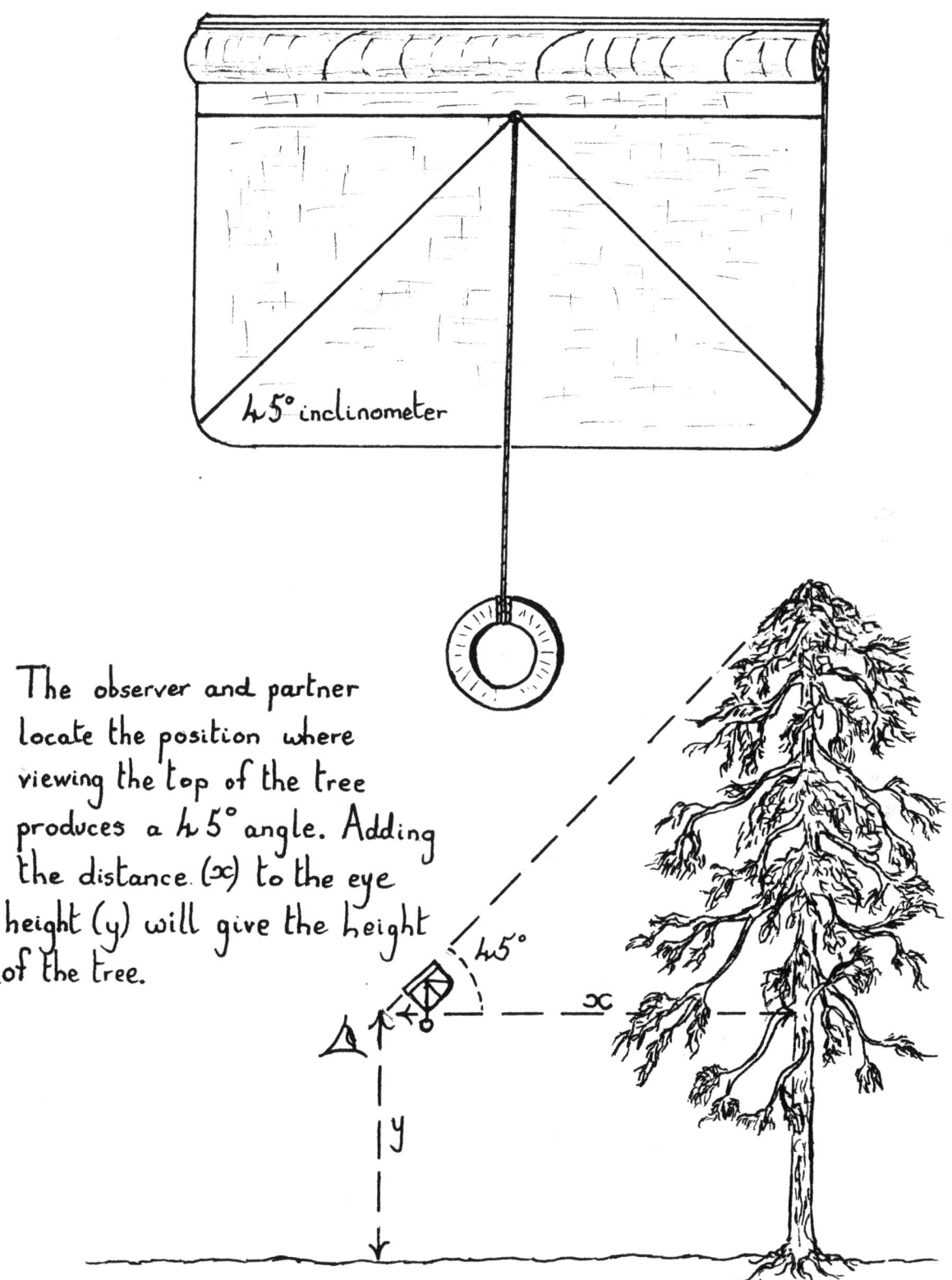

45° inclinometer

The observer and partner locate the position where viewing the top of the tree produces a 45° angle. Adding the distance (x) to the eye height (y) will give the height of the tree.

45°

x

y

9.5 Is weight an advantage in Tug-of-War?

Aim. To develop skills in collecting data for problem-solving. To develop skills in the interrogation of data.

In Brief. Tug-of-war teams are weighed and the weights compared with the outcomes of tug-of-war competitions.

What you will need:

A dry day to ensure your grass is suitable for tug-of-war.	Level ground – our experiments show that relatively minor slopes give an advantage to the lower team.
A tug-of-war rope of around 20m length and a minimum of 16mm diameter.*	Two sets of bathroom scales to weigh the teams. Paper, calculators etc.. to record results. A whistle to start and stop the tug-of-war.

* We use a special soft textured nylon rope to reduce the risk of rope burn.

Method.

1.   Introduce the activity to your group as a problem to solve – is weight an advantage in certain sports? Is weight an indicator of strength? How might tug-of-war be used to see if there is a clear relationship between strength and weight?

2.   Divide the class into groups of 4 with the task of deciding how they would tackle the problem. What equipment will they need and what information would they need to record? Explain that weights should be recorded anonymously to protect privacy. Different groups may come up with varying solutions, but encourage the need to collate different sets of data to confirm the outcome of the experiment.

3.   Discuss the methodologies the groups come up with and bring the class to a consensus on the method to be employed. Suggest that there might be the need to do some mixing and matching to achieve teams of significantly differing weight. Children usually love tug-of-war so it is important that whatever methodology is chosen everyone gets to compete at least twice!

4.   In case you are unfamiliar with tug-of-war management, I mark out the ground with 3 short pieces of rope , pegged down 3 metres apart to mark the movement of the rope. A piece of cloth is tied to the middle of the rope. Starting with the cloth over the centre rope, the first team to pull the rope 3 metres and over the outer rope on their side is the winner.

5.   On the sports field, weighing stations can be set up allowing the teams to be weighed and recorded in accordance with the chosen method. Teams of 6 to 8 are safer than larger teams and easier to manage. Each team can be identified by a name or colour and their aggregated weight. Then the tug-of-war competitions can begin and the win/lose outcomes recorded against a team's name and weight details. Allow time for at least 4 competitions. This means that with teams of 7, each student will experience competing twice in a class of 28.

Reflection. Compare the results of the different competitions. Are the results consistent and decisive? Did the heavier team always win? If the outcomes are not clear what conclusions might we reach? Were the weight differences between the teams significant enough?

9.6   Creating a planetarium on the school field

Aims. To give students insight into the distances involved in the solar system. To explore methods of creating a scale model. To create a sense of 'place' in understanding the relationship of the Earth to the rest of the solar system.

In Brief. Students make models of the different planets and set them out on the school field at correctly scaled distances.

What you will need: (This activity may take a number of sessions)

Ten 1m long hazel poles (or battening).	25 m tape measure.
Several cardboard boxes to make planets.	Scissors. Rubber mallet. Staple gun.

Method.

1. Introduce the solar system. Using a simple diagram on the whiteboard, discuss the problems of accurately illustrating the distances between planets. If we use a scale of 1cm per 10,000,000 miles, Mercury is 4.6cm from the sun, Venus 6.7cm, the Earth 9.1cm and Mars 20.5cm. Jupiter is 46cm away, Uranus 1.7m, and Neptune 2.8m. At its furthest from the sun, Pluto is 7.4m away!

2. The challenge is to make a scale model of the solar system showing relative size of the planets and their distance from the sun, using the full length of the school playing field or a nearby park. On completion, younger children in the school can walk across the solar system!

3. Divide the class into groups of 3 or 4. Each group (assuming 10 groups) is responsible for an individual planet or the sun itself. Head out to your chosen area with a couple of measuring tapes. What is the optimum scale they can use? For example, at 1metre per 10,000,000 miles, Neptune is 280m from the sun; the nearest star, Proxima Centauri, is 1,600 miles away!

4. *Make the Planets.* Groups paint suitably sized card circles to represent the different planets. It is useful if they can be to scale. On a scale of 1metre per 10,000,000 miles the sun would be 87cm across, Saturn would be a tennis ball, and the Earth, a pea. The groups should discuss and agree a practical scale and then work out sizes. Once complete and painted, attach the models to the poles (or battening) with a staple gun and hammer into the ground with a rubber mallet.

5. *Back outdoors*. Having agreed a scale, use the tape measure to position the planets in their orbits. If using 1 metre per 10,000,000 miles, distances from the sun are as follows:

    *   Mercury, 4.6 metres (46 million miles)
    *   Venus, 6.7 metres (67 million miles)
    *   Earth, 9.1 metres (91 million miles)
    *   Mars, 20.5 metres (205 million miles)
    *   Jupiter, 46 metres (460 million miles)
    *   Uranus, 170 metres. (1.7 billion miles)
    *   Neptune, 280 metres. (2.8 billion miles)
    *   Pluto, 280 metres (when closest to sun)*

    * Pluto is now generally regarded as one of the 70,000 or so Kuipe Belt objects, though at the time of writing it retains the status of a 'dwarf planet'.

Reflection. Share what the class has learned about the size of the solar system from the activity. What have they learned about the size of the solar system and the distances between planets? Share and discuss how a suitable scale for the model was worked out. Why is it difficult to represent the distances to stellar objects, such as stars and galaxies, with this kind of model?

9.7 Making a Giant Clock

Aim. To understand and apply degrees of arc using a compass. To develop skills in reading bearings and checking by taking back bearings. To support learning to tell the time with an analogue clock. To develop spatial awareness.

In Brief. Students use a rope and compass to set out the 30 degree intervals, and use the layout as a giant clock to support learning to tell the time by younger children.

What you will need:

An average, flat school field or tarmac playground.	A good, easy to read magnetic compass. A 25 metre length of rope.
13 one metre poles with different colour flags for the cardinal points e.g. 4 red flags and 8 green flags for the 30 degree intervals). Cones - as used in games - can work just as well.	

Method.

1. Remind students that, like a protractor, a compass, is divided into 360 degrees. Degrees are used to indicate a direction from a given point, with the compass held in position on magnetic north. With the older students, show how a compass is used to take a bearing, or, in this instance, determine magnetic north and the remaining three cardinal points. Compare a compass with the dial of an analogue clock. If midday is north, what time will east, south and west be?

2. *Set out the Clock.* One student stands in the centre of the clock and holds one end of the rope. A second takes the other end and paces out the length until taut. A third student with a compass gives directions to the others to orientate the rope on magnetic north. When he or she is satisfied with the accuracy of the bearing, the position at the end of the rope is marked with a cone or stake and flag. This will become Midday or Midnight and should be marked distinctively from the remaining points.

3. Now, using bearings, rotate the rope to mark East, West & North. Continue the procedure at 30 degree intervals – 30, 60, 120, 150 degrees and so on. When all positions are marked they can be checked by doing back bearings from the outer perimeter of the 'clock'. Thus, zero degrees north will yield a back bearing of 180 degrees south. Leave a marker, such as a cone, in the centre of the 'compass' or 'clock'.

4. *Use the clock to teach younger children.* Firstly, walk them round the 'clock' from midnight onwards, calling out the time as they arrive at each hour. Next demonstrate minutes. At 3.30 where will the hour 'finger' be standing and where will the minute 'finger' be standing?

5. Once you are satisfied that the group is aware of how the numbers stand in relation to each other, divide into two groups, say girls the hours and boys the minutes. Holding hands, they form two lines to act as fingers. Different times are called out and each group forms the finger pointing at the correct point on the dial. A more energetic and fun way to do it, is to have each group run to the correct position on the dial as you call out different times.

Reflection. Why are magnetic compasses and clocks so important? Make a list of the things they help us to do. Before there were clocks, how did people tell the time? Before there were compasses how did they navigate? What is the most important star for navigation? What is its special quality? Find out how to locate this special star in the night sky.

9.8 Fairground Probabilities Challenge

Aim. To develop and apply skills in calculating averages and probability. To reflect on methods of calculating business risk.

In Brief. Students run a variety of low tech fairground attractions to calculate potential profits based on throughput and the probability of customers winning the prize.

What you will need:

Access to a level area of school field, where several 'stalls' can be set up.

The material requirements for each fairground activity will depend on what the students come up with – but they can be confined to what is available from the school stores, or readily brought in. For example, cones or skittles that can be knocked over with a kicked ball or a tyre hung frlom a goalpost to throw a ball through.

Method.

1. Students discuss how probability is used in many contexts to calculate, and price, risk. For example, how much should an insurance company charge a 21-year-old to insure his car and what statistics will they work with? Discuss how probability might work in a fairground attraction based on a combination of skill and chance. If one in ten people win on a fairground attraction and the prize is ten times the stake, the stallholder will make no money. If we want to keep the 'big win', how might we reduce the incidence of winning, without losing customer turnover?

2. Set the challenge for groups of 4 students to design a fairground attraction that takes 60 seconds or less to complete. They must assesses profits based on throughput of punters and a tenfold return on a stake of 50p if the punter wins. How can profits be calculated? How many people would need to try out the attraction to establish the probability of someone winning?

3. When all the planning work is done and the equipment sorted out (balls, goalposts, skittles, hoops etc..) give each group a chance to try out their own attraction and tweak the chances of winning prior to bringing out the punters. A minimum of two students are needed to run each stall – one to manage the activity and a second to record throughput and numbers of winners. The other two in each group try out the various stalls. How many punters did you have in the 30 minutes? Calculate the turnover on the basis of 50p per punter. How many punters won the tenfold prize in that time? How much is deducted from takings to pay for winnings? Use multiplication to calculate your turnover in an 8 hour day. Multiply the number of winners by 16 (number of winners in your 30 minute run time multiplied to give the number of winners in an 8 hour working day). Subtract the winnings from turnover to calculate your profit.

4. Compare your profit with the other stallholders. Sharing information with all groups, compare the probabilities of punters winning each activity.

Reflection. Discuss how probability affects the way we live. What makes the National Lottery so attractive, even though the chances of winning the jackpot are less than 10,000,000 to 1? How might you make your stall more attractive and increase your profits at the same time? Reflect on other types of risk in our lives. Why is statistical probability not always a guide to risk? For example, why isn't everyone who drives a fast car or climbs a mountain subject to the same probability of an accident? Why do different fairground punters stand a much better chance of winning than others?

9.9   Investigating the Earth at your Feet

Aim. To develop investigative skills. To develop skills in identifying different types of stone and soil.

In Brief. Students collect soil and stone samples and sieve the collected materials for identification and classification.

What you will need:

A walking route, such as a farmland or woodland walk, to collect soil samples.	Plastic trowel and freezer bag for each student. Sample labels. Clipboards. Pens/pencils.
A couple of sieves to separate out smaller stones Plastic trays. Double-sided tape or glue stick	Water to clean stones. Card to make displays.

Method.

1.   Soil and stones can tell us a great deal about the history of a particular place. Soils vary a great deal. Some contain a lot of clay, some are coarse and contain a lot of flint, coastal soils may be very sandy, some very loamy (contain lots of humus) and some can be peaty. Stones can be even more varied – they can be chalk, limestone, slate, quartz or granite to name just a few. They can be rough and sharp – perhaps broken up by the plough or frost action – or worn smooth by river or sea action. Lots of gravel might indicate a glacial deposit (or human activity in the form of path or road-making!) Some may be man-made, such as bits of old brick or pottery.

2.   Divide the class into groups of 4. At each location on the walk one group member collects a sample. Consider the area - are we in a valley or on the side of a hill? What human activity is going on? (e.g. forestry or farming). Is there evidence of ploughing? Is there a river or stream nearby? Examine some of the stones and pebbles in situ. What do you think they are made of? Are they rough edged or worn smooth? Make notes about the area on your sample label.

3.   Look out for signs of past human activity, such as fragments of pottery, bits of coal or worn brick. What are the stones – flinty, chalk, sandstone etc..? Are there lots of smooth pebbles, indicating the presence of a stream or river in prehistoric times? Gravel and pebbles found on paths that aren't present on ground off the path may have been brought there from a quarry. We can still find out a lot. Broken gravel of a uniform colour may be crushed limestone from a quarry, very mixed rough gravel (different sizes and stone types), may be quarried glacial gravel from a gravel bed, smooth pebbles may be quarried from a beach or prehistoric river beds.

4.   Back at base, place the samples on separate trays for sorting. Wash stones and sift earth. With the help of illustrations sort and label the samples. Use the appropriate terminology.

Reflection. Your collection of earth and stones tell you something of the history of where you found them. Share the most interesting of your stones. What do you think are the messages they contain about the past? Study your soil samples. How would you describe them? Do you think it is good earth for growing things in? Reflect on where you found your sample. What human activity do you think has taken place there over the centuries? What was is the evidence for human activity in soil and stone?

9.10 Hinged Counterweight Trebuchet & Missile Trajectories

Aim. To develop understanding of the effects of gravity. To enable students to explore the forces involved in using stored energy to project a missile.

In Brief. A catapult or trebuchet is constructed that facilitates experimentation with different soft projectiles and their trajectories (*see fig 9.10*).

What you will need:

8 fresh hazel poles of around 1.3m in length and 3cm in diameter. 6 of the hazel poles need a pointed end, so they can be driven firmly into the ground.	
A tapering two metre pole of about 6cms in diameter for the lever or throwing arm.	One metre of dowelling or smooth hazel pole of about 2.5cms diameter for the pivot.
A matching diameter drill bit and brace to drill the hole for the pivot.	A cup, such as a small plastic food container to hold the projectiles.
A bradawl or small hand drill, screwdriver and 2 self-tapping screws to attach the cup to the throwing arm.	A ball of sisal string, scissors, and a mallet to hammer in poles and stakes.
For the projectiles - a collection of balls with different sizes and mass, such as a tennis ball, ping pong ball, a squash ball, golf ball etc. Try and get hold of a polystyrene ball if you can.	You will need to provide a 25 metre tape to measure the distance travelled by the projectiles.

Trebuchets are superb machines for demonstrating and exploring trajectories, gravitational forces, friction, and the multiplication of force using a lever. With the construction method described, a two metre pole is fixed to a pivot by drilling a hole through the pole and inserting a dowel rod. The pivot is secured to two tripods of hazel poles, firmly fixed to the ground. A cup is attached to the long end of the pole and a counterweight to the other.

Method.

1. Discuss how missiles of every kind are projected. What forces does a missile have to overcome in order to fly? How do those forces act against it (gravity, friction from air resistance)? How are missiles shaped and made to overcome these challenges?

2. Discuss examples of early projectile technology – throwing spears, bows and arrows, slingshot. Consider early machines, such as the ballista or trebuchet that made it possible to hurl heavy projectiles over greater distances. Discuss the energy used by the trebuchet – the force of gravity pulling the counterweight to ground. How might a simple large catapult be constructed to test some ideas about projectiles? How were Roman and Medieval catapults powered? One method was to construct a large bow out of flexible materials. Another was to use a giant sling on a pivoted lever powered by a heavy weight (trebuchet). The Romans used the tension from tightly twisted leather or sinew rope to power the ballista. The trebuchet could be a fearsome weapon. Some large trebuchets built in the middle ages were capable of hurling stones weighing more than a ton over 300 metres.

3. **Now get started on construction!** Provide laminated diagrams of a trebuchet for inspiration. Watch school-made trebuchets in action on YouTube.

4. **Begin with the throwing arm.** The pole should be about 1.8 metres in length and 6cms thick to allow for drilling a 2cm hole through to take the dowelling pivot. We select poles with a strong taper. The less weight on the projectile side of the throwing arm the better. Drill the 2cm pivot hole a quarter of the way along the pole at the thicker end (*see fig 9.10*). This multiplies the speed of the throwing cup by a factor of three relative to the speed of drop of the counterweight. Drill a second hole on the same axis at the thin end of the pole about 4cm from the end of the pole. Attach a strong piece of cord to this of about 3m in length. Finally, drill a hole on the same axis 4cm from the thick end of the pole. Attach a strong loop of cord. Now add the counterweight. We use a small Rhino (rubber) bucket containing a sandbag weighing 10 kilos full of sand, although the weight required depends on the thickness and weight of the throwing arm and may need to be adjusted. The sandbag is placed in the Rhino bucket, the bucket securely tied to the hole drilled through the counterweight end of the pole so that it swings freely. This free movement of the weight reduces recoil and puts less strain on the frame than a fixed weight would. Using a rubber bucket and sandbag counterweight reduces the risk of injury should it swing into a leg. Avoid using hard materials such as bricks for counterweights.On the same axis as the pivot and counterweight, attach the cup to the thin end of the pole. This might be, for example, a small square food container, drilled through and secured with two self-tapping screws.

5. **Next construct the two tripods.** These will be positioned to either side of the swinging arm. The gap between the tripods should be about 40cms to allow for the free swing of the throwing arm. They must be firmly embedded in the ground so that they don't pull loose. Tie the tripods such that they are of exactly equal height at the pivot axle. If need be, use guy ropes to provide extra stability to the tripods (a guy rope to front, rear and side). Next, rest the pivot on the tripods and secure with string. Check it swings freely. The counterweight must be clear of the ground when the throwing arm is in the vertical position.

6. **Test Missiles.** The sudden and unexpected movement of the swinging arm can cause significant injury. Ensure that all students are stood at least 3 metres to either side of the trebuchet (not to the front or rear) and out of the line of fire. Only use sports balls for projectiles. The trebuchet is cocked for firing by pulling down the swinging arm at the projectile end, using the loop of cord to pull on, until it is in the horizontal position. A second person places the projectile in the plastic cup. The person releasing the cord must stand back so there is no risk of their face being caught by the swinging arm or their body by the returning counterweight. If this cannot be comfortably achieved lengthen your pull cord.

7. **Now try out your various projectiles.** Which one goes the furthest? Measure distance travelled with a tape for each one. Also look at how they travel (parabola). Record your outcomes on a chart. Discuss the effect of size and weight during repeat firings.

Reflection. Discuss the forces that are at work in determining the distance the missile travels (the counterweight, gravity, friction, wind direction). Study your results. Which missiles flew the furthest and why? Find out how fast a missile would have to fly to go into orbit or escape the earth's gravitational pull altogether. What forces are involved in slinging the earth around the sun?

fig 9.10 Hinged Counterweight Trebuchet & Missile Trajectories

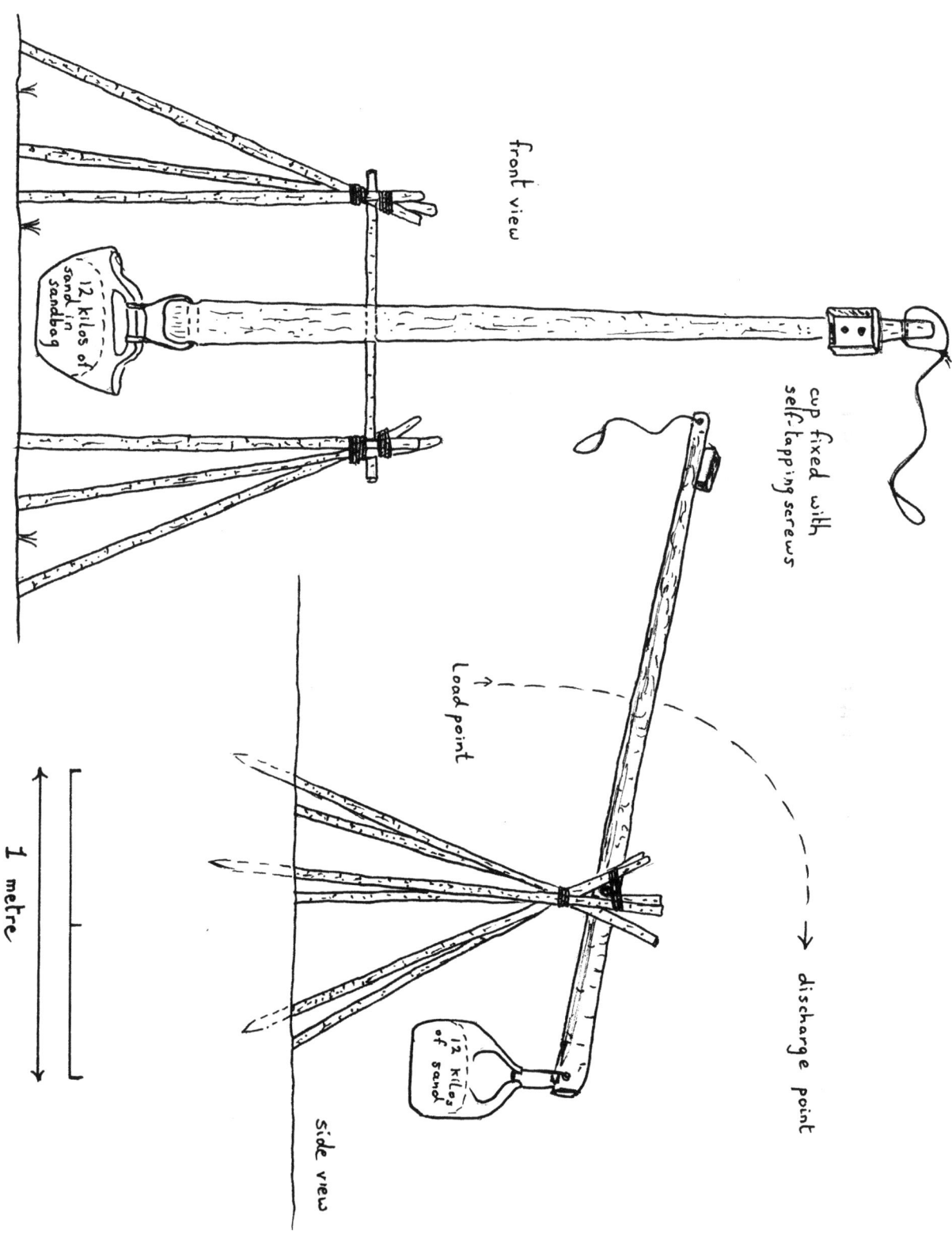

front view

12 kilos of sand in sandbag

cup fixed with self-tapping screws

Load point

discharge point

1 metre

12 kilos of sand

side view

9.11   Making a mini Ice-House

Aim. To explore different forms of insulation & their effectiveness in controlling heat loss.

In Brief. Students create a miniature ice-house and use ice cubes to compare the insulation properties of a variety of natural and man-made materials.

What you will need:

Average summer temperatures. Waste ground where each group can dig a hole approx. 30cm by 30cm by 40cm deep. Ice cubes sufficient to provide 4 per group of 4 students. A freezer box and freezer bags.	*Construction materials* depend on student research, they might include the following: roll of cooking foil, cardboard boxes, old newspapers, polystyrene packing chips and a bale of straw.

Tools: One spade per group, garden trowels, mini hacksaws to cut sticks to length, scissors, aluminium foil and string. A pile of sticks and a ball of string to construct a cover.

Method.

1.   Discuss the importance of insulation to regulate temperature in specific environments, such as homes and fridges. Consider the role of fridges and freezers in our lives, in shops, homes and refrigerated vehicles. Discuss the importance of the ice house in the past.

2.   Look at the material to be kept cool – ice. Weigh samples of 4 ice cubes from the freezer and then return them. These will be your control. They should be out of the ice-box about 10 minutes, so that they will be exposed to air a similar amount of time to those being carried to the mini ice-houses.

3.   Consider suitable locations for your mini ice-houses. Where might the ground be cooler? Look for north facing, shaded by trees, on a slope or bank of earth that gets very little sun.

4.   Once chosen each group of 3 or 4 students makes their mini ice-house by digging a hole, lining it (if that is their plan) with straw or other materials or keeping it empty. Suggest methods for lining the hole with aluminium foil, such as sheeting over panels of cardboard cut to match the hole.   Also consider suspending the ice-cubes in a foil bag in the centre of the ice-house. Decide how to construct the cover. Carefully record ice house structure for future analysis, including a drawing of the method of construction, measurements and materials used.

5.   When all is ready, quickly deliver the 4 ice cubes in small freezer bags to each group for burial. Leave a bowl of 4 ice cubes exposed to the open air to act as a second control. Leave for 2 to 4 hours, depending on ambient temperature.

6.   Open the ice house, and weigh the ice cube collections in turn, ensuring that residual cube weights and information about insulation techniques are recorded together. Weigh any remaining ice in the bowl left on the surface. Collate all the information and establish the most effective methods of insulation.

Reflection. Did you slow down the rate of melting by a useful amount? What are the advantages and disadvantages of modern refrigeration? (don't forget to discuss CFC gases and disposing of old fridges). Think about hot countries. When houses were built with thick mud brick or adobe walls they stayed naturally cool – how? How are modern houses kept cool in hot countries today and what are the problems?

9.12   Co-ordinates Game

Aim. To understand and use coordinates. To develop observational skills.

In Brief. Teams of students utilize a grid of coordinates marked out on a school field to plot coordinates and compete for accurate outcomes.

What you will need:

Access to field or playground .

Quality chalk if marking on tarmac, line paint if using a field.

Method.

1. The class should be familiar with plotting coordinates on graph paper. Discuss alignments with the students. Thus, 3 points on the precise 'X 5' axis can be said to be in alignment. Discuss how an alignment might be checked on open ground – surveying with a laser, theodolite, a cord stretched between two points, or two observers noting when an object or third person is positioned precisely between them.

2. On the field, use your students to set out the square. Using the corner of a football pitch or other alignment point, such as the sides of a building, set out your coordinates. The distances between points depends on the space available. A 50 metre square, for example, is marked out at 5 metre intervals around the perimeter to produce a 10 squares by 10 squares grid. If a 25metre square is available, the perimeter is marked out at 2.5 metre intervals. The squares themselves are not marked, but exist as 'sightlines'. Thus a stake marked 'X 3' is paired with another also marked 'X 3' on the opposite side of the square. To find a position, student observers stand at the opposing markers and hold their hands up to signal when a third student is stood in precise alignment between them. Thus two students stood at the opposing 'X 5' axis and another two students stood at the 'Y 5' axis will be able to guide a fifth student to the precise centre of the square. Expect this to take about 20 minutes.

3. Demonstrate and practice finding coordinates by positioning a student in the precise centre of the square, using 4 'sighters' as set out above. Practice further by directing groups of 4 'sighters', to position a student at different coordinates of your choice.

4. Divide the class into 2 teams. Each team will consist of 4 'sighters' and the remainder of each team will be positioned on the square. Give each team a different set of coordinates which are used to position their players. Teams should be able to position their players in 5 to 7 minutes. When all the players are in position, the teacher collects in the lists of coordinates.

5. In the next stage the teams of sighters calculate the position of the opponent's players in turn, starting with the player nearest the origin, with the teacher acting as referee. If the coordinates called out are correct, the player leaves the field. If the coordinates are incorrect, the player stays on the field and the team must try again on their next turn. The winning team is the one that correctly calls the coordinates of the opponent's positions with fewest errors.

Reflection. Coordinates are used for many important functions. Find out and discuss how coordinates are used by walkers, surveyors, builders, the army and drivers using satnavs. How accurate do they think the human eye is in fixing coordinates? Where do satnav coordinates come from?

10. TRADITIONAL TECHNOLOGY

Arrow-making, Willow bridges, Hurdles, Travois, Shadufs, Soakaways, Mill race, Building a school pond, Cob bread oven, Rope bridge.

The activities in this chapter are linked by their nature as craft activities. At the same time they throw light on simple, ancient and sustainable solutions to human needs – hunting, transporting things, managing water, making fences, and baking bread.

As a boy I made bows and arrows – hence the first activity – a skill that I acquired from I know not where. Kids love making bows and arrows, and as you watch youngsters at work, you begin to wonder if the craft has somehow worked itself into our genes. Countless generations have made hurdles to keep their animals safe. The same basic technique was used for making everything from baskets to fish traps. The occupants of the timber framed houses of the Tudors, the Saxon drinking halls and the Celtic roundhouses would all have been familiar with hurdles. Hurdles are usually made with hazel and willow. The techniques of working with willow are not complicated and can be learned with a little training and practice.

Woven panels of willow or hazel were also used as partitioning and wall material in timber-framed houses. The technique is often referred to as wattle and daub. It is what it sounds like. Sticks of whatever wood happened to be available, were cut and woven together to make the panels. These were fixed into place and plastered on both sides with a mix of clay, sand, chopped straw and water. As a traditional craft, making cob is accessible to children and a lot of (rather dirty) fun. In the old days, a large dollop of cow poo made the material even stonger. A great mixture for cob is 4 parts sand, 2 parts clay, 1 part cow poo and some well chopped straw or horse hair. The result is a wall that could last for centuries if suitably painted and protected from the elements. It all sounds a bit primitive – but there is a lot of science in exploring what makes cob so versatile. Dried clay or mud is brittle and inflexible – but mix some sand and chopped straw or horsehair with it and daub it onto a willow hurdle and you have a walling material that is both flexible and strong. It is popular today as an innovative building material with a very low carbon footprint. In hot countries houses built with thick walls of mud or adobe don't need air-conditioning because thick mud walls keep a house warm at night and cool in the day.

Working with natural materials, in short, embeds basic lessons about getting the best out of any material. The fabric of innovation (and therefore wealth creation) lies in the ability to see the potential of the materials and technologies available to us. And natural materials have the advantage of being cheap, relatively low in carbon footprint, and bio-degradable.

Water. This chapter has three water related activities – making and utilizing shadufs, soakaways and school ponds. The activities were developed in response to schools doing topic work on water. A working shaduf can be made in a single lesson and is a great Science or Geography activity. At the other end of the scale, the pond project requires a significant investment in time and resources and is a whole school commitment.

School ponds can be a real focus for bringing the Science curriculum to life. We have also seen ponds neglected, abandoned and filled in. Some of this is to do with the type of pond and its location. A pond needs to be large enough to sustain the full range of pond life, be relatively self-maintaining, and close enough to the school buildings for supervision and regular access in all weathers. It is also about pond activities.

Teachers need a structured programme of pond activities, such as recording seasonal changes in the pond, studies of wildlife and flora in the immediate area, and regular visits to map the life cycle of specific species. Pond-dipping will be a part of this, but should not be a daily activity if you want your pond life to thrive.

10.1 Arrows

Aim. To explore aspects of aerodynamics. To practice the craft of fletching.

In Brief. Students make an arrow with hazel or willow and fletch it with feathers they have found (*see fig 10.1*).

What you will need:

Good, straight sticks approx. 1cm in diameter and 75cm long, one per student. Woollen thread or a fine green sisal garden twine to bind the flights. Safety knives. Scissors. Mini hacksaws with wood cutting blades. Log stumps to saw on. PVA or good glue stick to hold flights to the shaft. *	Loppers - if you intend to harvest your material from the tree. If you wish to experiment with straightening arrows, have a small fire available. If a patch of coppice hazel or willow is available students can select and cut their own with loppers (*use of loppers by students requires 1:1 supervision*). If willow or hazel is not available, consider buying a bundle of withies from a fencing supplier (approx. £15 to £25 per 100).

For the flights: The wing feathers of most large birds are good for fletching. One 20cm long feather will fletch an arrow. Goose and turkey wing feathers are perhaps the best. Easiest to find are pigeon feathers and they make perfectly good flights. Encourage pupils to collect and bring in feathers ahead of the activity.

* To make safety tips, provide a couple of old bicycle inner tubes - see step 12.

Method.

1. Discuss the antiquity of the arrow, one of the earliest forms of hunting missile, and how it works. What is the purpose of the flights and why is a weight needed at the front? Discuss other forms of missile. Missiles usually have flights of some sort, even space rockets. Flights create drag, thus preventing tumbling and impart a certain amount of spin that improves accuracy in flight. The straighter the shaft of the arrow and the more symmetrical the flights the straighter the arrow flies.

2. **Prepare the shaft**. Have the students check their arrow for straightness by looking along its length. Green wood arrows can be gently bent into shape by flexing the arrow in the opposite direction to the bend. A small amount of applied warmth, even hand warmth, helps to soften the wood. More properly, the section to be bent can be heated briefly (a few seconds) above a small fire to make it supple.

3. Remove any protrusions with a safety knife. To facilitate flight attachment, carefully peel off the bark from the last 15cms of the shaft. If the bark is 'ringed' first this can be done very neatly.

4. **Prepare the flights**. This is a good time to discuss the construction of a flight feather. The quill or shaft of a feather is hollow for lightness, but contains a cellular framework to strengthen it. The branches or barbs of the feather have tiny hooks holding then together, so stroking a feather can repair it where the barbs have come apart.

5. If you are using feathers with very thick quills, such as goose, these will need splitting down the length of the quill. Cut off the quill tip (the bit that goes into the bird) and cut along the length of the quill with scissors to split the feather in half. If the quill is thick and hard, use a log stump and safety knife. For smaller feathers, simply strip away the barbs on the short side of the feather by hand.

6. Students now select three flights. They should look for feathers with an identical profile – that is, the barbs curve in the same direction.

7. From each feather, select the 14cm length that will become the flight. Very carefully, strip away 2cms of barbs above and below the flight so it can be tied to the shaft. Repeat this with the next feather until three flights of near identical profile have been produced.

8. Cutting the nock. Cutting a nock or notch for the bowstring enables the flights to be correctly positioned. The flight end of the shaft is held firmly on the log stump by a gloved student whilst the second cuts a neat 'V' in the end of the shaft no deeper than the mini hacksaw blade. A deep 'V' may cause the arrow to split in use.

9. Attaching the flights. Finish the preparation of the flights by smearing a small amount of PVA glue or glue stick along the rear of the quill where it will come into contact with the shaft. Also smear glue on the twine or wool used to tie the flight to the shaft. Carefully position the flights so they are parallel to the shaft, equally spaced and perfectly level with each other.

10. The flights are tied to the shaft by wrapping thread round the stripped area of bare quill at the top and bottom of the flights (see fig 10.1). This should be done neatly. Avoid overlapping of the thread. Ensure the entire length of the quill is in contact with the shaft.

11. Additional glue can be added by using a twig to apply PVA to the quill once it is tied to the shaft. PVA needs 30 minutes to become touch dry on a warm day. It is solvent in rain until completely dry.

12. Making the tip. It should be stressed to the students that they must never throw the arrows at each other. They can easily break skin even with a blunt end and, at worst, could blind someone. Use a safety knife to trim the edges of the point to produce a rounded profile. Re-enactment suppliers sell rubber tips (Red Heads Blunts), which can be used to weight the ends. At 80 pence each, however, they are expensive. An alternative is to use a piece of old bicycle inner tube cut into 5-10cm lengths. These can be slipped over the end of the shaft, folded over and in, and secured with twine.

13. Trying out the arrows. The arrow can be tried by throwing by hand so that it achieves an arched trajectory. The end result is judged not just by distance but quality of flight. Does the arrow wobble or obviously fly off course? Alternatively, a couple of temporary bows can be assembled using green hazel and twine to test them. We do not make bows with students to be taken away.

Reflection. What qualities do you need to make a good arrow? Are you pleased with your results? Discuss with a partner if you found this an enjoyable activity and what aspects you found easy or difficult.

Fig 10.1   Making Arrows

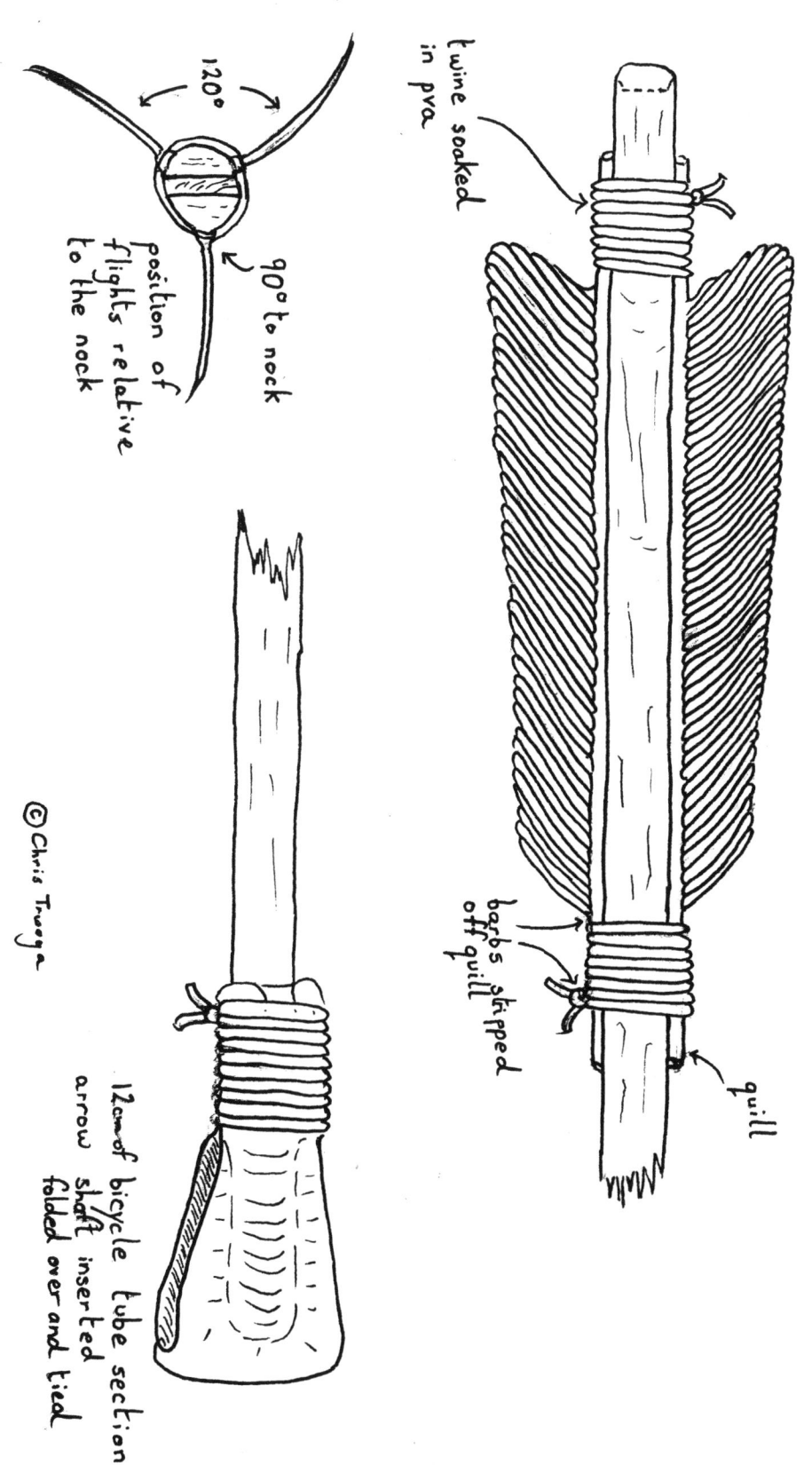

120°

twine soaked in pva

90° to nock

position of flights relative to the nock

© Chris Trooga

barbs stripped off quill

quill

12cm of bicycle tube section arrow shaft inserted folded over and tied

10.2 Miniature Willow Bridges

Aim. To develop understanding of forces by constructing suspension and arched bridge forms. To develop skills in working effectively as a team.

In Brief. Students construct bridges out of withies and twine capable of being loaded with 10 kilos at the centre of the span (*see fig. 10.2*).

What you will need:

Per group of 4 – 6 students: a bundle of 25 thin hazel sticks, garden canes, or withies, average length of 1m and a diameter of 1cm.	A bundle of 20 short, thinner sticks (diamter less than 1cm) of about 30cm in length to support a variety in construction techniques.
A ball of two ply twine, a pair of safety scissors, a dozen or so steel tent pegs and a rubber mallet. Sharpened sticks and mallets are useful for making holes if the ground is hard.	*For the groups to share*: 10 kg of weight-training discs to test the bridges. We also supply a metre ruler to ensure the bridge conforms to the span requirements.

Method.

1. The group should already be familiar with different methods of making a load-bearing bridge; suspension, arched and box section bridges being the most common. Discuss how the forces are distributed through such structures under load and in what manner and direction they are communicated to the ground. Explain the activity. The task is to construct a bridge with a typical ground clearance of 50cms and a span of one metre, capable of taking a 10 kilo load at the centre. The bridge must provide a suitable platform at the centre on which to place the test 10 kilo weights.

2. Discuss possible structural forms, such as arches, box sections and suspension bridges. Alternatively, you may wish to restrict them to a specific structural form, such as the suspension bridge. Provide any necessary guidance with basic construction techniques with thin willow, such as constructing tripods. With younger groups you may wish to practice with towers and knot tying before they begin their bridges (*see fig 4.3*). To ensure structure reflects real designs, do not allow several sticks to be bundled together. A well made withy suspension bridge will take the weight comfortably with only two 5mm withies for the actual bridge span.

3. Observe the groups and allow sufficient time for the bridges to be constructed with care and attention to appearance as well as form. Encourage neat knot tying.

4. Once the bridges are complete, test with the 10 kilo weights. If a bridge fails allow time to discuss the causes of failure. Explore with the students how the load is being distributed and where the forces are being transferred.

Reflection. Did making the bridge help you understand the distribution of forces in such structures? The Victorians built bridges of brick, stone and iron. Which of these materials do sticks behave like? Think about the impact on bridges of modern traffic. Why do bridges have to be regularly checked? Why is a fixed load not a proper test for a bridge that carries road or rail traffic?

Fig 10.2   Miniature Willow Bridge

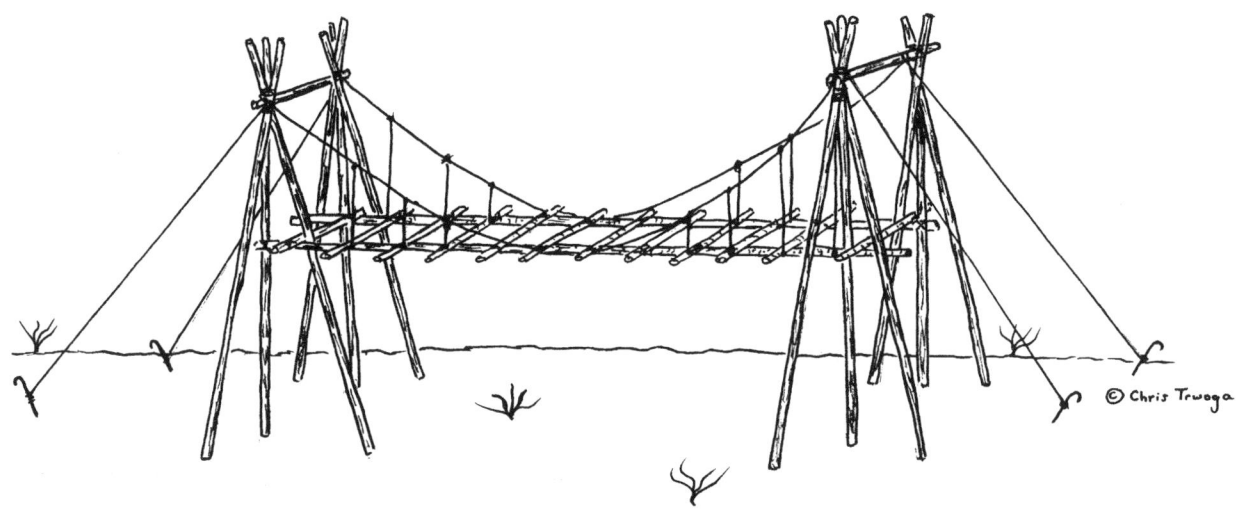

Twine and Willow Suspension Bridge
Castle Cary 2010

10.3 Hurdles

Aim. To practice the craft of hurdle making & appreciate its traditional applications.

In Brief. Students make a hurdle, miniature or full-scale, for a practical application.

What you will need: (To make a hurdle 1 metre wide and 75cm high).

6 relatively straight hazel sticks, 1m in length and about 2cm diameter - these are your "sails". Bill hook or loppers to sharpen sail ends. A bow saw to cut sails to length, loppers or secateurs to trim willow (*adult use only or 1-1 supervsion*), string for temporary tying, and a light, wooden mallet or piece of wood for tapping down the weaves.	For the weaving material, or weft, use willow (approx. £15 for a bundle of about 100). Alternatively, harvest in your woodland space for thin willow, hazel and other trees producing thin, straight sticks. The willow should be a centimetre or under in thickness for ease of weaving.

Tip: It is just as much fun to make mini-hurdles at 50cm sq for decorative purposes.

Method.

1. Discuss the role of walls and fences in settled lifestyles. Explain how hurdles are made by a weaving process and are probably the oldest form of fencing. What will your hurdle(s) be used for?

2. Once you know the size and number of hurdles you require, source your hazel or willow sails. The distance between them will depend on the width of the panel. The traditional distance is 9 inches. For a 1m wide panel 20cm is about right and requires 6 sails or uprights.

3. Push or tap the sails into the ground at the required distances apart. For a 75cm high hurdle go 20-25cm into the soil. Fence-makers use a 'mould' - a block of timber the length of the hurdle, drilled at 9" intervals (see *fig 10.3*). With the uprights in place, begin weaving!

4. Weave from the top. Once the withy is woven between all the sails, carefully push or tap it down with a mallet to the base of the uprights. This first weave and every fifth weave thereafter should project 25cm beyond the sails so it can be woven back on itself and round the second sail. This is known as a twist (*see fig 10.3*). To make the twist easier, start with the thinner end of your withy to the left. The second withy starts with the thin end to the right and the twist will be on the right. Thus the twist is applied to every fifth pair of withies.   By alternating the direction you weave from with tapering withies, the hurdle will weave level and create a more attractive appearance.

5. As they are doing the first few weaves ensure the students check the sails for straightness and correct as necessary. If you are making a continuous fence, such as round a pond, it is only the end sails that need to be secured with twists. The first few weaves are the hardest, and if sticks aren't secure in the ground they will move about and the hurdle may fall apart. Once the hurdle is complete, ensure that the top weave is firmly woven twisted back on itself. For strength the top withy should be woven downwards into the last three weaves. Leave the last 8cms or so of sail clear so that the last weave cannot easily slip off the top.

Reflection. Hurdle-making was once a vital rural craft. Discuss all the modern materials and processes that have replaced hurdles. Do hurdles have advantages over the modern versions? How do you feel about learning this skill? What qualities do you need as an individual to do this well? How might those qualities apply to other areas of life?

Fig 10.3   Making Hurdles

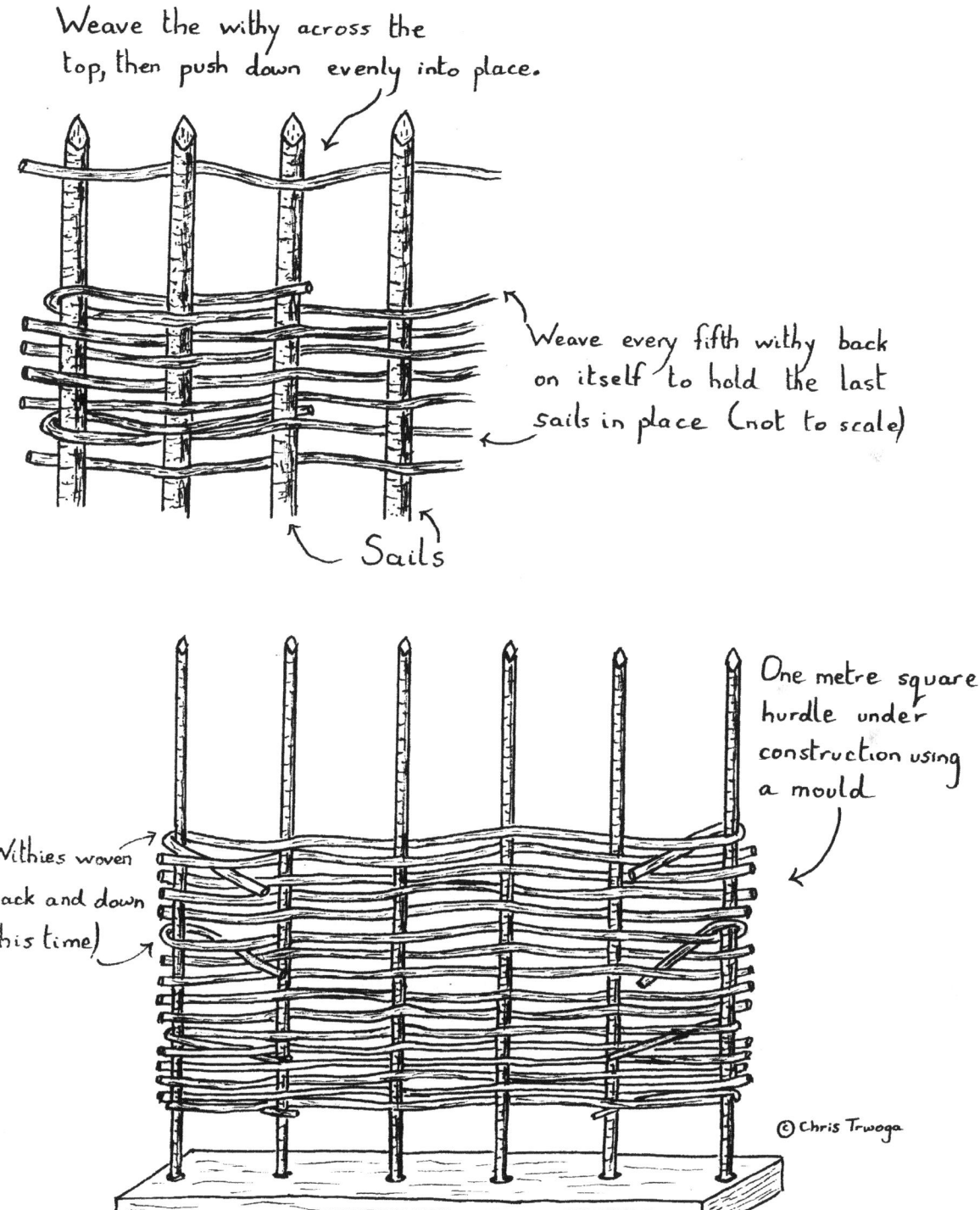

Weave the withy across the
top, then push down evenly into place.

Weave every fifth withy back
on itself to hold the last
sails in place (not to scale)

Sails

One metre square
hurdle under
construction using
a mould

(Withies woven
back and down
this time)

© Chris Trwoga

235

10. 4 Travois Races - Native American Transportation

Aim. To solve problems associated with moving heavy objects. To develop construction skills & problem-solving as a team. To gain insights into Native American culture.

In Brief. Students make two or more travois capable of carrying a person, which are tested in a race (*see fig 10.4*).

What you will need: (one travois kit per 4-6 students is ideal).

*For one travois kit with ready cut poles: * * 4 poles 3.5m long and 5cm average diameter. 8 poles 1.2m long and 3cm average diameter. A bale of 2 – 3 ply twine.*** Safety scissors.	We often run this activity alongside tipi making (*activity 1.6*), and making dream-catchers (*activity 5.9*), so that a full class can be involved in a carousel of activities with a Native American theme.
* A travois, capable of carrying a person, can be made by a team of 4 – 6 students in 30 mins or less. *** Note, this activity may use several metres of twine per travois.*	

Method.

1. Discuss non-mechanized modes of transport, including horse, cart and sled. Consider the role of the wheel. What forms of transport were available prior to the wheel? Look at forms of sled, including travois, that would have been widely used until recent times. For a nomadic people the advantage is simplicity of construction and availability of all the necessary materials.

1. Rather than provide detailed diagrams, as shown opposite, we use laminated photographs of Native American travois. This makes it more of a problem-solving activity as students have to come up with their own construction method. For inspiration look up 'travois racing' online. At time of writing, a YouTube video was posted under 'travois races'.

2. Study the images of travois and how they are pulled. Traditionally travois are pulled by horses, dogs and people. What would be the best design if it is being pulled by 2 – 4 people? Look at how the frame might be braced to provide rigidity. Practice knot-tying.

3. Issue the pole kits. Explain that if the long poles are likely to bend too much under load to consider doubling up. Then leave them to it. ***Note: as a Forest School activity, students can source their own wood and cut poles to size themselves.***

4. Once the travois are complete encourage the teams to check the sturdiness of the frame and the quality of the knots. If okay, test for a short distance carrying a person. The travois can now be raced against each other, with matched teams of two to four pulling one passenger. A good travois will stand the strain. If knots, design or materials are substandard, the travois will come apart.

Reflection. Why is transport so important to us? What important human activities does a basic transport system like a travois facilitate? Study the travois. What are its advantages over simply carrying something on your back? Reflect on your enjoyment of the activity. What factors contributed to your enjoyment?

Fig 10.4   Making a Traditional Travois

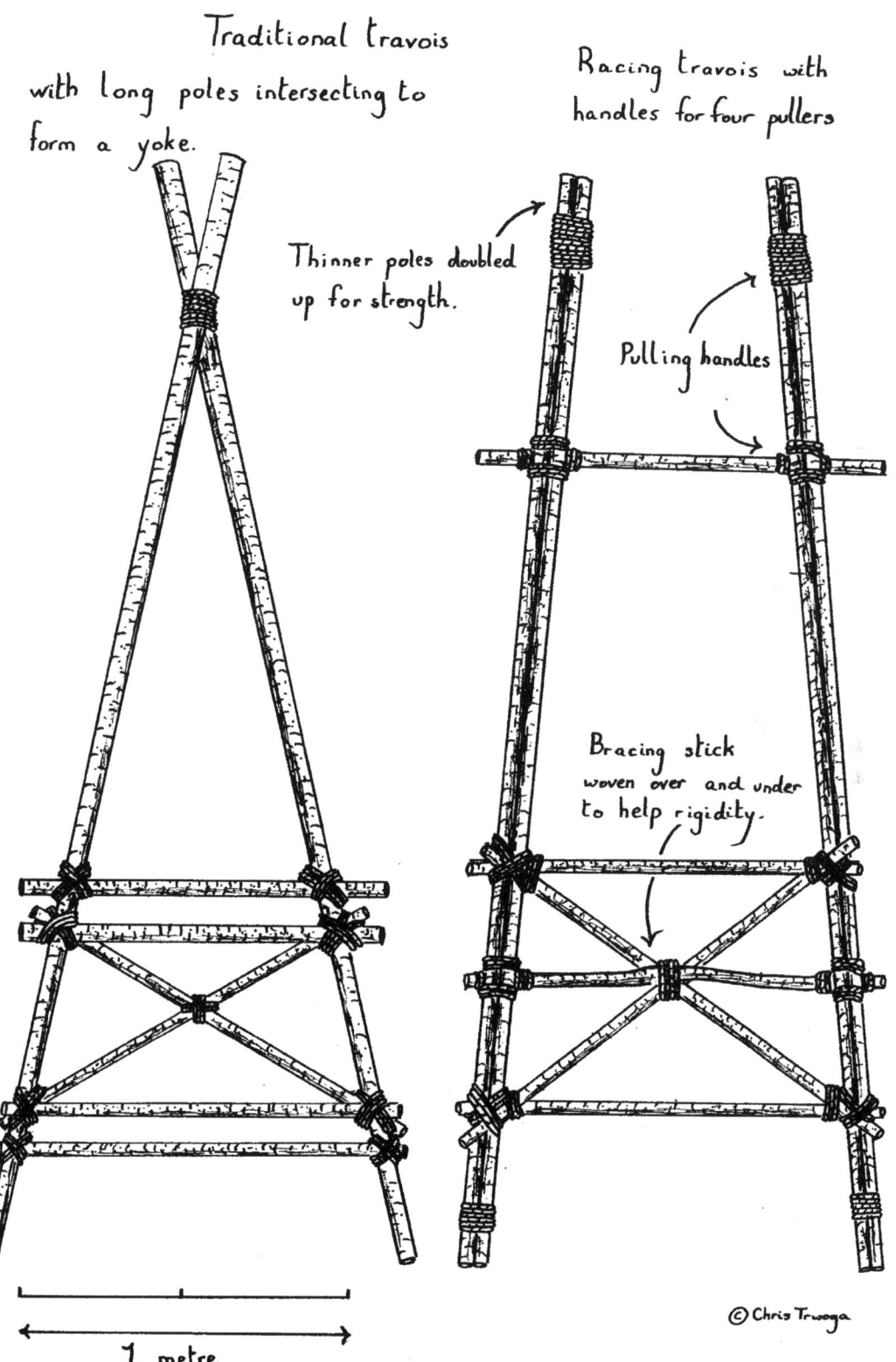

Traditional travois with long poles intersecting to form a yoke.

Racing travois with handles for four pullers

Thinner poles doubled up for strength.

Pulling handles

Bracing stick woven over and under to help rigidity.

1 metre

© Chris Trwoga

10.5 Water: Making a Shaduf

Aim. To explore early technologies for raising water and irrigation. To study the use of counterbalances and levers to raise heavy objects.

In Brief. Students make a working half-scale shaduf (*see fig 10.5*).

What you will need: (4 to 6 students per shaduf).

*For one shaduf kit with ready cut poles:**	
1 reasonably straight pole - about 3m long and 5 to 7cm thick.	A small flexible bucket or similar
7 poles about 1.2m long and 4cm thick with sharpened ends for hammering into the ground.	A bale of two-ply sisal twine.
	Safety scissors and a rubber mallet.
A hessian sandbag filled with sand.	Laminated photographs of Egyptian shadufs for design inspiration.

* As a Forest School activity the shaduf might be made from scratch, with the students sourcing the timber materials. For this you need to provide bow saw and saw horse to saw your poles to length.

Method.

1. In class, study different methods used for raising water before the invention of motorised pumps. These include waterwheels, Archimedes screw and a bucket on a rope.

2. Identify your water source or provide an artificial source, such as a large tub of water.

3. First make the fulcrum on which to balance the pole (lever). This needs to be about 1.2m from the ground and sturdily supported on two tripods, 75cm apart, made from the 1.2m poles. For each tripod drive 3 poles into the ground to form a triangle with 30cm sides. Bend them in and tie together very firmly. Rest the fulcrum pole across the tripods and lash it firmly to both tripods. Check the structure is very stable and capable of supporting 25kg.

4. Position the lever in the middle of the fulcrum with the thinner end of the pole facing the water source. Tie the pole to the fulcrum so that it is firmly held but can swing up and down. The pole is not balanced but has one third of the pole on the counterbalance side and two-thirds on the water carrier side. Attach the bucket or water carrier to the end of the pole. The bucket should be able to swing freely so that water does not tip out as it rises and falls. Ensure the carrier sinks into the water. This can be achieved by weighting it (see fig 10.5).

5. Now, counterbalance the pole. Wrap the sandbag round the short end of the pole tie firmly. The pole (lever) should be balanced such that the pole has to be pulled down towards the water and the counterweight should be capable of lifting the bucket part-filled with water. Adjustment can be made by sliding the pole (lever) backwards and forwards across the fulcrum.

6. Use the shaduf for several minutes. How does is compare in effort with raising a bucket of water by hand? Continue to adjust the pole and weight to minimize effort.

Reflection. Why do some people describe water as 'precious'? Do you think we treat water with enough respect? Along the Nile, the sound of petrol-powered water pumps for irrigation is now very common. Pumps are used around the world to get water out of the ground. How can this affect the water table? Find out how water pumps can transform a community's standard of living? But for how long?

Fig 10.5   Making a Shaduf

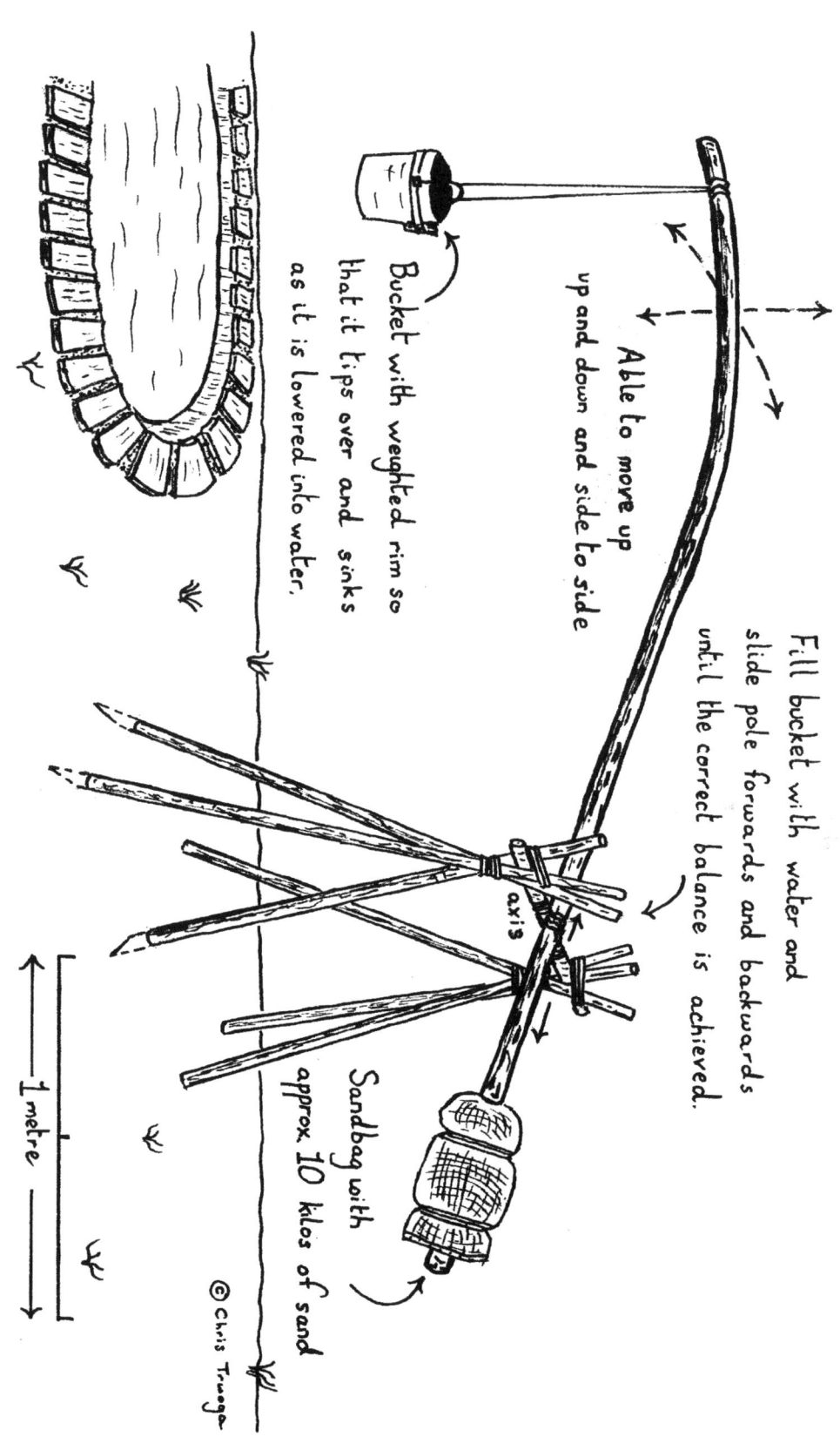

Able to move up and down and side to side

Bucket with weighted rim so that it tips over and sinks as it is lowered into water.

Fill bucket with water and slide pole forwards and backwards until the correct balance is achieved.

axis

Sandbag with approx. 10 kilos of sand

1 metre

© Chris Truega

10.6 Water: Digging a Soakaway

Aim. To gain insight into water management and drainage. To understand how storm water from domestic roofs is disposed of so that it does not overload the sewage system. To provide a practical solution to a water drainage issue.

In Brief. Students make a soakaway by digging a trench, filling it with gravel and crocks and covering it over.

What you will need:

Tools: Spades of appropriate size for your students* Hard plastic trowels for younger children. Flexible buckets for soil removal.	*Materials:* About 50 kg of gravel. A couple of buckets of large clay crocks. A 65cm length of soil pipe or gutter downpipe. A tarpaulin to store soil on.
*Use Hard hats, protective gloves & reinforced toe boots if digging with steel spades.	

Method.

1. Discuss why drainage is important in any built-up area. Why does rainwater have to be taken away from buildings? (damage to foundations and localized flooding).   Explain soakaway construction - the principal is to create a highly porous sub-soil layer to speed up the process of water soaking away without saturating the surface soil. They are constructed under grassed areas, such as playing fields or gardens, to improve drainage.

2. Take the group on a tour of the school site and identify where soakaways may already be in use. Identify a location where it might be useful to construct one - carry out a soakaway experiment. Alternatively, construct a soakaway to take waste water from the end of a mill race (see 10.7).

3. Dig the trench. For safety reasons only a limited number of students can dig at the same time, Teamwork is therefore needed with other children carrying the soil away. If digging a grassed area, carefully remove the turf in 20cm squares so that it can be replaced. Dig the hole to your chosen dimensions. Remember to cover the hole with a board and mark with cones, or surround with temporary fencing if an unfinished hole is to be left unsupervised.

4. Pour the gravel or small grade hardcore into the hole. Ensure there is at least 30cm of space left above for crocks and backfill. Carefully tamp down the gravel or hardcore without compressing it into the subsoil. This is to prevent subsidence. Use a suitable timber post. Take care to avoid injury to feet and shins and only one post should be in action at any one time. Place the crocks carefully over the gravel or hardcore. If you are going to use a drainpipe insert it at this point so that it drains into the gravel and the end is covered with crocks to prevent soil entering. Backfill the hole with soil and replace the turf as necessary. Alternatively, the hole can be topped up with gravel to surface level to make a garden drain. Trial your soakaway by pouring several buckets of water into it. Compare with just pouring water onto the ground. How effective is it?

Reflection.   Many gardens and playing fields need soakaways. Discuss why they are considered good for the environment? What else can we do with rainwater so that it doesn't go into our sewers? Consider the measures you used to work safely. Why are they important? Did your project go smoothly? What were you pleased with? How might you improve on how you worked as a team?

10.7 Water: Constructing a Mill/ Marble Race

Aim. To explore the dynamics of moving water in a raised watercourse. To provide a device to support a variety of water based experiments.

In Brief. Students make portable supports from hazel poles to support a water course constructed of reclaimed plastic guttering (*see fig 10.7*).

What you will need:

Materials (per frame):	Tools:
4 hazel poles approx 80cm long	A bale of 2 or 3 ply twine .
6 hazel poles approx 60cm long.	Scissors.
a length of guttering approx 2m long.	Mini hacksaws and log stumps or saw horse to -
Make 4 - 6 frames for a decent run.	if cutting poles in situ.

Method.

1. Discuss the use of open guttering - e.g. on houses to transport rainwater. On water mills a timber water course or 'race' would deliver the water to the waterwheel. The Romans transported water on stone aqueducts or in lead or timber channels.

2. Construct the frames. Demonstrate the frame construction technique (*see fig 10.7*). Two of the 60cm sticks are tied firmly together in the middle to make an 'X'. The two 80cm uprights are laid on the ground parallel to each other and about 35cms apart. The 'X' frame is then firmly tied to the sticks at the four crossover points. Finally, another 60 cm stick is tied between the two uprights to give the frame extra rigidity. I suggest to the students that the final stick can be woven between the uprights and the 'X' frame prior to tying as this tightens the frame and makes it much more rigid. In groups of 3 or 4 now construct a pair of frames. They should aim to make their frames identical in height such that the two 'X's match up nicely.

3. The final construction stage is to tie the two frames together at the top of the uprights such that they can hinge in and out like an 'A' board. Finally, a length of string is tied between the two bracing sticks to limit how far the 'A' frame can be opened. Graduating the height of the frames. The guttering, or water channel, rests on the 'X' within the frame. The heights of your series of 'A' frames can be graduated by positioning the 'X's higher or lower on the uprights. The frames should be made to achieve a gradual downward slope. We usually find that natural 'error' results in differing heights.

4. Once the frames are complete, they can be spaced out and the guttering rested in place with the upper guttering overlapping the lower. Water can be supplied from a slow-running hose pipe, or a shaduf (*see activity 10.5*) to raise water from a ground based supply. A gentle gradient is best for sailing toy boats or irrigation. A slightly steeper slope provides a suitable slope for experimenting with the speeds of rolling objects

Reflection. In Britain, we often describe rain as 'bad' weather. In other parts of the world, lack of rainfall is a matter of life and death. Think of the things that would disappear from our lives if we lived in a desert country. In many major cities around the world, from Las Vegas to Mexico City and Bangalore, water shortages are a severe problem. Find out about water shortages in one of these cities. Do you agree when some people say that water is our most precious commodity?

Fig 10.7   Mill / Marble Race

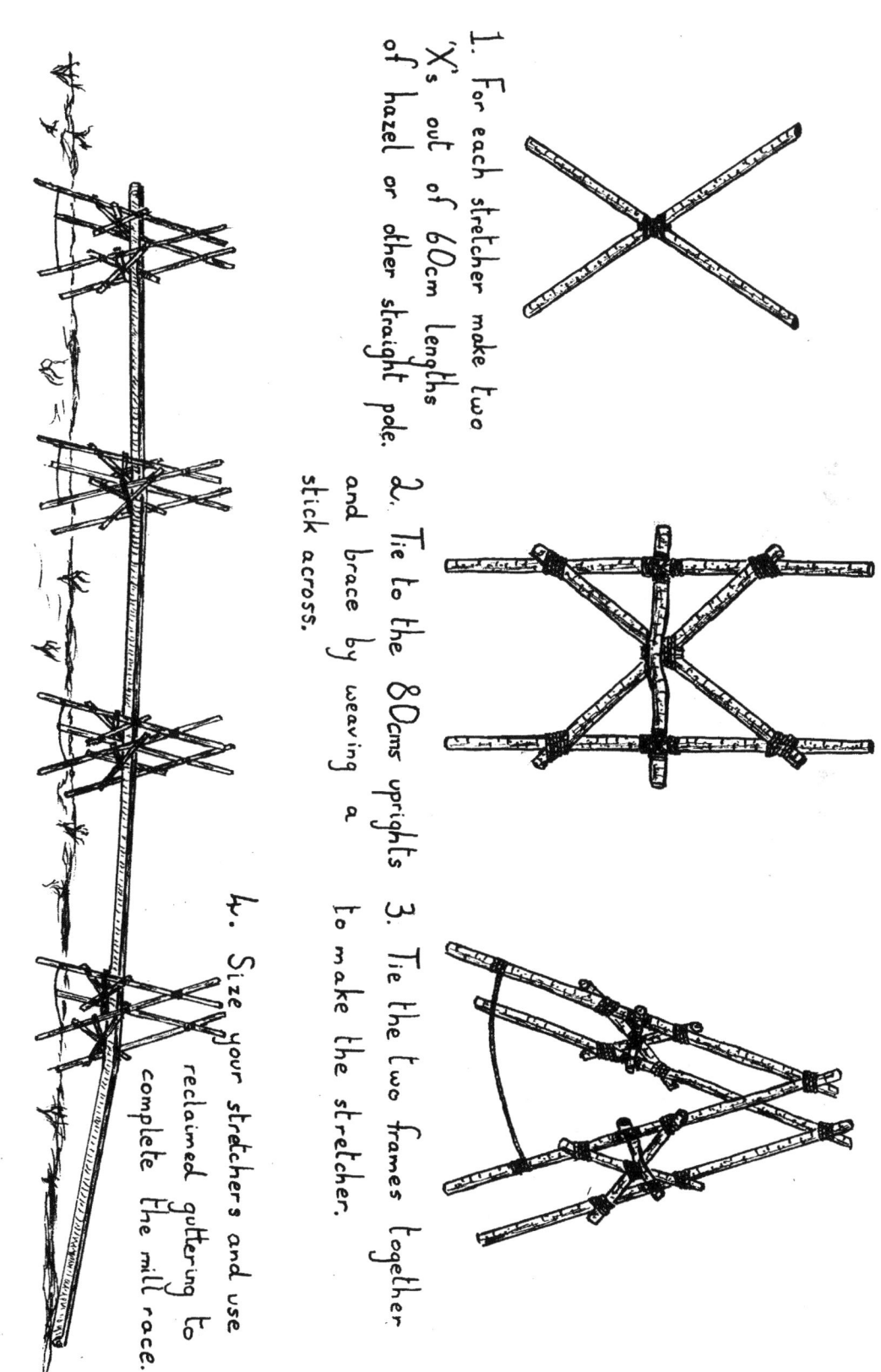

1. For each stretcher make two 'X's out of 60cm lengths of hazel or other straight pole.

2. Tie to the 80cms uprights and brace by weaving a stick across.

3. Tie the two frames together to make the stretcher.

4. Size your stretchers and use reclaimed guttering to complete the mill race.

10.8 Building a School Pond

Aim. To enable students to design and make a school pond to improve their school environment. To explore related environmental & biological themes.

In Brief. Students design and make a viable school pond.

What you will need:

For the pond liner. Do not use cheap PVC liner. Use .75mm thick butyl rubber (approx. £7.45 per sq m online). Alternatively, use an Epalyn liner at 1mm thick (approx. £6 per sq m online). *	
Pieces of old carpet to cover the pond basin before placing the liner - natural materials only.	
Materials: 20 or so second-hand paving slabs 50cm sq. 120 recycled bricks to support slabs. Sacks of large pebbles or similar to fill gaps between paving slabs and for your marsh area. Permanent fence with gate when complete (see activity 10.3)	*Tools:* 25m tape measure. 25m rope/hose pipe Steel spades of appropriate size for your students. ** Hard plastic trowels for young children. 6 small flexible buckets for soil removal. A couple of wheelbarrows.
*Don't buy your liner until the pond is dug and you are satisfied with the size and shape. ****Use Hard hats, protective gloves & reinforced toe boots if digging with steel spades.**	

Method. *(See also notes on p252)*

1. All ages can be included in this activity. Younger students usually love digging and will wallow in a muddy hole with abandon if you let them!

2. Talk about the importance of ponds as part of an ecosystem. Why do people make them? Take the group for a walk around the school grounds or garden to see if a suitable space exists. What would be an ideal size? Small ponds rarely thrive; a minimum size is around 3m by 2m with 50cm depth. Consider the practical issues. Is there good access from the school building? Are there nearby trees? - roots can be a problem, falling leaves will pollute the water.

3. **Explore pond design**. A wildlife pond is deep at one end and then rises to a marshy shelf at the other. The pond surround can be divided into an area with paving slabs that is used for pond-dipping and other access activities, and an area that is fenced off and never walked on to encourage natural vegetation and provide a mini wildlife reserve. Draw a plan with the students. Indicate the different depths, perhaps from 50cm to 40cm and then 30cm (a pond floor should not be built as a slope, but a series of levels to facilitate planting in pots).

4. **Start the dig!** Students mark out the pond shape with a rope or garden hose and the outline is cut through the turf. The turf should be removed in small easy to carry squares. The same applies for general digging. Younger children are happy to dig with mini-spades and trowels, but need help to loosen stones or break up hard patches. The topsoil beneath the turf often comes away easily, but expect harder stuff lower down. After a couple of digging sessions you will get some idea of how long it is going to take, given the nature of the ground.

5. **Prepare the pond for lining**. Once the hole is dug to the agreed dimensions, students check the surface carefully for sharp stones or any projections that might stress the lining. These are eased out. The surface can then be tamped down by foot. Lay your pieces of old carpets on the pond floor and sides to protect the lining. Dig a shelf, 15cm deep and 30cm wide to take the bricks that support the paving slabs around edge of the pond.

6. **Measure for the liner**. Using a piece of string stretched across the pond, find the longest axis and put two stakes in the ground 25cm from the edge to mark it. Do the same for the widest point. Lay a 25m tape loosely between the two long axis stakes so that it follows the contours of the pond and is in firm contact with the ground. Take the measurement at the second stake, thus allowing for the liner to hug the bottom of the pond and overlap by 25cm on both sides. Repeat the process between the two stakes that mark the maximum width. Buy your liner. Carefully unfold and place your into the hole. Now fill the pond.

7. **Create the paved area**. The paving slabs will rest on a shelf of bricks. For greater stability, the bricks face the pond, end on. The liner passes underneath the bricks. A layer of carpet or spare pond liner should be laid on the liner edge before the bricks are positioned. Place slabs around half the pond at the deep end. Leave the shallow, marshy area to develop as a wildlife reserve. Try to use slabs small enough for students to handle. If not, adults place and level them, students fill the gaps with pebbles. Tamp down the earth around the remainder of the pond with the flat of a spade. Now comes the fun bit! Obtain appropriate pond plants and plants for the marsh area. Concentrate the plants away from the paved area to allow viewing and pond-dipping. Use cobbles and water-worn pebbles to provide an attractive surface for your marshy area.

8. **Fence the pond.** Consider making a hurdle fence to a height of 1m (*see activity 10.3*), with a picket gate. I have also made and erected picket fencing with ten to fourteen year olds. Buy loose pickets and nail the palings together in 6ft sections. Students can dig postholes, help with leveling, hammer palings together. Mature students can use battery powered drills and screwdrivers to attach palings to posts. Be guided by your own risk assessments. Hurdle fence-making is recommended for the primary setting.

Reflection. Ponds create an opportunity for life. What other things can we do to encourage wildlife in our garden and school environment? A pond will thrive only if it becomes a successful ecosystem. Explore the things that need to be in place for your pond to support plants, insect life and amphibians. Tell the story of how the pond was made. Keep a diary if you can. What things went well? What difficulties did you have to overcome?

Pond building notes

Ponds are best positioned close to school buildings so that they can be readily accessed in most weathers and do not become neglected as a result of being in a remote and invisible corner of the school. Making a pond can be achieved in a week as part of a special curriculum event or over time as part of regular outdoor activities.

You will need a suitable site that can be fenced off. It should connect with other green spaces to facilitate the migration of amphibious pond life. Avoid overhanging trees as leaf litter is bad for water quality. Be clear about where the soil waste will go, bearing in mind that much of it may be heavy subsoil unsuitable for your school garden. Separate the topsoil and subsoil, so that the topsoil can be recycled. If you plan a large pond (say 5 metres by 4 metres and 60cm deep in the middle, and you want to save a lot of back-breaking work, hire someone with a small mechanical digger to do the main scoop. This job can often be done in a couple of hours.

10.9 Cob Bread Oven

Aim. To learn about a traditional building material and its manufacture and composition. To explore uses for the material by constructing an earth oven.

In Brief. Cob is produced from sand, clay and chopped straw and used to construct an oven on a 'wattle' frame (*see fig.10.9 p255*).

What you will need:

For weaving the dome frame: 12 thin withies of no more than 1cm in thickness and a bundle of thinner, green withies. A ball of twine to tie the frame to shape. Tarpaulin to protect your work from rain during the construction phase.	*Tools:* Steel spades* for mixing the cob (plastic trowels for small children), A couple of buckets, loppers or secateurs (adult use only) to trim the hazel or willow.
For the cob: A source of good heavy clay - it is very useful if you live in a clay area! A small amount of water. At least a 100 kg of sharp sand (source from any D.I.Y. store or builder's merchant) . A few carrier bags of chopped straw.	Wellies and waterproofs - working with cob is messy! *For the oven floor:* a firm area of ground and a dozen or so reclaimed bricks.

**Use Hard hats, protective gloves & reinforced toe boots if digging with steel spades.

Making a cob oven is a project that takes a number of sessions to allow the cob to dry and complete the work. Getting the cob right isn't always easy, and an apparently well-made oven can sometimes develop cracks or simply disintegrate.   Cob ovens are often built on a raised platform of bricks or concrete slabs. In the British climate, these structures have a limited life-span unless covered with a canopy, as they are eroded by rain. Cob houses in Britain are protected by very wide eaves that keep the rain off the walls.

Method.

1. Discuss the type of fire you are making with your group. A cob or bread oven is the most ancient form of oven and has been in use for thousands of years. There are still many parts of the world where they remain in use. In this type of oven, a fire is lit inside the oven and allowed to burn to ashes. The ashes are raked out and the bread placed in the oven. The heat retained in the mass of the oven walls cooks the bread. The advantage of this type of oven is that it produces a moist bread, as combustion is no longer happening in the cooking space. In a typical village setting there will be one very large bread oven that is heated up overnight. Early in the morning, the villagers will bring along their loaves to bake in the communal oven. Dried clay cracks and breaks up very quickly. Explore how cob is made to overcome the problem of cracking. The mixture is similar to that used to make earthenware pots, or even cement, where silica (sand) is added to bond the material. Practice making a small amount of cob and make small bricks with it. Does it crack as it dries or does it hold together?

2. **Mix the cob on an old tarpaulin**. The soil you use should be 'clay rich', the kind that sticks to your boots in thick layers. Add sharp or coarse builder's sand; that's the type that's used to make

concrete. The amount of sand you add depends on how gritty the clay soil is, but an average mix is 75% sharp sand and 25% clay. Cob only works if it is properly mixed. This is best done by mashing it for some time by treading all over it in wellies. The texture you're aiming for is something that looks and feels like horse dung. If needed, add enough water so that it can be moulded into a ball of cob that holds together nicely. If the cob is the correct mix it will dry without cracking. Normally, chopped straw is added too. When making a cob oven, however, the inner layer of cob is usually mixed without straw.

3. **Make the frame**. The function of the woven frame is to support the oven structurally whilst it is being made. The frame will be burned away once the oven is in use. Mark out a ring of 10 holes to form circle of around 60cms diameter. Insert the hazel or willow, bend over and tie off in pairs to make a dome. Strengthen by weaving thinner withies around the dome and by further tying. Next, decide where the door is going to be, trim away the withies with secateurs or loppers and re-tie any material that springs out of shape.

4. The door needs to be about 30cms wide and 25cm high, so you can slide in an average baking tray. A good way to get the shape right is to make the oven door at this stage. To retain heat the door needs to be made of material that is at least 3cms thick (a 30 cm length of old scaffolding plank is ideal). Nail a piece of battening across one side of the door to act as a handle. The inner face is then lined with tinfoil to reflect the heat. This should be nailed to the oven door and the edges snipped to shape so it can be bent round and nailed to the sides.

5. **Make the floor**. Begin by placing a line of bricks across the oven door (*see fig 10.9*). The bricks should be half way across the doorway to make it easier to slide the baking tray in and out. The willow frame can be covered in old cotton fabric or newspaper tied with tape or string to prevent the cob falling into the oven space.

6. **Now comes the dirty work**! Apply the cob, to the floor first, building up a layer to the height of the bricks. Now start to shape the oven. Start at the base and work up. Press the cob firmly into the willow to achieve a good key. Apply the cob in a 6cm thick layer. Press downwards, not inwards, to avoid damaging the frame. Once the first layer is in place, wet the surface of the cob and apply a further layers until you achieve a thickness of about 10cm.

7. For the next layers add chopped straw to your cob to strengthen it and resist cracking. The chopped straw should be about 10cms in length and mixed in to the kind of quantity you would find in horse manure. You are looking to add enough cob to your oven dome to achieve an average thickness of 30cm.

8. Give the oven several days to dry before use. This helps to prevent cracking when the oven is fired for the first time. A bread oven works by heating up the whole oven, raking out the ashes and then inserting the dough. In ancient times, the loaves would have been slid into place on a wooden paddle – as they still are with a pizza oven – on a bed of leaves to stop them sticking to the oven floor. Use the oven door, so that the air temperature inside rises.

Reflection. Research the many traditional uses of cob, mud brick and adobe. Discuss why modern industrial societies don't use these materials. What has replaced them? What are the advantages and disadvantages of more modern materials such as concrete blocks and cement? Find out why some people have gone back to using cob and similar materials in construction work.

Fig 10.9 Cob Bread Oven

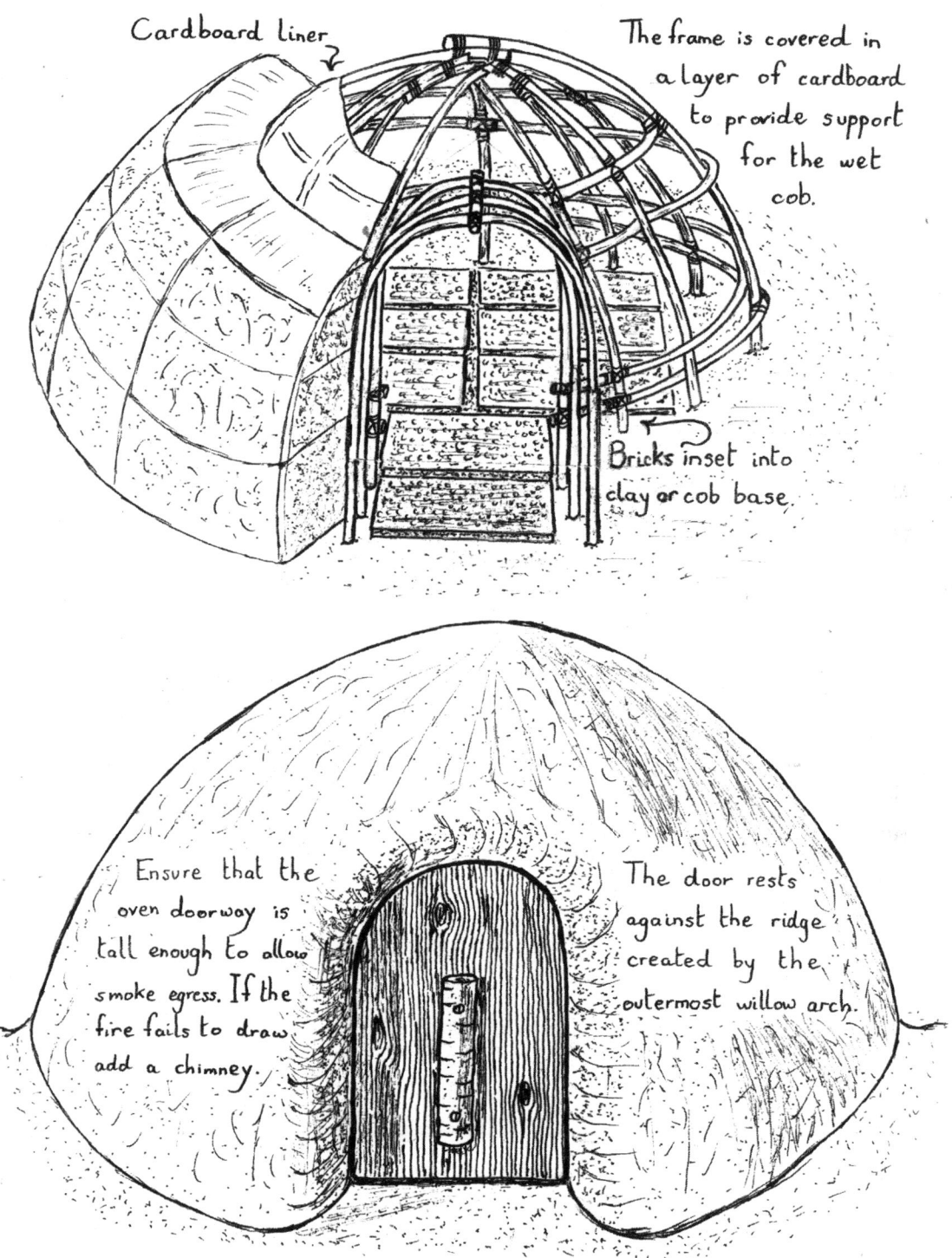

Cardboard liner

The frame is covered in a layer of cardboard to provide support for the wet cob.

Bricks inset into clay or cob base.

Ensure that the oven doorway is tall enough to allow smoke egress. If the fire fails to draw add a chimney.

The door rests against the ridge created by the outermost willow arch.

10.10 Rope Bridge

Aim. To develop team spirit in fulfilling tasks requiring the combined strength of the group. To develop skills in tying and tensioning ropes.

In Brief. Students construct a suspension bridge out of 16mm sisal rope or similar, capable of taking the weight of an adult (*see fig. 10.10*).

What you will need:

2 mature trees, about 4m apart, with a minimum 40cm girth at point of tying.
3 ropes of around 25m in length and between 12mm and 16mm in thickness.
A bale of three ply sisal twine for the vertical suspensions.

Tools: Safety scissors.

Safety tip: we recommend the wearing of sturdy gardening gloves for this activity.

Method. (usually take 45 minutes to an hour.).

1. If students are not already familiar with the concept of suspension bridges, use illustrations to explain how they work. In this activity the bridge is constructed between two trees; the load, therefore, must be transferred to the tree trunks. For safety reasons the lowest rope of the bridge is fixed no more than 75cm from the ground - above an area free of stumps or rocks. The most important aspect of a successful rope bridge is the tensioning of the ropes and good tying off. If a rope is slack or starts to work loose the bridge becomes unstable and unsafe - refer to the diagram for how to ensure good rope tension.

2. Attach the lower (foot) rope to the first tree so that it departs from the centre of the trunk at a height of around 75cms. Pass it round the trunk several times before tying off. Test the rope with several students pulling on it to make sure it can't work loose. Take the rope to the second tree. In tug of war fashion, use every available student to pull on the rope to tension it. With the rope under full and constant tension, the group walk it clockwise round the tree several times and tie off in the way shown opposite. The rope should be bowstring tight.

3. Next, tie the first 'handrail' rope to the tree about 75cm above the foot rope - this can be adjusted to the suit the average size of your children. Tie off in the way shown in the illustration to ensure that it stays to the left side of the trunk. Keep as much tension on the rope as possible whilst wrapping it round the tree; ensure there is no slackness in the coils or the knot tying. Under tension, tie the rope to the second tree. Repeat the process for the right-hand rope.

4. Once all three ropes are attached they should have a 'V' shaped profile. Now attach the suspension twine at 35cm intervals. Each piece of twine is tied to the left hand handrail, wrapped round the foot rope (not just passed underneath it) and then tied to the right hand rope. The twine should be taut without pulling up the foot rope.

5. Once finished trial it with one student crossing at a time. It is important that students are taught to place their feet in the 'V' of the suspension strings. This will stop their foot slipping off the rope. Once they are confident try crossing blindfold or holding a cup of water.

Reflection. Share what you enjoyed most about the activity. Evaluate your teamwork. Think about the procedures that went well and not so well. How could you improve next time? What have you learned about suspension bridges as a result of making the rope bridge?

Fig 10.10   Rope Bridge

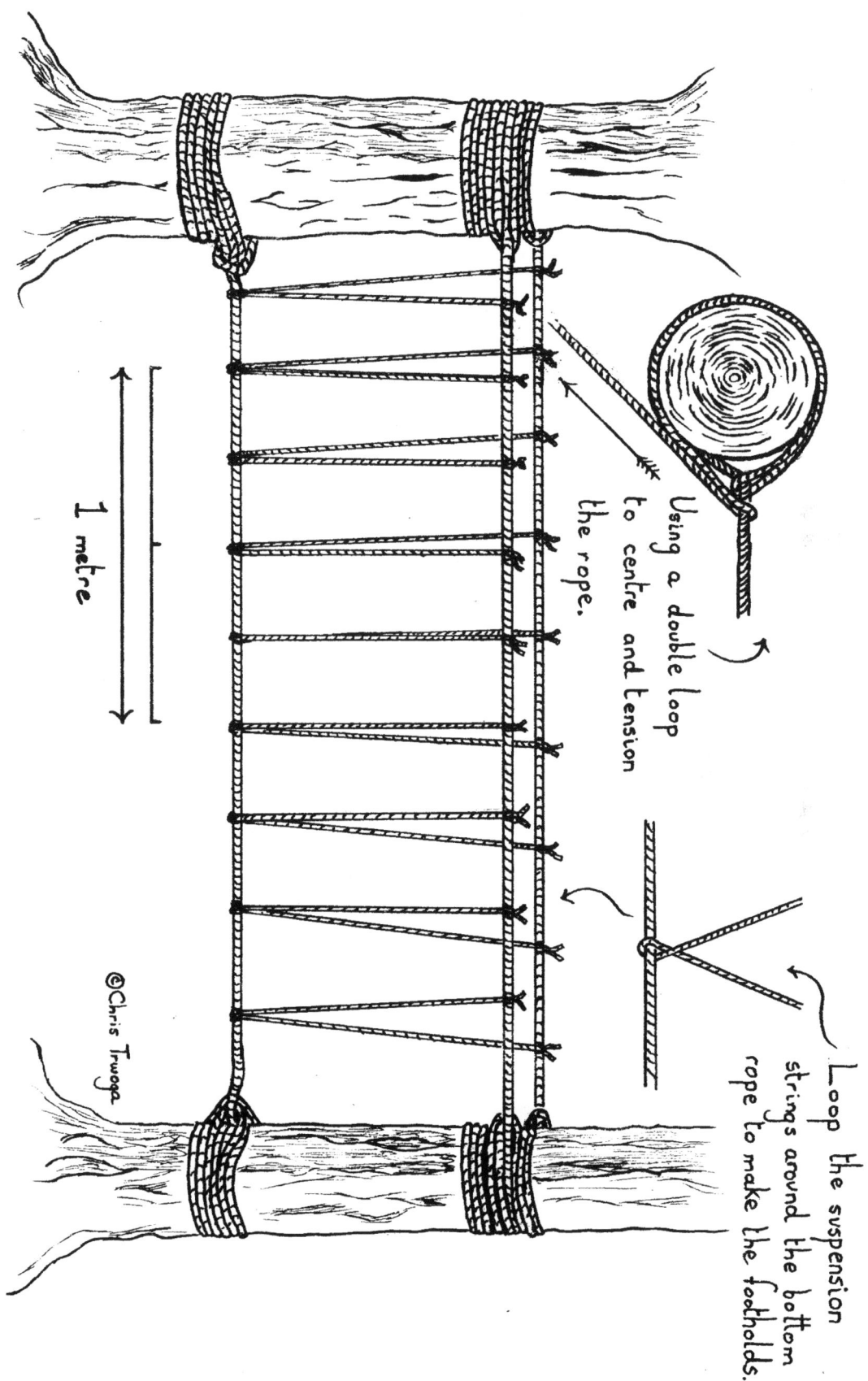

1 metre

Using a double loop to centre and tension the rope.

©Chris Truoga

Loop the suspension strings around the bottom rope to make the footholds.

References

i. Five Reasons for Learning Outdoors

1. Wendell Berry (quoted in Richard Louv, Last Child in the Woods. Saving our children from Nature Deficit Disorder. Algonquin Books, 2006)
2. Raisuyah Bhagwan. International Journal of Children's Spirituality, Vol 14, No.3 Aug 2009, 225-234
3. An overview of child well-being in rich countries – A comprehensive assessment of the lives and well-being of children and adolescents in the economically advanced nations. UNICEF Innocenti Research Centre, Florence, 2007.)
4. Lord Layard, conference speech, 'Happiness and its Causes, London 2007
5. Daniel Nettle, The relationship between Material Prosperity and Happiness, conference speech, Savoy Place, London, 13th October 2007). Also Daniel Nettle, Happiness – The Science behind your Smile, (O.U.P., 2006)
6. Healthy Schools in Somerset Outcomes, NHSS audit tool, 2009)
7. see Tony Eaude – International Journal of Children's Spirituality Vol 14, No.3, August 2009, 185-196.)
8. Edward O. Wilson, Biophilia: The Human Bond with other Species. Cambridge: Harvard University Press, 1984
9. Edward O. Wilson, Biophilia and the Conservation Ethic, in The Biophilia Hypothesis, Edit., Stephen R. Kellert, Island Press, 1993.
10. ibid: P33 – 34
11. Richard Louv, Last Child in the Woods: Saving Our Children from Nature-Deficit Disorder, Algonquin Press, 2005
12. Sue Palmer, Boys need to be boys for all our sakes, Sunday Times article, 2010
13. Dr. William Bird, Natural Thinking, A Report for the Royal Society for the Protection of Birds investigating the links between the Natural Environment, Biodiversity and Mental Health, June 2007
14. ibid P.10
15. Chris Trwoga, Forest Schools Support - Observations carried out during the Autumn Term 2007 and The Glastonbury Trust – Spirituality in Schools Project, website archive; 2007
16. Dr. John W. Fisher, Spiritual Health: It's nature and place in the school curriculum, Doctoral Thesis Dept/ of Science & Mathematics Education, The University of Melbourne, 1998)
17. ibid: P.24
18. ibid: P.24
19. D. Hay & R. Nye. The spirit of the child. London: Fount/Harper Collins, 1998, P.9ff)
20. see Religious Education in English schools: Non-Statutory Guidance 2010. Department for Children, Schools and Families (DCSF)
21. William Bird, 2007, P.15
22. Mihaly Csikszentmihalyi: Flow: the Psychology of Optimal Experience, Harper & Row, New York, 1990.

23. Marny R. Hauge & Douglas A. Gentile, Video Game Addiction Among Adolescents: Associations with Academic Performance and Aggression. School on Professional Psychology, Argosy University National Institute of Media and the Family, presented at Society for Research in Child Development Conference, April 2003, Tampa, Florida, USA.
24. David Derbyshire, How children lost the right to roam in four generations, Daily Mail Online, 15 June 2007.
25. For a non-technical explanation see: Andrew Curran, The Little Book of Big Stuff about the Brain, Crown House Publishing, 2008. Dr. Curran is a practicing paediatric neurologist.
26. Dr William Bird, 2007. P.9
27. Fleming, N.D. & Mills, C. (1992). Helping Students Understand How They Learn. The Teaching Professor, Vol. 7 No. 4, Magma Publications, Madison, Wisconsin, USA.
28. Susan Greenfield, Times Educational Supplement Magazine, 29th July 2007.
29. see Hugh Lafferty, Dr. Keith Burley, Do Learning Styles exist? 2009, http://www.learningstyles.web.com
30. see Cathy Nutbrown, Threads of Thinking: Young Children Learning and the Role of Early Education, Paul Chapman Publishing, 1999

ii. Being Practical.

1. The Guardian, Monday 11th March 2002
2. The Guardian, Saturday 3rd October 2009

1. Special Places

1. William James, The Varieties of Religious Experience, Fontana edition, 1982, P97.
2. see Christopher Tilley, The Phenomenology of Landscape, (Berg, 1994)

7. Art in Nature

1. see Mihaly Csikszentmihalyi, Flow: The Psychology of Optimal Experience, Harper Perennial Modern Classics, 2008
2. see www.miecat.org.au
3. Vivienne Mountain. Educational contexts for the development of students's spirituality: exploring the use of imagination .The International Journal of Students's Spirituality, Vol 12, No 2, August 2007, P196
4. ibid pp191-205

8. Story and Landscape

1. Jane Sahi, Education for Peace, Akshar Mudra, Pune, India, 2000, P.133

Further Reading

Goleman, D. Emotional Intelligence, New York: Bantam Books, 1995
E M Hallowell (2002) Happy Child, happy adult: The childhood routes of adult happiness.
Vermillon: London

REPORT OF THE COUNCIL ON SCIENCE AND PUBLIC HEALTH CSAPH Report 12-A-07 -
Subject: Emotional and Behavioral Effects, Including Addictive Potential, of Video Games,
Presented by: Mohamed K. Khan, MD, PhD, Chair.
Minnesota Longitudinal Study of Parents and Children (1975 to date)
http://cehd.umn.edu/ICD/Parent-Child/default.html

Noddings N. 2003. Happiness and education. Cambridge, UK. C.U.P.,2003
Sue Palmer, Toxic Childhood, How the Modern World is Damaging our Children and What
We Can Do About It, Orion, 2006

Martin Seligman (1995). The Optimistic Child. Harper Perennial: New York.)

Starratt R. J. (2004) The spirituality of presence for educational leaders, in C. Shields, M.

Edwards, A. Sayani (Eds) Inspiring spirituality and educational leadership (Lancaster PA,
ProActive), 67 - 84.

Andrew Wright, The Child in relationship: towards a communal model of spirituality, in
Education, Spirituality and the whole child, edit. Ron Best, Cassell 1996, P.139 – 158.